EMPLOYMENT AND WAGE POLICIES IN POLAND, CZECHOSLOVAKIA AND HUNGARY SINCE 1950

The book deals with employment and wage policies in Poland, Czechoslovakia and Hungary from the start of economic planning. The book is divided into two parts: the first part discusses employment and wage policies on a general level and the second shows how the principles which governed these policies were applied in the four individual phases into which the whole period is divided. Besides the historical dimension the book has also a comparative one: it examines how differences in the systems of management in the three countries affected employment and wage policies.

The book shows how the three countries have managed to achieve and maintain full employment despite recent declining economic growth (in Poland a deep political and economic crisis). It also examines reasons for the various negative phenomena, such as overemployment, hoarding of labor, labor shortages, low labor discipline, which coexist with full employment, and the extent to which they are the by-product of full employment. Finally it discusses the methods countries use to cope with these problems.

The book also discusses the reasons for the rise of a policy of low wages and its reflection in the relationship of wage growth to productivity growth. It examines the evolution of wages in individual phases and the impact of the internal political situation, economic reforms and economic growth on the growth of wages. It also analyzes the evolution of wage differentials and the reasons for their becoming gradually narrower.

Jan Adam is Professor of Economics at the University of Calgary, Calgary, Alberta, Canada. He was born in Czechoslovakia and in 1959 he joined the Department of Political Economy at Charles University, Prague, where he was Associate Professor (Dozent) from 1964 to 1968. After the occuption of Czechoslovakia in 1968 he emigrated to Canada, where his first appointment was Visiting Professor at McGill University, Montreal.

He is the author of *Wage, Price and Taxation Policy in Czechoslovakia, 1948–70*, and *Wage Control and Inflation in Soviet Bloc Countries* and the editor of, and contributor to, *Employment Policies in the Soviet Union and Eastern Europe*.

EMPLOYMENT AND WAGE POLICIES IN POLAND, CZECHOSLOVAKIA AND HUNGARY SINCE 1950

Jan Adam

St. Martin's Press   New York

All rights reserved. For information, write:
St. Martin's Press, Inc., 175 Fifth Avenue, New York, NY 10010
Printed in Hong Kong
Published in the United Kingdom by The Macmillan Press Ltd.
First published in the United States of America in 1984

ISBN 0–312–24457–6

Library of Congress Cataloging in Publication Data

Adam, Jan, 1920–
  Employment and wage policies in Poland, Czechoslovakia,
and Hungary since 1950.

  Bibliography: p.
  Includes index.
  1. Manpower policy—Poland.   2. Manpower policy—
Czechoslovakia.   3. Manpower policy—Hungary.   4. Wages
—Government policy—Poland.   5. Wages—Government policy
—Czechoslovakia.   6. Wages—Government policy—Hungary.
I. Title.
HD5797.7.A6A3   1985   331.12′042′0943   83–40125
ISBN 0–312–24457–6

To Vili and Bözsi and the memory of my parents

Contents

List of Tables and Figure

Tables

Figure

Acknowledgements

I would like first to thank the Social Sciences and Humanities Research Council of Canada for the extended grant which enabled me to work on this study.

I am obliged to those who read the original draft, part or whole, and whose comments enabled me to improve the final version of this book. I would like to pay special tribute to Professors W. Brus, S. Peitchinis and Dr T. Vais. I greatly benefited from consultations with scholars in the field. I am especially obliged to Professors W. Brus, B. Csikós-Nagy, R. I. Gábor, J. Kovács, F. Levcik, G. Révész, J. Timár. Of course, the sole responsibility for the views expressed in the book or any remaining errors is mine.

Most of the materials for this book were collected in libraries and institutes in Europe and the USA. My thanks are due to the libraries and their workers: to the Weltwirtschaft Institut in Kiel, Radio Free Europe in Munich, Osteuropa Institut in Munich, Library of United Nations in Geneva, Bundesinstitut für Ostwissenschaftliche und Internationale Studien in Cologne, Statistical Board in Budapest, Institute for Comparative Economic Studies in Vienna and Harvard University in Cambridge, Mass.

I also wish to record my appreciation of the help contributed by my research assistants: Mmes K. Lukasziewicz in compiling statistical tables, S. Gruszczynska and J. Vértes-Ádler in collecting, processing and evaluating materials. Special thanks go to Mrs B. Blackman for the care and patience with which she improved the English of my typescript. To Mrs M. Samuels as well as to Mrs S. Langan I am obliged for their care in typing the several drafts of the study. To my wife Zuzana, who encouraged me in my work and helped me to collect and process materials, I am very much indebted.

A small part of the material in the book was published earlier in a study, 'Regulation of Labour Supply in Poland, Czechoslovakia and Hungary' *Soviet Studies*, no. 1. January 1984. I wish to thank the editor of the journal for allowing me to use a part of the material contained in my article in this book.

Calgary
December 1983

J. A.

Abbreviations

a. For countries:
   CSR   Czech Lands
   CSSR Czechoslovak Socialist Republic

b. For journals and papers:
   GP   *Gospodarka Planowa* (Polish)
   PiZS   *Praca i Zabezpieczenie Społeczne*
   TL   *Trybuna Ludu*
   ZG   *Życie Gospodarcze*
   HN   *Hospodářské noviny* (Czechoslovak)
   PH   *Plánované hospodářství*
   PaM   *Práce a mzda*
   KSz   *Közgazdasági Szemle* (Hungarian)
   MSz   *Munkaügyi Szemle*
   TSz   *Társadalmi Szemle*
   ESE   *Economic Survey of Europe* (Annual Report of
          European Economic Commission)

c. For national statistical yearbooks:
   MRS   *Maly Rocznik Statystyczny* (Polish pocket yearbook)
   RS   *Rocznik Statystyczny* (Polish)
   SE   *Statisztikai Évkönyv* (Hungarian)
   SRC   *Statistická ročenka CSSR* (Czechoslovak)
   ZGN   *Zatrudnienie w Gospodarcze Narodowej* (Polish employ-
          ment statistics)

d. For miscellaneous matters:
   CMEA Council for Mutual Economic Assistance
   FAZ   Fund for occupational activation
   FE   Full employment
   FYP   Five-year plan

JEC   Publications of the Joint Economic Committee of the US
Congress, ed. by J. Hardt

NEM   New Economic Mechanism

RE   Rational employment

Introduction

Despite declining rates of economic growth in Czechoslovakia and Hungary and a deep economic crisis in Poland, all three countries have managed to maintain full employment. Questions are warranted: How have socialist countries managed to achieve full employment? How do they understand full employment? What do they do in order to sustain it? What is the role of the socialist economic system? And what is the cost of full employment? In this book all these and related questions are examined, and an attempt is made to contribute to their elucidation.

Since employment policy is in many respects intertwined with wage policy the latter is also discussed, but to a much lesser extent because some aspects of wage policy have been dealt with by me in another book.

In the book employment and wage policies are first discussed on a general level (Part I), then examined by periods, from the introduction of central planning to the present (Part II). Part I is thus a study of the principles which have governed employment and wage policies, and Part II an examination of how these principles were applied in individual periods.

The book has two dimensions – comparative (the three countries discussed have for long been marked by different management systems) and historical – to some degree interrelated. The first enables the study of how systemic differences have affected employment and wage policies and the second how economic development and changes in the system of management in individual periods affected these policies.

I was much troubled with the problem of how to structure Part II. I was confronted with two possibilities: to discuss the topic by periods or to split it into several subtopics and examine them separately, regardless of periodisation. Both approaches have their advantages and disadvantages.

I have opted for the first approach, but not in a consistent way. The four chapters (7–10) dealing with the applied employment and wage policies and other related topics are discussed by periods, since it is felt to be important to examine them in close association with economic

xv

development and their other determinants. In addition such an approach seems to be in line with the historical method. The two remaining chapters, especially Ch. 12, are discussed according to the second method because it is felt that the reader will by then have benefited from the historical context of the previous chapters.

The period under review is divided into four phases. The main criteria used for periodisation were the following: major changes in general economic policy, the start of major reforms and great changes in economic growth. The first phase is the shortest and deals primarily with the dramatic years 1950–5, which were characterised by the start of the industrialisation drive as reflected in the first medium plans, but also by a slowdown in the drive, needed to cope with imbalances generated by overambitious plans and to ease the pressure on the population (1954–5). It is also the period of the laying down of the foundation of the centralised system of management of the economy.

The second phase starts with 1956, the year of great events in the history of socialist countries: the 20th Congress of the Soviet Communist Party, at which Stalin was denounced, an event which opened the gates for a widespread criticism; the Polish riots and Hungarian uprising followed. The period 1956–65 is also a time of timid reforms and great disappointments (in the beginning of the 60s) which paved the way for the major reforms of the 60s.

The third phase starts with the commencement of a major economic reform in Czechoslovakia (1966) which was followed by one in Hungary in 1968. The Polish reform was instituted only later. It is the most successful period in terms of economic growth and improvements in the standard of living.

The fourth phase commences with 1976, which can be characterised as the year of the start of the economic downturn, if its evolution is viewed in terms of FYPs. All three countries have suffered a slowdown in economic growth, which in the 80s has turned to stagnation. Poland, in addition, has been going through a deep political crisis which has compounded the economic crisis.

Each of the two parts of the book is made up of six chapters. In the first chapter the objectives and determinants of employment policy in the real socialist system are examined. Among other things the role of the adopted strategy of economic development in the shaping of the direction of employment policy is stressed. One of the objectives of employment policy is full employment, the achievement of which has been accompanied by overemployment, labour shortages, low labour discipline, etc. Ch. 2 examines the causes of these phenomena, which, naturally, the countries try to cope with in order to improve labour economy. For this purpose they regulate employment. The methods used to regulate demand for and supply of labour and the extent of systemic influences are analysed in Ch. 3. In Ch. 4, which is an appendix, the views of the East European economists on full employment and rational employment are discussed. Wage policy, its objectives and determinants, as well as the wage system, are discussed in Ch. 5. The next chapter, which is the second appendix, discusses the views of East European economists on distribution according to work, which is said to be the principle governing income distribution under socialism.

The first four chapters of Part II (Chs 7–10) are devoted to an examination of employment and wage policies as they were practised in individual phases. In addition employment regulation, placement policies, unemployment compensation and wage determination for individual workers are discussed. Ch. 11 is focused on the analysis of wage differential policies in the whole period under review. Ch. 12 is a hybrid; it discusses wage and labour productivity growth and changes in employment structure.

The book deals with a topic which has not had much attention in the West. Even in the East there is little literature of a comparative nature with a historical dimension on employment policy. Therefore I have had to carry out pioneering work in some respects. For this and other reasons the book does not pretend to be an answer to all problems raised about employment and wage policies, but is rather a modest contribution to research on a topic of great importance, which will hopefully be followed up with further research.

My book relies heavily on the official documents and economic literature of the countries discussed. Despite effort I have not managed to obtain access to all the information deemed important for this study. This is also due to the fact that some of the problems discussed in this book have been neglected in the literature, particularly employment policy; there is a much richer literature on wage policy. In the CSSR in the 50s very little was published on employment policy, as if it were a taboo topic. Employment problems started to be researched in a systematic way in the 60s. In the second half of the 60s and the early 70s, the first-known books on employment were published. Very little has been published on employment regulation, far less anything of a comparative nature.

The figures indicated in this book are, for economies of space, much fewer than those used for the analyses. The comparability of the indicated figures for the three countries is quite good, but not as perfect as one would expect considering that these countries belong to one political bloc and are engaged in very close economic co-operation. There is insufficient co-ordination between the countries in the definition of concepts, classification of statistical variables and rules for the compilation of data. The best example of the first case is that the working-age population is defined differently in each country. The economically active population for statistical purposes is not defined in all three countries in the same way, and, what is worse, the countries do not stick to one definition. Employment figures published by the Hungarian *Statistical Yearbook* refer to the beginning of the year, whereas in Czechoslovakia and Poland they refer mostly to the annual average. In Poland and Hungary real-wage figures are compiled from net wages, and in Czechoslovakia from gross figures.

Before the Introduction is brought to an end some definitions of terms used in this study should be given. To begin with planning and management of the economy, I distinguish the term 'management' in both a narrow and broad sense. Management in the narrow sense means the execution of planned targets, whereas management in the broad sense is an activity which also includes planning. A system of management of the economy (management in the broad sense) defines the role of planning in the direction of the economy and of other tools to be used. In this book management, unless otherwise indicated, is used in the broad sense. What has been said about management, in my opinion, also applies to regulation *vis-à-vis* planning.

National income is used in its marxist concept as it is understood in the countries examined; it is what is called in Western literature net material product. For the purpose of this study it is, in the author's view, the only possible approach.

Many economists use the terms 'wage-fund' and 'wage-bill' as synonyms. In this book the term 'wage-fund' is used for the economy as a whole and, in order to distinguish it from the wage-bill which is reserved for enterprises and associations, the wage-fund is usually provided with the adjective 'global'. Wage-fund and wage-bill always refer to wages paid out during a year.

In socialist countries the national economy is divided into – what I call – sectors, and industry as one sector is divided into branches. Industry is understood to include manufacturing and mining. Construction is regarded as a separate sector. In this book the socialist classification is used.

The term 'economically active' covers all who perform some gainful civilian activity, whether in the state sector or in the co-operative and private sectors. The term 'employed' refers only to those who are in an 'employment relationship', which means who work in the state sector or even in co-operatives and in the private sector, as long as they are employees there. The term 'labour force' includes all those who are economically active.

Part

Part I

1 Factors Determining Employment Policy in the Real Socialist System

1 OBJECTIVES OF EMPLOYMENT POLICY – DEFINED

My intention is to discuss not the objectives of employment policy generally, but specifically the objectives of the real socialist system as it exists in the three countries under review. Such an approach is warranted since the socioeconomic setup in the socialist states has a far-reaching impact, particularly on employment policy; it should not be forgotten that the three countries have centrally planned economies (though differently applied) and are committed to full employment.

The problem regarding the objectives of employment policy caught the attention of economists only in the 60s and in Poland at first. In the first years of planned economy the endeavour was directed primarily to a mobilisation of potential workers for ambitious investment projects without proper regard to economic efficiency. Achievement of the full-employment goal was a by-product of this expansion drive. With the passage of time, concerns for efficiency increased, and due to difficulties in the labour market calls for rational utilisation of labour have come into the forefront. And with them arose the interest in the objectives of employment policies. Nowadays one can read different definitions of the objectives of employment policy. Taking what these definitions have in common, one can briefly define the objectives as an endeavour by the state authorities to achieve through proper provisions a rational management of manpower resources corresponding to the economic and social needs of the country and at the same time to ensure full employment. Employment policy and manpower management should be distinguished. The objective of the latter is usually to bring about the most rational[1] utilisation of existing manpower resources in accordance with quantitative and qualitative needs of the economy in its existing

3

structure. Employment policy in its objectives is a much broader concept, implemented through manpower management. To achieve the objectives of employment policy the government must accordingly co-ordinate many other policies, as educational, population, old-age pension, wage, incentive, investment and price, to mention the most important (Pogány 1969, pp. 167–8).

The given definition of the objectives of employment policy is, of course, too general; for the elaboration of this definition Gy. Pogány's (1969, pp. 183–9) views are used as a departure-point. He maintains that employment policy follows four objectives: (1) to reproduce manpower, (2) to determine rules for distribution and redistribution of labour which vary depending on the system of management of the economy, (3) to determine methods for the best utilisation of the numerical capacity as well as the quality of the already employed labour force, (4) to make sure that the right to a job is implemented.

The last three objectives are self-explanatory; only the first needs some elaboration. 'Reproduction of manpower' is a term from Marxian political economy. Some economists understand the term very broadly; in brief it includes everything which is connected with manpower management including theory of employment. This approach has been used primarily in the USSR, but also in other countries, mainly Czechoslovakia in the 50s. Gy. Pogány includes in manpower reproduction all provisions requisite for a generation of a manpower which could meet the needs of the economy. To him it includes three components: provisions for a biological reproduction of the population (a population policy), for a promotion of the skills and culture of the manpower and for a continuous reproduction of the work force through supply of consumer goods.

This breakdown of the objectives of economic policy is not a dogma. One can imagine a more detailed breakdown or one with quite a different structure. What is important is that the objectives of employment policy – if they are to be effective – should not be arbitrary; they must be based on or reconciled with the functions employment plays in the economy. This does not mean that a socialist state cannot attribute certain objectives to employment for reasons other than economic.

In the socialist countries three functions are usually attributed to employment: (1) growth, in that it is a factor of economic growth, (2) income, in that through employment workers gain a share in the produced national income. These two functions are surely acceptable to all economists (socialist or non-socialist) regardless of their ideological bias. (3) The third function which is much stressed in socialist countries is more controversial. M. Kabaj (1977, p. 44) calls it social and results from Marx's view about the importance of work for society and human beings. People work not only because they expect remuneration in order to make a living, but also because this is the way they assert themselves as equal members of society and because many seek self-fulfilment through work.

Not only may the objectives of employment policy as defined and the functions of employment conflict, but there may be a conflict between the objectives themselves and the functions likewise. Optimisation of economic growth may be in conflict with the effort for full employment. Employment of more people than the economy requires is contrary to the objective of rational utilisation of labour. The income function as well as the social (which in the final analysis means a right to a job) may conflict with the growth function. Fast growth of incomes may hamper economic growth and vice versa. In the following chapters I will try to show the kind of conflicts resulting from government policies and the methods used to cope with them.

If employment policy is to achieve its objectives it must be harmonised with other policies. Of course, employment policy does not relate to all the components of the complex of policies the government must act upon in the same way. In relation to some policies it is in a subordinated position whereas to others it is in a more or less interrelated position. Once employment policy is determined it acquires a certain autonomous position which is reflected in its ability even to influence the policy it is subordinated to.

Employment policy is in a subordinated position to and must serve the economic system, the general economic policy and the system of management of the economy (which is an economic subsystem definable succintly as a strategy of applied methods for achieving the objectives of the general economic policy). The general economic policy is geared to short-term and long-term objectives. Viewed as a long-term policy directed to the development of the economy it is usually known as the strategy of economic development and/or under the related term, strategy of economic growth.[2]

In the following pages the impact of the most important factors on employment policy and manpower management will be discussed on a very general level. The statements made here will be elaborated in later chapters.

2   STRATEGY OF ECONOMIC DEVELOPMENT

All three countries adopted the Soviet strategy of economic development. Without going into great detail it is possible to characterise the Soviet strategy in the following way: industrialisation (within it heavy industry) is the main focus of development, carried out at the maximum possible pace, and financed by agriculture and consumers. As to the strategy of economic growth, so-called extensive growth has been characteristic; labour has been used to a great extent as a substitute for capital.

The Soviet strategy of economic development was greatly influenced by military considerations; one of its chief goals was to create an industrial apparatus for armament. East European countries shaped their first medium-term plans according to the Soviet pattern; military spending got high priority, mainly in the modified plans of 1950–1. The outbreak of the Korean War – the first transformation of the cold war, which was raging between West and East, into a hot war – accelerated the armament race between the USA and the Soviet Union. The Soviets did not hesitate to involve East European countries on their side in this race. Huge funds were diverted for military programmes; Hungarian economists (Balogh and Jakab 1978, p. 175) estimate their extent in Hungary at 20 per cent of the national income in 1950.

This strategy had a far-reaching impact on demand for labour, the effectiveness of its utilisation and on the implementation of the commitment to full employment. Since in the three countries, but mainly in Poland and Hungary, capital was scarce, while labour, particularly unskilled, was abundant, labour was, according to the Soviet pattern, destined to play a decisive role in the implementation of the industrialisation drive. In more concrete terms this meant that East European countries followed a policy of applying the most advanced production techniques accessible to them to the basic production processes in heavy industry and labour-intensive methods to auxiliary production processes and administration (cf. Ellman 1979). The planners apparently believed that by using scarce capital for the basic production processes output could be maximised since in this way more factories could be built. At the same time the chosen production technique meant a tremendous increase in demand for labour which substantially reduced open and hidden unemployment. The demand for labour was strengthened by the fact that most of the investment funds earmarked for productive purposes were channelled into the construction of new factories and very little into the modernisation of the existing ones

(Höhmann and Seidenstecher 1977, p. 41; Vachel 1965).

The strategies, including their military aspects discussed here briefly, have survived to a great extent up to now. Needless to say, such strategies could only be carried out at the cost of inefficiencies, including inefficiency in the utilisation of labour.

3   THE REAL SOCIALIST SYSTEM – RESOURCE CONSTRAINED SYSTEM

In the capitalist system firms must operate on their own account and at their own risk. A capitalist firm must maximise profit if it wants to survive and expand. Under market conditions maximisation of profit presupposes products being produced in a composition demanded by buyers. But it also means expanding employment only to a point at which the value of the contribution by the last worker to the product is at least equal to the labour costs involved. If the demand for his product declines the capitalist will not hesitate to contract output and dismiss redundant workers. We may say that a capitalist economy is demand constrained.

A socialist enterprise is, in fact, operating on the state's account and with the state taking the risk; if it gets into financial trouble the state will bail it out. This is primarily true in the traditional socialist system. In Hungary, and recently in Poland, there is an endeavour to make enterprises financially independent, self-financing; yet this is still far from reality, and who knows whether it will ever be achieved. The socialist enterprise maximises output, whether gross (as it was for a long time in the traditional system) or net (as in Hungary despite profit being the evaluation indicator) is of no great relevance in this case. Maximisation of output is a product of the strategy of economic development which is geared to maximum growth and of the system of management which serves this strategy. (I have in mind here primarily the fact that the incentive system is linked to growth.) There are, of course, other factors contributing to the maximising function of output: e.g. managers' interest in managing large enterprises for pecuniary and social status reasons. In conditions of maximisation of output enterprises are not exposed to the employment constraints characteristic of a capitalist firm; as long as a socialist enterprise grows, managers may expand employment beyond the point at which the contribution of newly hired workers is equal at least to the labour cost involved, provided that they add to the output of the enterprise. This behaviour of enterprises is, of course, sanctioned by the central planners who view economic efficiency as a macroeconomic concept and therefore take apparently the position that in many cases it is more efficient to let people work – even if their contribution is below labour costs – than to support them. It would, however, be wrong to conclude from this that the central planners view full employment as an end in itself; they have always viewed it as a way to expand the nation's wealth.

The only constraints to maximisation of output are resources, including manpower resources. The socialist system is thus in contrast to the capitalist system, supply oriented or, as J. Kornai (1980, p. 26) calls it, resource constrained.

After explaining the objective function of the economic actors it is possible to define rational employment as it is understood in socialist countries. This is a utilisation and distribution of labour which brings about the maximum possible level of national income. This implies that labour is as much as possible fully and optimally used. By fully I mean that workers perform jobs for which they have qualifications and by optimally that they work in enterprises where their potential can be maximally used. Rational employment in a socialist economy is a macroeconomic concept which means that individual enterprises, being output maximisers, may use labour even beyond the limits for a capitalist profit-maximising enterprise as long as it contributes to the growth of national income (cf. Kabaj 1972, pp. 41–5). Rational employment is an ideal which socialist countries strive to achieve.

4 MANAGEMENT OF THE ECONOMY

The most important aspects of the management system which have an influence on manpower management at the enterprise level are the following: (a) methods used for making enterprises meet national plan targets; (b) indicators used for measuring the performance of enterprises; (c) wage determination and regulation system; (d) incentive system and (e) investment system. It will be shown later that the management system in some of its components stimulates maximisation of output and thus maximisation of employment.

(a) **Methods used for making enterprises meet national plan targets**

This is the most important aspect of a management system because in it is reflected the substance of the management system and through it is determined the nature of the four other aspects. The Soviet system of management the three countries took over was and is a centralised system. To put it briefly, in a centralised system the central planners use primarily administrative methods, the main one being the annual plan which contains output targets binding on enterprises. In such a system the central planners endeavour to have economic activities including employment in enterprises under strict control. Employment control has been exercised differently in different periods. For a long time enterprises were assigned limits for employment for individual years. Growth of employment was also controlled by regulating the wage-bill and average wages and by assigning targets for increases in productivity for individual enterprises. This is not to say that all these provisions present an effective control over employment; on the contrary, they are – as will be shown – to an extent counterproductive. Here it should only be stated that labour rationing – which these controls amount to – stimulates enterprises to hoard labour.

The reforms introduced in the second half of the 60s in the CSSR and Hungary brought about substantial economic autonomy for enterprises which manifested itself in a far-reaching elimination of the system of annual plans with binding output targets and its replacement by indirect methods. Such a decentralisation of the system of management could not but affect the system of employment regulation. Direct control of employment at the enterprise level does not square well with economic autonomy. It was therefore no surprise that the two countries dropped the assignment of direct limits for employment. (Poland did the same in its reforms in 1973 and 1982.) However, the emergence of labour shortages prompted even Hungary, which went the farthest in its reforms, to apply some elements of administrative controls. With regard to white-collar workers there has always been a tendency to apply more stringent methods.

(b) Indicators used for measuring performance

The methods used for making enterprises achieve national plan targets predetermine the nature of indicators selected for measuring perform-ance and, what is even more important, the role of indicators. In a centralised system indicators measure the extent of fulfilment of plan targets whereas in a decentralised system they measure the performance of enterprises mostly compared to the level of the previous year.

The centralised system in fact was for a long time concerned primarily with the achievement of quantitative targets without due regard to cost and quality. Quantitative targets were expressed in gross value of output which also served as the main indicator. Gross value of output was also used for the determination of the size of wage-bill for enterprises and for computation of labour productivity. In assigning employment limits to enterprises the expected increases in productivity as well as the planned targets for output were taken into consideration. As will be shown, enterprises are interested in getting plan targets which could be easily fulfilled and overfulfilled. Therefore enterprises try to obtain slack targets for output and maximum numbers of workers. Since it lends itself to manipulation in different ways, gross value of output as an indicator made enterprises' efforts easier. Recently there has been a tendency even in Czechoslovakia, which has a traditional management system, to get away from gross indicators.

A decentralised system which puts great stress on the use of elements of market mechanism and attaches great importance to efficiency must necessarily apply net sales indicators. This is not to say that the use of such methods makes a system a decentralised one. But what is an option in a centralised system becomes a *sine qua non* in a decentralised system. Since in a decentralised system limits for employment are not usually assigned to enterprises, indicators are supposed to play primarily an indirect role through their impact on the performance of enterprises.

(c) Wage determination and regulation

It has been mentioned that one of the functions of employment is an income function and is realised through the wages workers receive for their productive services. Therefore efforts to achieve a rational employment policy depend very much on wage policy. Of primary importance in this respect are the methods used: for the determination of the wage-bill of enterprises including the control of drawing funds for wages, for the determination of wages for individual workers including pay forms, for the adjustment of wage differentials and their actual state. The methods used are to varying extents conditioned by the nature of the system of management. In practice the determination of the wage-bill, due to its central importance for the control of wage growth, is, of the three problems mentioned, the most influenced by systemic consider-ations. Aspects of wage-bill determination such as – how is the size of this wage-bill determined? What is the role of the plan and market elements in this respect? How is the control of wage growth exercised, administratively or through economic levers? – are solved differently in a centralised and in a decentralised system of management. The concrete resolution of these questions have an influence on the way regulation of employment growth is exercised and the methods used for promoting labour economy. (For more see Part II.)

(d) Incentive system

Manpower management can also be influenced by the incentive system. Of great importance in this respect are the methods used to determine the size of the bonus fund (mainly whether or not it depends on plan targets), the nature of indicators, particularly the role of profit, and to what extent allocation of bonuses depends on meeting employment limits. Of course, the incentive system, mainly its first aspect, depends on the system of management of the economy.

For a long time the three countries did not use special incentives geared to restraining employment or to inducing enterprises to a better utilisation of labour. Expansion of output and employment got priority. Only in the second half of the 50s, indirectly in Czechoslovakia and in the 60s in the other two countries, when greater stress began to be put on economic efficiency and when shortages started to show up attention was then given to special incentives.

(e) Investment system

Manpower management is significantly affected by the way the following questions are dealt with: who makes decisions about the size of investment outlays and their structure, and how is investment financed? Again the solution to these questions is conditional on the system of management of the economy. Up to the mid 60s in the traditional Soviet system almost all investment decisions were concentrated in the hands of the centre and financing was done by free interest grants from state revenues. Since this system led to great waste, *inter alia* to excessive demand for and under-utilisation of labour, it was subject to some modifications: 'decentralised' investment was substantially expanded and the burden of financing was shifted to a certain extent to enterprises. The Hungarian decentralised system went the furthest in this respect.

To induce enterprises to practise a rational investment policy and thus greater labour economy it is necessary to really tie the financial situation of enterprises to their performance. This is a precondition if money incentives and disincentives, geared to labour economy, are to work.

5 POLITICAL AND IDEOLOGICAL ASPECTS

To understand their impact on employment policy one must consider the role employment played in the Marxist critique of capitalism and particularly in the propaganda of the communist parties when they were still in open or underground opposition to the capitalist establishment. As it is known, Marx considered unemployment (the industrial reserve army) not only a product of the capitalist system, but also a necessary precondition for the working of the capitalist system. Unemployment was – according to Marxists – so inherent in the capitalist system that its liquidation could be achieved only with the elimination of capitalism itself and its replacement by a socialist system. The communist parties pledged that once they had seized power, unemployment, the plague of capitalism, would be eliminated and full employment instituted. This pledge has become an important article of communist ideology. With the seizure of power after the Second World War communist parties were confronted with the necessity of fulfilling the pledge – *Hic Rhodus hic salta*. No wonder full employment was put high on the priority lists of the communist programmes.

The way socialist industrialisation was carried out, full employment was – disregarding some temporary difficulties – not only facilitated but – as will be shown later – was its natural outcome. The industrialisation and armament drive absorbed not only the unemployed and the partly employed, but also attracted into the work-force groups of population which had never before been economically active.

The commitment to full employment and, what is even more important, the ability to honour this commitment after a certain period of time (regardless of its price) is a powerful trump in the hands of the communist leaders, particularly nowadays when capitalist countries are plagued by high rates of unemployment. But full employment as a trump has its limitations. Due to the long-lasting propaganda the working classes identify socialism *inter alia* with full employment and see the incorporation of the right to a job in the constitution as something natural and to be taken for granted. Unemployment belongs to a short list of phenomena (as currency reform, substantial decline in real wages, increases in prices without proper compensation, excessive tightening of work norms) which, if present even in mild form, might destabilise the regime. The legitimacy of the socialist system – unlike that of advanced capitalist countries which is based on democratic institutions – relies on the ability of the communist leaders to make the people believe that the system fulfils a certain social function which cannot be met by any other system – namely ensuring full employment, and a much more equal distribution of income, to mention just the most important. Once it turns out that the leaders are not able to honour their promises the socialist regime may be dangerously destabilised. Communist leaders are very well aware of this danger and therefore employment problems obtain preferential attention. Not only this, but whenever economic considerations conflict with the objective of full employment, usually the latter gets priority. Expansion of employment in contest with wage increases is handled similarly. The planners feel that slower wage increases are less damaging to the system than unemployment. In addition they expect that increased expansion of employment results in greater output.

6 LABOUR RESOURCES

Up to now the discussion has concentrated on factors on the demand side which determine or influence employment policy. Now consideration will be given to factors on the supply side, again on a very general level.

(a) Demographic factors

Among demographic factors the most important for purposes of this study are: the current and future percentage of population of working age and the rate of participation in economic activity. Evolution of the working-age population in the long run depends on the growth rates of the population as well as on its age-structure. The working-age population is always larger numerically than the active labour force without workers of pensionable age. Some cannot join the labour force for health reasons. The main reasons for the difference, however, are that some working-age women prefer to take care of their children or cannot find jobs. Also the vast majority of young people are preparing for future jobs; over a considerable period their number was not only absolutely but also relatively increasing. Because of this, increments in the working-age population are not translated right away into employment increases. These in annual terms depend on the difference between the number who enter the labour force and the number who leave it; the balance thus arising constitutes the net increment to the labour force. The entrants consist primarily of graduates of schools (vocational, high schools and universities), teenagers after finishing compulsory attendance at school (this is the case in the CSSR and Hungary where the working-age group starts at the age when compulsory schooling ends), housewives who decided to join or rejoin the labour force, discharged conscripts, women returning from their short- or long-term maternity leave and retirees. Some of the school graduates do not take jobs after completing their education (estimated to be 20 per cent in the CSSR) because of military service, marriage and pregnancy. The decrement in the active labour force results from natural reasons (death, disability, retirement) and other reasons (start of military service and maternity leave).

The higher the participation rate the lower the potential net increment to the labour force (assuming all other factors remain unchanged) and vice versa. Disregarding some minor fluctuations, the participation rate in the three countries increased steadily up to the second half of the 70s (in the CSSR even in the beginning of the 80s) thus reaching almost the maximum possible level. Further increases in employment could come primarily from increments in the working-age population, which was declining in the three countries to different extents and thus contributing to the existing labour shortages.

(b) Female employment

Growth of female employment depends on labour demand and the willingness of women to join the labour force. The latter has been influenced by two factors: ideological and economic (financial). In the beginning of the 50s the authorities exerted ideological pressure combined with a propaganda barrage to make women take jobs. Even when the ideological pressure abated, and the governments were no longer interested in the intensification of female employment, the economic one did not cease. In the initial planning period wages were set at a level which forced great numbers of housewives to take jobs simply to contribute to the family income. Wages thus played an important role in generating female labour supply.

The absorption of women into the labour force was not a smooth process. As will be shown, in various periods female unemployment, mainly in Poland but also in Hungary, persisted and the planners had great difficulty in coping with it. In some few areas even now there are no suitable jobs for women.

High female participation rates combined with the elimination of abortion prohibition laws and great shortages in housing had an adverse effect on birth-rates and on the bringing up of the new generation. To counter the adverse effects all three countries resorted to some provision aimed at promoting the growth of the population.

(c) **Working retirees**

Labour supply also depends on the willingness of people beyond working age (retirees) to continue working. Disregarding the retirement age (which is relatively low nowadays in the CSSR and Hungary) the participation rate of retirees depends primarily on the provisions of the pension law; by its adjustment it is possible to regulate the labour supply of retirees. (For more see pp. 49–51)

Considering the participation rate of retirees one should not forget that for a long time collective farmers (and in Poland private farmers) were not eligible for pensions from state revenues. And this was also the reason why the participation rate of agricultural retirees was high. Once agricultural retirees achieved the same pension rights as their colleagues in other sectors their participation rate started to decline and this has necessarily also affected employment in non-agricultural sectors.

Finally, the participation rate of retirees depends on job opportunities in the private sector regardless of its legal status. The more work available in the private sector, which pays better than the state sector, the greater the attraction to continue working.

(d) **Agriculture**

It is known that with the development of the economy the number of economically active in agriculture declines not only relatively but also absolutely. The pace of exodus from agriculture in the socialist countries has been conditioned by several factors – the extent of hidden unemployment in agriculture, job opportunities outside agriculture, the level of wages in jobs outside agriculture compared to the possible earnings in agriculture, the pace of collectivisation, supply of food in cities, etc.

With the industrialisation drive after the Second World War many job opportunities were created in the non-agricultural sectors, primarily in industry and construction, and agricultural workers seized these opportunities. The drive for a speedy collectivisation of agriculture, combined with inhumane methods of implementation in 1949–53, accelerated the exodus from agriculture. When the pressure for collectivisation eased and the demand for labour outside agriculture declined, the exodus slowed down substantially and some peasants even returned to work in agriculture.

Changes in the number of economically active persons in agriculture influences the supply of labour available outside agriculture and thus the growth rate of employment. If the exodus from agriculture fluctuates extensively this may also bring about an extensive fluctuation in the growth of employment outside agriculture. If the migration out from agriculture is too heavy it may even cause unemployment (e.g. in Hungary in 1959).

2 Causes of Overemployment and Labour Shortages

1 DEFINITION OF TERMS

From reports on employment coming from East European countries it is clear that full employment, overemployment, labour hoarding, low labour discipline and labour shortages all coexist in these countries. The emergence of labour shortages has not eliminated the other three negative phenomena; on the contrary it contributes to their spread in a sense. In this chapter the causes of these phenomena are analysed. First most of the terms must be explained in order to avoid misunderstanding.

Full employment is a state in which everyone who wants to work can obtain a job; if he wants a full-time job then one is available. Does this mean that jobs in which workers are not fully utilised (because they perform jobs which do not use their skills or because their productivity is low) are also counted towards full employment? In this author's view the answer should be affirmative because an underutilised worker is still an employed worker and contributes to the growth of the social product. By the way, statistical institutions all over the world also count underutilised people as employed.

For the definition of overemployment I use M. Kabaj's definition as a point of departure. To him (1972, p. 233) overemployment arises if enterprises or non-profit organisations expand employment beyond the numbers needed to meet production targets at a given level of technology and average labour intensity. It is a situation in which the marginal productivity of a certain group in an enterprise is zero or close to zero, or lower than what is regarded as the proper limit for rational employment in the existing conditions. Thus M. Kabaj does not use the relationship of marginal productivity to labour costs involved as a criterion for overemployment as a capitalist profit-maximising firm does. Such an

17

approach is not surprising if one realises that M. Kabaj agrees with the commitment to full employment and apparently views rational employment under socialism in macroeconomic terms.

M. Kabaj's concept of overemployment is flexible, but also loose because of the qualification attached to the last part of the definition (which did not exist in the original one (Kabaj 1960)), namely, that he makes overemployment dependent on the current perception of rational employment. He probably takes such a position because it enables him to set a stricter criterion for overemployment under conditions of full employment than under conditions of unemployment.

To what extent should overemployment include employment resulting from the use of out-of-date production techniques and/or inefficient organisation? There is a difference between the two factors under central planning; the first is believed to be determined mostly by exogenous and the second by endogenous agents. One could therefore argue, as M. Kabaj does, that not the potential but the applied production technique should serve as a criterion for the definition of overemployment. Yet this author believes that enterprises (more so after the reform of the 60s than before) have always been in a position to improve on the first factor if they wished to do so. Thus overemployment also means an expansion of employment which could easily be avoided by a better organisation of the production process and related activities, and by improving the techniques of production if the personnel of the enterprises, particularly managers, were interested in doing so. My definition has, however, the disadvantage that it makes the estimate of the number of redundant more difficult, a reason why Kabaj takes the level of technology and labour intensity as given.

Labour hoarding is a special case of overemployment; it is more or less the result of a conscious decision by managers and is practised for a certain purpose. It includes hoarding in order to ensure labour for peak economic activities during the year as well as for potential future demand. It also includes hoarding which results from the desire of managers to gain some financial advantages (for themselves and/or for their employees) which the wage regulation and/or incentive systems allow (usually unintentionally).

Overemployment, whether it results from a conscious or unconscious decision, means an underutilisation of labour. Under conditions of full employment it is a cause of lower economic growth, since it produces shortages of labour. Underutilisation of labour results not only from overemployment, but also to an extent from low labour discipline.

Overemployment means the some groups of workers are underutilised. In my opinion depending on whether we approach the problem from the viewpoint of enterprises (and the whole economy) or workers, one can talk of overemployment or underemployment. M. Bornstein (1978) uses the term 'underemployment' or 'disguised unemployment' for a situation where workers have jobs but are underutilised. I prefer to use the term 'overemployment'.

Labour shortage exists when the demand for labour in some sectors of the economy cannot be satisfied. It is not an absolute state in the sense that all potential labour supply (not yet absorbed in the economy) or internal labour reserves are entirely exhausted. Labour shortages are usually combined with and result from overemployment in the same or other sectors of the economy.

Even with the definitions given here it is not easy to draw a strict line between labour hoarding and overemployment, and between under-utilisation of labour resulting from overemployment and that resulting from other sources. This is all the more true since the terms 'overemploy-ment' and 'labour hoarding' are concepts rather than strictly defined phenomena which can be easily quantified. Therefore in the following pages various phenomena which generate underutilisation of labour – and lead to overemployment and often to labour shortages – will be discussed even if not always categorised. First I will discuss what I regard as the main causes of overemployment and of labour shortages, namely the resource-constrained nature of the socialist system and the applied strategy of economic development.

2 RESOURCE CONSTRAINED SYSTEM AND STRATEGY OF ECONOMIC DEVELOPMENT

J. Kornai believes that the socialist system, primarily the traditional, being resource constrained produces shortages including labour short-ages. Such a system must sooner or later absorb all the people willing to work. The primary mover of this process is the *'expansion drive and closely related almost-insatiable investment hunger'* (1980, p. 260). Shortages are a permanent accompaniment of the system; they cannot *'be eliminated by an increase in supply – as long as the inner regularities of the economy make demand almost-insatiable.* Increased supply is also *finite –* while the demand facing it is always driven by insurmountable inner tendencies towards *infinity'* (1980, p. 264).[1]

J. Kornai's conclusions are, on the whole, correct; however some comments are warranted. In this author's view the same process which brings about full employment and labour shortages leads also to overemployment and low labour discipline. Moreover underutilisation of labour, as mentioned, also produces labour shortages which in turn adversely affect utilisation of labour. Historically overemployment arose first, at the earliest stage of central planning when full employment had not yet fully materialised, whereas evident labour shortages arose only in the 70s (in Czechoslovakia earlier, primarily due to the post-war expulsion of the German population), when the countries achieved very high employment participation rates and were and are exposed to an unfavourable demographic development. (For more see also Adam 1982, pp. 123–9.)

It should be emphasised that the achievement of full employment was not always an automatic process. In Ch. 3 and in Part II it will be shown that in different periods governments undertook various measures aimed at coping with unemployment. (Here it should be mentioned that the investment policy was geared to the needs of employment. Retraining programmes, financed by the government and enterprises, have always been available for workers who lose their jobs.)

Finally the strategy of economic development adopted by the Soviet leaders in the 30s and embraced in the late 40s by East European countries was instrumental in the introduction of the resource con-strained system. If it had not been for the chosen strategy, who knows whether a resource-constrained system would ever have been introduced in the way it exists nowadays. The Soviet leaders resorted to it in the belief that only this system could help to fulfil their ambitious industrialisation plans. Had the economy been left to the working of the market mechanism, fast industrialisation in the structure desired (preferantial development of heavy industry) would not have ma-terialised, at least not in such as short period of time. It was no accident that E. Preobrazhenski (1965), who designed the industrialisation model used by Stalin, called for a restraining of the law of value during the industrialisation process in Russia.

This is not to say that if not for the strategy of economic development the Soviet planners would have opted for a demand-constrained system. The adoption of such a system, mainly in its pure form, would have been contrary to the tenets of the Marxist labour movement and would have exposed the economy to recessions, unemployment and inflation, phenomena which the movement pledged itself to eliminate once it seized power.

The process of overemployment started with the expansion drive (combined with the production technique choice as explained in the preceding chapter) in the period of the first medium-term plans. The ambitious industrialisation plans brought about a massive influx of labour into the economy. Many of the newly employed could not be put to the most productive use (Baka 1979), partly because they had first to be trained even for the simplest jobs (a great many of them were peasants who were not familiar with factory work and its rhythm) and partly because tremendous organisational problems arose with the placement of people in suitable jobs. Even if these initial difficulties were gradually overcome, the great army of workers (primarily auxiliary) and administrators continued to grow. The socialist system is not equipped with a mechanism which allows redundant or inadequately used workers to be quickly transferred to other jobs (Kabaj 1960).

The central planners did not mind the great influx of labour. Maximisation of output was their primary goal, but at the same time it brought the planners close to fulfilling their commitment to full employment.

3 POLICY OF LOW WAGES

Such an employment policy in itself could not be favourable for a policy of high wages. The huge influx of labour, mainly unskilled, had an unfavourable effect on productivity growth. Even the effect of the shift of labour from agriculture to industry where productivity is higher could not change this very much. The situation was compounded by the circumstance that, at the same time, many skilled workers left factories for jobs in governmental departments and agencies, and many unqualified housewives, self-employed people and employees of the service sector were recruited (sometimes against their will) for factory work. If, in addition, one considers the planners' obsession with maximum economic growth, reflected in increasing investment ratios and relegation of personal consumption to a residual, it is clear that average wages could only be low relative to *per capita* national income (see also Ch. 4). Increasing military expenditures due to the cold war also worked in this direction. Therefore it is no wonder that in all the countries under review real wages in the period of the first medium-term plans dropped. Even when real wages started to increase in the following FYP periods, a policy of letting wages lag far behind productivity has been followed as a matter of principle. Departures from this policy came about in periods of high political tension or their aftermath or in periods of economic reforms. For more see Ch. 12.

The policy of low wages (I call this the phenomenon of low wages regardless of whether or not it was a deliberate policy) contributed to an expansion of employment, mainly female, beyond the real needs of the economy. It exerted pressure on people to take jobs, since only by taking jobs could the standard of living substantially increase. In many middle-class families, which before the war had made a decent living from one employment income, the housewife was now forced to take a job to supplement the family budget.

B. Fick (1970, pp. 80–1) maintains that there is a close relationship between the dynamics of real wages and female employment. In 1956–60 when real wages grew fast (29.1 per cent for the whole period) female employment increased by 17 per cent, whereas in 1961–5 when real wages rose only by 8 per cent, female employment increased by 31 per cent. In 1955–60 female employment as a percentage of total employment rose to 34 per cent from 33.3 per cent, and in 1961–5 to 36.9 per cent.

B. Fick is not oblivious to the known experience that increases in the wages of breadwinners cannot stop the growth process of the female participation rate for ever. There is, namely, no absolute limit for satiation; even if consumption reaches a relatively high level, new needs can make taking a job attractive to housewives. Nowadays housewives are no longer inhibited by conventional considerations from taking a job. Increases in real wages may, however, slow down the increase in the female participation rate.

The policy of low wages which has served to mobilize women into jobs has turned out to be a two-edged sword, as it has also provided the impetus for pressuring the authorities into creating job opportunities often simply for social reasons, a fact which has frequently contributed to a surpassing of employment limits (Kruczkowska 1979, p. 148) and to overemployment. The pressure was all the more successful because enterprises did not resist employment expansion.

The policy of low wages contributed to investment overstrain and had an adverse effect on spatial allocation of investment projects. In order to satisfy the local demand for employment, plants were often established, even though non-utilised capacities for the same products existed in other regions. The principle gained ground to a great extent that investment has to be mechanically channelled into areas where people desire to work (Sucharda 1967, p. 99). The desire to satisfy social employment was one of the main reasons why inefficient plants, sometimes even plants which produced unsaleable products, continued to operate.

There is a two-sided interrelationship between the policy of low wages and employment. Expansion of employment, mainly if it is in excess of the plan limit, strengthens the policy of low wages. The global wage-fund is usually not adjusted fully to the rate of employment increase resulting from exceeding plan limits, and therefore part of the wages for new employees is taken from the funds earmarked for wage increases (Fick 1970, p. 95; Tomášek 1967, p. 13). This policy is due to the inflexibility in planning consumer goods and the desire to avoid a disequilibrium in the market for consumer goods. In turn the resulting low increases in wages stimulate pressure for an expansion of employment. B. Fick (1970, p. 21) talks about an employment wage-bill spiral, the activity of which results in weakening the dynamics of wage increases.

The policy of low wages also contributed to an excessive narrowing of wage differentials. (It is excessive in the sense that such wage differentials do not act as a sufficient incentive.) Under conditions of low wages, especially if at the same time there is a justifiable desire to improve the lot of low-income groups, the only way to do so is at the expense of better-paid income groups.

Low average wages combined with narrow wage differentials act as a disincentive to increases in qualifications and productivity and are one of the inducements to managers to solve the problem of fulfilling higher output targets by expanding employment.

4 POLICY OF LOW WAGES AND SUBSTITUTION OF CAPITAL FOR LABOUR

The policy of low wages has also had an adverse effect on the substitution of capital for labour. Low wages are the main reason that labour is inexpensive compared to prices of machinery in East European countries,[2] and therefore enterprises are not very interested in striving for an improvement in the methods of production by substituting mechanisation for labour-intensive methods. This was evident, primarily after the start of the economic reforms of the second half of the 60s when enterprises received greater authority over investment decisions. This is not to say – as is usually believed – that before the economic reforms cheap labour had no impact at all on the substitution of capital for labour. Had enterprises been materially interested in such substitution, a little progress could have been made, since, even before the reforms, some funds for minor investments were at their disposal. East European countries, along with the adoption of the Soviet system of management, had introduced a Soviet-type Director's fund (later called the enterprise fund), part of which could be used to finance the introduction of new techniques and modernisation (Sielunin 1971, pp. 102–3).

Most East European economists agree that the cheapness of labour has a negative impact on substitution of capital for labour. But many of them, for ideological or other reasons, do not like the idea of linking the aversion of enterprises to substitution with a policy of low wages. They rather stress the fact that enterprises do not pay all the costs of the 'reproduction of the labour force', and that, in the microeconomic calculation of labour costs, many costs are omitted or only partly accounted for (Kabaj 1977, p. 62, and 1975; Sipos 1980; Kalinová 1979, p. 28; Pick 1980). The classical case in point is the cost of education most of which is borne by the state budget; mention should also be made of health care, old-age pensions, etc., paid from state funds. There are also labour costs borne by enterprises which are not fully included in the production costs.

No doubt the underestimation of labour costs because of the neglect of social costs as explained above makes substitution less attractive. On the other hand it should not be forgotten that neither are all labour costs – as indirectly explained above – included in the costs of products in the West; nevertheless there is a strong tendency to substitution. The different approach in the West and East to substitution is no doubt, to a great degree, due to the different level of wages.

Regardless of the reasons for the reluctance of enterprises to substitute capital for labour, once such a reluctance exists (and this is generally admitted) it necessarily feeds the demand for labour.

5   MANAGERS' INSUFFICIENT INTEREST IN LABOUR ECONOMY
(Reasons for labour hoarding and thus for overemployment)

The insufficient interest has its origin in many factors, which have a common denominator in the system of management, more precisely in the way targets are assigned to enterprises, and wages and bonuses are determined and regulated, a process which affects directly or indirectly the pecuniary interests of managers.

Due to lack of reliable data for the setting of output targets for enterprises, supervising authorities in the traditional system use a very simple method. The performance of the current year serves as a basis for setting targets for the next year. Since authorities believe that enterprises have some reserves in productivity, the new targets are supposed to be taut compared to the performance in the current year. Yet enterprises know exactly the authorities' approach; they therefore try hard not to be deprived of reserves. Under such conditions enterprises cannot be sufficiently interested in labour economy. Should they in one year practise such a policy they may be penalised in the next year by the planner's imposition of targets which cannot be met.

In the bargaining process with central planners enterprises have an advantage with regard to employment. If they insist on their inability to fulfil assigned productivity targets and thus the output targets without allocation of further labour, the authorities will be confronted with the choice of reducing output targets or increasing employment. If there are no great shortages of labour the authorities will opt for the second alternative. A decrease in output targets may reduce the chance of meeting targets within the branch for which the supervising authorities are responsible, and, in addition, may affect the output of other enterprises, while an increase in employment means only a recruitment of more labour which may be readily available.

Even in a decentralised system where the enterprises are not assigned plan targets their performance is evaluated by net indicators; therefore they are interested in having labour reserves which enable them to increase their performance from year to year without being entirely dependent on productivity increases.

Regardless of the system of management, enterprises are interested in having enough labour to fulfil and overfulfil annual plans (in Hungary the enterprises' own plans are meant), even if increases in the plan targets may occur during the year. In all three countries the fear that a shortage of labour may deprive the personnel of bonuses is a strong stimulus for hoarding in enterprises.

Uneven spread of the workload during the year due to disruptions in the supply of materials and/or shortcomings in planning is another reason for hoarding. Usually at the beginning of any year or month, economic activities are slow, while at the end of the year and month enterprises try to catch up with the plan targets through increased activity ('storming'). Such a work rhythm provides a strong incentive for not allowing employment to drop much below the needs of the period of peak activities. Even in Hungary, where output targets are not assigned, enterprises behave in the same way (Munkácsy 1978).

Up to now I have discussed the impact of the assignment of output targets to enterprises. It should be added that the assigning of employment limits in itself, which amounts to labour rationing, also contributes to hoarding. Enterprises react to such a provision as consumers react to goods rationing.

A further factor contributing to labour hoarding is the government practice of obliging enterprises to make workers available for various special labour 'brigades'. Though these are mostly brigades for short-term seasonal work in agriculture, they are also used in mining and construction (usually for a longer period), in brief, in sectors of production where normal recruiting remains below the plan target.

6 THE EFFECTS OF WAGE REGULATION AND INCENTIVE SYSTEMS
(Further reasons for labour hoarding)

In a centralised system, such as Czechoslovakia has, overfulfilment of output targets motivated by the wage regulation system provides such an incentive for labour hoarding. In such a system the actual wage-bill in profit-making enterprises depends on the extent to which assigned output targets are fulfilled. Overfulfilment of output targets was particularly attractive in the 50s when the actual wage-bill was permitted to exceed the planned one in exact proportion to the percentage of overfulfilment. Even with the less than proportionate adjustment now in effect, many enterprises still find it materially advantageous to overfulfil output targets. When overfulfilment can be achieved through better organisation, improved production techniques, juggling the wage regulator, etc., the wage-bill can be increased by more than the additional costs involved. Often the possibility of overfulfilment depends on the availability of labour reserves – hence the stimulus to hoard labour. Moreover overfulfilment of the output plan legitimises the exceeding of employment limits.

Labour hoarding can also be encouraged by setting a ceiling for average wage growth or levying a tax on the growth of average wages. Regardless of the reason for the ceiling or taxation, enterprises will try to circumvent it by hiring new workers who can be paid wages below average. In the case of a ceiling such behaviour is usually motivated by the desire of management to have funds for raises for certain experts, who would otherwise look for jobs in other enterprises. Even a decentralised system, as Hungarian experience from 1968 to 1971 shows, is not immune from such hoarding (for more see p. 152).

Setting wage ceilings for individual workers, a practice which has been applied in all three countries, particularly if their remuneration is based on piece rates, may have a similar effect. A ceiling dampens increases in productivity, and this is, in turn, translated into a need for more workers.

The incentive system can also be an inducement to hoard labour. Whenever bonuses are linked to a target which can be achieved more easily by expanding employment, and when enterprises are not under sufficient pressure to be concerned with economic efficiency, there is a tendency to go this route. Linkage of bonuses to quality of products, which is nowadays a common indicator in Czechoslovakia and the USSR, and was in the past in Poland, may have such an effect. Since changes in technology take place slowly and their introduction may frequently endanger the fulfilment of the plan targets, the most convenient way to achieve improvements in quality of products is through hiring more labour. Even profit as an indicator can act in such a direction, provided the indicator is the amount of profit which can be expanded by more labour.

The way wage-rates are determined and changed may also be a reason for overemployment. In all three countries wage-rates as well as basic salaries were and are set by the centre. With the exception of Hungary since the 70s, wage-rates and basic salaries have changed only after long intervals. The prolonged rigidity of wage-rates means that their share in average wages declines between two adjustments. The difference is bridged by slackening performance norms in the case of piece-rate workers and by introducing supplementary bonuses for time-rate workers. The slackening of performance norms leads in the final analysis to an increased demand for labour. The same can be said of piece rates if they are combined with performance norms, which can be, for whatever reason, easy to fulfil; in such a case workers resent mechanisation, and this contributes to higher employment (Fick 1970, p. 154).

If the level of enterprise employment is an important factor in determining managers' basic salaries and/or bonuses, there is a further reason to hoard labour. The closer the actual size of an enterprise to the next larger size of employment classification, the stronger the stimulus for hoarding. In all three countries earnings of top managers depend on the size of enterprise they manage as measured by value of output and total employment as well as on its economic importance. Salary differentials stemming from these factors are quite substantial in Hungary. Since the size of bonuses is usually set as a percentage of basic salaries, the level of employment also influences bonuses and total earnings (Szávai 1979). Similar arrangements exist in Poland (Jacukowicz 1974, p. 63) and in Czechoslovakia (Pokorná 1979). Like their colleagues in the West, East European managers are interested in maximising economic growth in the enterprises entrusted to their management for reasons of social status and prestige as well as for pecuniary benefits (Zelko 1976).

7   UNDERUTILISATION OF QUALIFICATIONS

Rational employment presupposes a full utilisation of qualifications of professionals as well as those of skilled workers. This requires matching the qualifications of the job-holders with the qualifications required for the jobs. It also requires that the job-holders predominantly perform work which is proper to their qualifications, and do not engage in work which could be done by persons with lower qualifications.

The first requirement was not much respected in the aftermath of the seizure of power by the communists; rather they were concerned with the consolidation of their power and with the establishment and strengthening of what they call 'the dictatorship of the proletariat'. In the Marxist tradition the building of a new revolutionary system called for the destruction of the old state apparatus. In practice this meant replacing old political institutions with new ones, rebuilding the repressive apparatus into a force which would serve the new regime, purging the state administrative apparatus of real or assumed political foes, and filling important positions with persons who were faithful to the new system. In the implementation of these principles thousands and tens of thousands of highly qualified and experienced professionals in government departments, local governments, the economy, universities, etc., were dismissed. Their positions were frequently given to people who had only one asset – willingness to follow Party instructions faithfully. Many jobs requiring university education were filled by people who often had only elementary schooling. Opponents of the regime with non-technical education were exposed to the harshest treatment; in the universities many professors, primarily of social sciences where ideology plays a great role, were dismissed. Many intellectuals were put to manual work; in the vicinity of Prague there is a permanent witness to this policy – a bridge built by lawyers, called popularly the bridge of intellectuals. The known Chinese slogan 'redness instead of expertness' triumphed in all the countries, and perhaps most of all in Czechoslovakia, where the party had a great following among the intelligentsia and therefore believed that it could afford to treat its opponents harshly.

Of interest is the finding that even in the 60s most of the top managers of enterprises in Czechoslovakia had no university background. In Czechoslovakia in 1966 only 29.2 per cent of all the directors of enterprises and plants and their deputies had university education.[3] Since, in the nomination of directors, political considerations played a much greater role than in the case of their deputies, it can be assumed that a much smaller percentage of directors had a university education. In Poland the situation was apparently better; in 1968 51.8 per cent of directors and 70.4 per cent of their technical deputies had university education.

The purge of the state and economic apparatus was not confined to the period of seizure of power by the communists. Whenever cuts in the number of white-collar workers were made, but primarily in the 50s and 60s, they were used to eliminate 'unreliable' elements. A tremendous waste of expertise and talent was experienced. Since many sophisticated jobs were performed by people with no proper qualifications, quantity had to compensate for quality. One reason for the fast-growing white-collar category of workers lies in just what is called in Eastern Europe 'cadre policy' as described above.

In the 60s and 70s the matching of the qualifications of job-holders with the qualifications required improved substantially. Jobs have been increasingly filled by qualified candidates, partly because university and high-school education in East European countries has expanded rapidly. The talents of children of certain social groups, which before the war were indirectly discouraged from higher education, have consciously been tapped in new conditions. On the other hand, the application of class criteria for admission to universities for a long time has led to a waste of many talents, mainly among children of the intelligentsia.

Table 2.1 reveals that in the 70s the number of jobs requiring university and high-school education exceeded substantially the number of job-holders with such education. In this respect the situation was the worst in Czechoslovakia, where the demand for workers with university education exceeded the supply by 55 per cent in 1970 and 49 per cent in 1973. In Poland in 1973 the difference was even lower than in Hungary in 1971 (14 per cent against 15 per cent) but in 1977, for unknown reasons (modernisation of industry?), increased to 43 per cent. The figures indicate that jobs requiring university education were filled by people who did not have the necessary qualifications; in Czechoslovakia in 1973 this was the case with 33 per cent of such jobs, in Poland in 1977 with 30 per cent and in Hungary with 13 per cent of the jobs. The differences between the countries were quite large; it seems, however, that the figures have no great comparative value, since it is doubtful that equal criteria

TABLE 2.1 *Matching of qualifications of salaried workers with job requirements*[a]
(in thousands)

	1 — Number of jobs requiring education		2 — Number of persons with education		3 — 1 : 2 in %		4 — Number of persons with university education performing jobs requiring education		5 — Number of persons with high-school education performing jobs requiring education		
	A university	*B high school*	*A university*	*B high school*	*A*	*B*	*university*	*lower*	*university*	*high school*	*lower*
Poland											
1973	698	2472	611	2366	114	104	508	103			
1977	1113	2662	778	2935	143	91	748	30	28	2028	879[b]
CSSR											
1970	422	803[c]	272	683[c]	155	118	239	33	113	466	104[b]
1973	479	893[c]	321	757[c]	149	118					
Hungary January											
1971	205 (112)	863	178 (95)	689	115	125	166 (88)	12 (7)	29 (9)	528	133[e]

[a] The Polish figures refer to the socialist sector, whereas the Czechoslovak and Hungarian refer to the whole economy.
[b] It is clear that they performed blue-collar jobs, but it is not clear to what extent these were unskilled.
[c] Refers only to technical schools, equivalent to a high school.
[d] Numbers in parentheses refer to schools which are between high schools and university.
[e] 83 000 were skilled jobs.

SOURCES Poland   – Spiš . . . 1979, pp. 2, 51, 90, 220, 236, 242, and Kabaj 1977, p. 70.
              Czechoslovakia – Kalinová 1979, pp. 131–4.
              Hungary   – Olajos 1978, p. 104.

were used for determining the qualifications needed for certain jobs, apart from some exceptions.

Table 2.1 also shows that at the same time some holders of university and high-school diplomas did not work in jobs requiring the same level of education. The figures for university graduates were not, however, dramatic.

The figures in the table are aggregate figures and conceal the quite great differences in mismatches among sectors of the economy and among industrial branches. For example in Poland, in 1977, in education 47.6 per cent of jobs reserved for university graduates were filled by persons with lower qualifications. In transport and communications the figure was 43.1 per cent, in industry 21.2 per cent and in health care and social welfare only 5.8 per cent. The best match by professions was found – as one would expect – among physicians and pharmacists (99.8 per cent) and the worst in arts, journalism and education (*Spis* . . . 1979, pp. 236–42, 2–3, 51–3).

With the exception of Poland the data indicated in Table 2.1 refer to the first half of the 70s, and it can be assumed that in the meantime changes have taken place, probably in a positive direction.

Data indicated in Table 2.2 show that some of the skilled workers do not perform jobs for which they have training. No doubt many of them perform white-collar jobs, but it is also known that not a negligible number are performing unskilled jobs (as the indicated Hungarian figures demonstrate), the reason being that they are well paid and have little responsibility attached to them. On the other hand many unskilled workers perform skilled jobs. In Czechoslovakia in 1974 the number of unskilled workers who performed skilled jobs for more than five years reached 17.3 per cent of the whole blue-collar work force (Kalinová 1979, p. 137). This is not to say that unskilled workers who work in certain jobs for more than five years cannot do as good work as skilled workers. However unskilled workers, who in this case can be characterised as semi-skilled, have the disadvantage of not possessing the convertible skills of skilled workers who can, if necessary, or if they want to, work in a related trade without the need of any retraining.

There are only fragmentary data on the way the workday is used by highly qualified professionals. In Poland at the end of the 60s, such a study on engineers found that 20–25 per cent of the working time of engineers was used for work which does not require engineering training. If the time wasted by poor organisation and meetings is added it turns out that 35–6 per cent of working time is lost (Kabaj 1977, p. 73–4). In Hungary studies have shown that only 40–50 per cent of engineers (with

TABLE 2.2 *Matching of qualifications of skilled workers[a] with job requirements*
(in thousands)

	Number of skilled workers	Number of skilled jobs performed by skilled workers	in %	Other jobs performed by skilled workers	
				white-collar	semi-skilled or unskilled
CSSR, 1967	1577	1058	67.1		518
1974	1923	1260	65.5		663
Hungary, January 1971	977.2	699.4	71.6	55.0	222.8

[a] Workers with journeyman certificate.

SOURCES CSSR – L. Kalinová 1979, p. 137.
Hungary – A. Olajos 1978, p. 104.

university education) perform jobs which really require engineering skills (Szikra 1978).

8 UNFAVOURABLE STRUCTURE OF THE LABOUR FORCE

In all three countries the view is widespread that the percentage of white-collar workers in the labour force, because of the excessiveness and overstaffing of managerial and administrative work, is too high. The same is true of auxiliary blue-collar workers, mainly those engaged in handling materials within enterprises (transportation, sorting and shelving). No doubt a reduction in the mentioned categories of workers could ease the problem of labour shortages and improve efficiency.

Figures on the expansion of the white-collar workers are available, though not entirely comparable between countries. As Table 2.3 shows, the ratio of white-collar workers to the labour force grew dramatically. But this is a general phenomenon. Some economists maintain that this ratio is a reflection of the level of economic development, and that in advanced capitalist countries which have achieved a higher economic development than the socialist countries it is higher (Olajos 1981). This does not mean that systemic differences have no effect at all on the structure of the labour force. No doubt the lower growth of the tertiary sector (a topic discussed in Ch. 12) in the socialist countries than in advanced capitalist countries, a phenomenon which has a systemic association, has had some impact. It is known that this is the sector where white-collar workers are the most strongly represented. Only a special study could answer – if at all – the extent of this impact. Considering the factors which contribute to a smaller percentage of white-collar workers, it is worth while mentioning that some occupations connected with the market mechanism (e.g. such as stock-brokers) do not exist in socialist countries. On the other hand the centralisation of management of the economy contributed to the fast growth of the white-collar labour force, probably more in the past than nowadays (J. Timár 1981, p. 109). The authoritarian nature of the socialist political system, backed up by a sizeable oppressive apparatus, has acted in the same direction.

There are no time series available about the evolution of the managerial and administrative staff. Only recently have the three countries started to publish data on the structure of the white-collar labour force, and only the Czechoslovak and Hungarian figures can be said to be comparable to some extent. From figures listed in Table 2.4 it is

TABLE 2.3 Social structure of economically active population in %

	Poland					CSSR[a]				Hungary				
	1931	1950	1960	1970	1980	1950	1961	1970	1980	1941	1949	1960	1970	1980
Blue-collar workers	25.3	43.9	33.5	39.3	45.9	56.4	56.3	58.2	57.7	54.0	38.8	50.8	57.1	57.8
White-collar workers	4.1		18.2	22.0	24.2	16.4	27.9	26.5	30.9	7.0	8.3	16.0	22.3	27.4
Collective farmers		0.4	0.2	0.2	0.1	0.0	10.6	9.0	8.8	0.0	0.3	12.0	17.4	12.0
Other co-operative producers		1.3	2.3	2.3		0.0	1.2	1.6	0.9					
Private farmers	60.7	52.6	44.0	33.7	23.7	20.3	3.5	1.2	0.3	25.8	42.6	18.7	1.6	1.6
Small private businessmen	9.5	1.6	1.5	1.3	2.3	3.8	0.5	0.1	0.1	8.8	8.1	2.4	1.6	1.2
Capitalists						3.1	0.0	0.0	0.0	4.4	1.9	0.1	0.0	0.0
Rest and unknown	0.4	0.2	0.3	1.2	3.8	0.0	0.0	3.4	1.3					

[a] Refers to the structure of the population by social groups of the chief breadwinners.

SOURCES Poland – Zagorski 1976, p. 282. Figures for 1980 are taken from ZGN 1982, pp. 1–2, and they are not comparable with the other figures.

CSSR – Průcha and Kalinová 1982, p. 37. Figures for 1970 and 1980 come from SRC 1982, p. 96, and they are more or less comparable with other figures.

Hungary – Bálint 1983, p. 29.

TABLE 2.4   *Structure of the white-collar labour force*
(in per cent) [a]

	CSSR		Hungary	
	1977	*1981*	*1970*	*1980*
1. Technicians	31.3	31.8	15.9	20.4
2. Workers in health, culture and education [b]	25.9	27.1	24.0	25.2
3. Workers in science and research	2.4	2.6		
4. Workers in management and administration	40.4	38.5	60.1	54.4
5. In state administration and management			8.1	35.2

[a] The degree of a congruity in classification is not known.
[b] The Hungarian source refers only to health and culture.

SOURCES CSSR   – SRC, 1982, p. 218
Hungary – Bálint 1983, p. 76.

clear that in 1981 the managerial and administrative workers made up 38.5 per cent of the total white-collar labour force in the CSSR and 54.4 per cent in Hungary (in 1980). According to one source 20 per cent of the Polish labour force in 1970 consisted of administrative workers (Zagorski 1976, p. 285). These figures in themselves do not prove that the number of managerial and administrative workers is excessive. There is, however, some evidence to support such an assumption. In all three countries there is a shortage of manual workers[4] and rather an excessive interest in administrative and managerial jobs, though their number has been declining relatively in recent years. Furthermore it is generally accepted that there is plenty of room for cutting down administrative and managerial work by better organisation and more mechanisation.

Research into the role of auxiliary workers within enterprises is hampered by the lack of appropriate figures. True, Czechoslovakia and Hungary have recently started to publish such figures, but again they are only comparable to a small extent due to the use of different classifications. From time to time figures which pop up in economic literature are so different from official figures that it is really difficult to draw any conclusions. One Czechoslovak economist (Kozár 1977) maintained in 1977 that in Czechoslovakia approximately 1.3 million workers were engaged in handling materials (transport, sorting and shelving), whereas the *Statistical Yearbook* mentions 345 000 for 1977. However all economists dealing with this topic agree that the number of auxiliary workers is excessive. An inquiry in 282 Czechoslovak engineering enterprises in 1976 revealed that workers in the basic production processes exceeded the numbers of auxiliary workers by only 23 per cent. 21.3 per cent of the auxiliary workers were directly engaged in handling materials (Votava 1979). According to experts mechanisation of handling of materials which reached only 20–22 per cent in the CSSR (against 80 per cent in the USA and West Germany) and better organisation could release 100 000 workers (Mikeš and Steinich 1975), and thus ease labour shortages.

9   UNDERUTILISATION OF THE POTENTIAL WORK TIME

It is known that all three countries suffer from a gross underutilisation of the potential work-time fund, which results to a great extent from low labour discipline. Some of the time losses, such as full-day absenteeism, can be easily quantified, but others, e.g. losses at the workplace, can only be estimated. Therefore views on the extent of losses differ substantially. For example, in Hungary some put the losses in the range of 10–15 per cent, but more pessimistic authors maintain that they are rather in the range of 20–30 per cent of the potential work time (Hatlacki 1976; J. Timár 1976). Usually the authors are not very specific about what is included in the losses. At any rate the losses are so huge that if they could be reduced by half, a huge army of workers could be gained.

The Polish minister of labour and social affairs claimed that a reduction in absenteeism could mean a labour army of 100 000, and 50 per cent better utilisation of working time in industry alone would mean the output of 180 000–240 000 workers (*ZG 1978*, 10 Dec). In an interview the same minister stated that in industry time lost by workers directly involved in production is 8–10 per cent, whereas for those who service production the loss is in the range of 20–30 per cent (*ZG 1978*, 29 Dec).

Tests in thirty-three industrial and construction enterprises in the CSSR revealed that in 1976 only about 70 per cent of the potential work-time fund was utilised; of the time wasted, 52 per cent was caused by technico-organisational shortcomings, while the remaining 48 per cent was caused by individual workers (Rybovičová 1978).

The causes of these huge losses in working time can be classified in three groups according to whether they are the result of: (1) deficiencies in the planning and organisation of the production process, (2) which can be called lack of discipline at the workplace, (3) legitimate or unauthorised partial or full-day absenteeism.

To a great degree the first two causes are intertwined. Workers, who frequently see that their work is not well organised due to the negligence of their superiors and that they must stand idle for hours because the supply of the material to be processed is not smooth, or because equipment and documentation are missing, etc., do not feel that they violate the moral code if they waste time in a different way (by extending breaks, visiting friends for a chat, leaving the workplace before termination of the shift, etc.).

It will exceed the scope of this study to engage in a detailed discussion of the reasons for the deficiencies in planning and organisation. Suffice it to mention here only some of the reasons. One of the reasons for deficiencies in planning is the taut planning, i.e. the tendency of planners to impose on enterprises very demanding targets which result in a shortage of materials. Deficiencies in organisation result from the lack of a mechanism which would make managers highly attentive to organisational needs. Shortage of organisational experts and lack of strong incentives for the introduction of organisational innovations are surely also to blame for the deficiencies (Penc 1980).

Unauthorised absenteeism is relatively small. In Hungary in 1979 in industry it amounted to a loss of 0.2 per cent of the work-time fund and in construction, where it is the highest, 0.5 per cent. A similar situation existed in Poland; no figures are available for the CSSR. This kind of absenteeism is used for many purposes: e.g. 'peasant workers' use it for performing urgent work at their farm or plot; some use it for moonlighting, and others for running errands.

Unauthorised absenteeism would be much higher if not for the possibility of getting legal leave of absence even with pay for legitimate reasons or under false pretences. These losses in working time are quite large and result partly from the abuse of sickness insurance. Statistical figures for Poland and Hungary show that the number of people incapacitated by sickness and accidents has increased substantially since 1960. In that year in all three countries it was almost the same: in Poland 4.0 per cent (referring only to those employed in industry), in Czechoslovakia 4.03 per cent and in Hungary 4.05 per cent of all employed. In Poland in the following years, apart from some fluctuations, the figure steadily increased and in 1978 reached 7.0 per cent and in 1981 8.1 per cent. In Hungary the number collecting sickness benefits (which is equal to the number of sick) reached 6.1 per cent in 1975 and 5.9 per cent in 1982 of all employed. In Czechoslovakia no great changes have occurred.

These relatively huge increases in the number of sick people indicate that sickness insurance is partially used to cover up unjustifiable absenteeism. Perhaps the best proof of this assumption is the following interesting fact from Hungary: when the government introduced in 1975 some provisions to curtail abuses in sickness insurance, the decline in the incidence of reported sickness was accompanied by an increase in the number of other justified or non-justified absences (Somogyi 1978).

10 LABOUR TURNOVER

In discussing the factors which lead to underutilisation of labour one cannot ignore the impact of labour turnover. It should be stated right away that this factor was given much greater attention in the past than it deserved. Few topics were as confused – to a great extent intentionally – as this one. Many of the problems plaguing the economy were blamed on labour turnover which was portrayed onesidedly, as if it were only a liability, disregarding the fact that it is also a precondition for structural changes in the economy. This approach apparently resulted from the authorities' preference for having everyone stay in his job, with changes in jobs (except for health, marriage reasons, etc.) limited to those in accordance with the needs of the economy as determined by the planners.

Only at some time in the 60s did economists start to distinguish between useful and harmful labour turnover on a macroeconomic and microeconomic level. On the macroeconomic level every job change which furthers needed structural changes in the economy is regarded as useful. Venyige (1975, p. 155) regards as harmful labour turnover which 'in size and direction deviates from the socially necessary . . . '. In an enterprise labour turnover which does not serve its interest may be regarded as harmful even if it is useful from a macroeconomic viewpoint.

Harmful turnover is so termed since it involves social cost in terms of lost working time, qualifications and funds, and runs against the trend in structural changes. The performance of workers who make up their minds to look for new jobs usually declines in the last month and is lower for some time in the new workplaces too. In the transition period between old and new jobs several working days or even weeks may be lost. If, in addition, the worker changes not only his workplace but also his occupation, then investment in skills may be lost and new funds must be spent for his retraining.

In practice it is very difficult to draw the line between useful and harmful labour turnover. Nevertheless, some fractional figures exist. A Polish economist maintains that in 1975 the incidence of harmful turnover corresponded to 6–7 per cent of the total labour force (20 per cent of all job changes) (Penc 1977). It seems that Czechoslovak figures in 1976–9 were higher; for four ministries the available figures were in the range of 6.3–13.8 per cent (Bobošiková 1981).

11   FULL EMPLOYMENT AND OVEREMPLOYMENT

The implementation of the commitment to full employment (FE) in socialist countries was not without cost to the economy. Once the policy of FE is adopted and put into effect, it is only natural that employment considerations often get priority over economic efficiency and that job opportunities are frequently created for social reasons. (After all public works carried out during recessions in capitalist countries are also governed more by employment considerations than by economic efficiency.) Such an approach seems justifiable as long as it remains within tolerable limits; unemployment with its moral and psychological, not to say economic, hardships, is also costly to society and may cost even more than the restoration or maintenance of FE.

It is also natural that under conditions of FE policy the authorities cannot easily relocate workers according to the needs of the economy and enforce labour discipline. If one considers in addition that the resource constrained system and the system of management stimulate various phenomena of underutilisation of labour, then it is clear why full employment in the countries under review is accompanied by overemployment, labour hoarding, labour shortages and low labour discipline.

This does not mean that the FE policy in itself must necessarily lead to all the adverse phenomena mentioned; one can argue that the conditions under which it was put into effect including the political system and the way the principle was implemented are more to blame for them. The low level of labour discipline is a case in point. The difficulties in enforcing labour discipline in socialist countries result not so much from the FE policy as from the nature of the political system. If the system were based to a greater degree on the consensus of the population, the authorities could enforce more labour discipline, since they would not have to be afraid that unpopular measures could endanger the regime.

12 CONCLUDING REMARKS

I have indicated various kinds of phenomena which generate underutilisation of labour and thus overemployment. No doubt overemployment is an important factor of labour shortages and so is the slow level of mechanisation of manual work. This does not mean, however, that should the authorities manage to ease overemployment (it is deeply entrenched in the system and therefore to expect its complete elimination would be unrealistic) labour shortages will be eliminated. Labour shortages in some sectors are caused by unpleasant working conditions there (mining, construction) and may not attract labour to a sufficient extent as long as other job opportunities are available. But they are also caused by discrepancies between the structure of the labour force and the requirements of the economy. Finally the unfavourable demographic development has also played an important role. Easing of overemployment does not mean that the countries are threatened by unemployment. Primarily in the service sector, which has been long neglected, enormous job opportunities can be created. In addition potential unemployment could be mitigated by shortening the workweek.

3 Methods of Planning and Regulating Employment

A PLANNING OF EMPLOYMENT

In the effort to make employment policy a reality two instruments are used: the planning and the regulation of employment. The purpose of planning is to set aims within the bounds of employment policy, whereas the purpose of regulation is to ensure that the plans will be achieved by using also other methods than planning. The examination starts with planning on the macroeconomic level; planning for and in the microsphere is discussed in the framework of employment regulation.

Employment is planned with the help of manpower balances which mean nothing else than balancing demand for and supply of labour. In addition to differences in terminology there are some differences in the way balances are compiled and classified in the three countries; what they have in common is that they compile aggregate balances and special balances. The first are balances affecting the whole country and as such are an integral part of supreme national economic balances and the second cover some aspects of the aggregate balances (sectoral, industrial, regional, the demand for and supply of labour skills, etc.). From the vantage-point of their occurrence we distinguish statistical and planned manpower balances. Aggregate balances of manpower resources in their statistical form refer to certain actual processes in the past and the present. They indicate the evolution of labour resources (changes in the number of the working-age population as well as in the number of working retirees) and their utilisation, broken down by sectors of the economy. The number of economically active is usually smaller than the manpower resources; therefore the balances also give an account of the position of the rest of the resources. Finally, manpower resources are related to the population size, broken down by age groups, from the viewpoint of possible economic activity.

Of the same importance are so-called balances of needs and resources

41

of manpower. If they are planned their purpose is to balance the demand for new workers with the potential supply. In compiling these balances the planners must also consider on the demand side the replacement for people who may pass away during the planned period, for the number of people who may retire and also for those who may quit for other reasons – health, etc. On the supply side the potential number of youngsters joining the labour force for the first time and the number of housewives and retirees who may be attracted into the labour force and placed must be projected. If the balances are broken down by sectors, the number of 'drifters'[1] must be considered on the demand side as well as on the supply side. (For more see J. Timár, 1981, pp. 200–2; Kováčová 1980, pp. 187–211; Vais 1981, pp. 242–5).

Needless to say, the planned balances can be designed for planning periods of different duration: for one year, five years or even longer. Of course, the longer the planned period the greater the probability that the reality will deviate from the envisaged targets. On the other hand, balances for a longer time, say five years, can incorporate tasks (for which annual ones are not suitable) such as balance of skilled workers (including their training).

Of great importance in the manpower planning process is the planning of education and training of professionals and skilled workers. Since the training of some professionals lasts 5–6 years, planners must have a good idea about the future development of the economy and its structure. Finally mention should be made that the planners also compile plans of recruitment and distribution of labour.

Planned manpower balances are drawn, *inter alia*, on the basis of the following information: statistical manpower balances, demographic forecasts and data about employment obtained from ministries and enterprises (Olędzki 1978, p. 227). The achievement of the planned targets for employment depends among other things on the fulfilment of plan targets in other areas (productivity growth, recruitment, training, relocation of workers, etc.), on the accuracy of demographic forecasts and the expected reaction of people still outside the labour force. Thus the translation of planned manpower balances into practice requires that both sides of the balances, the demand and the supply of labour, be correctly estimated.

B   REGULATION OF EMPLOYMENT

It refers to the regulation of labour demand (meaning the number of persons employable in enterprises) and also to labour supply.

1   Regulation of Labour Demand

Socialist countries, regardless of their management system, are reluctant to leave the evolution of employment in enterprises to the decisions of enterprises themselves. In the traditional Soviet system the planners endeavour to have all important factors of production under control, and employment is no doubt one of them. This is all the more important because there is no guarantee that enterprises will voluntarily follow the objectives of the planners with regard to employment, the main reason being – as has been shown in Ch. 2 – that the objectives of the central planners and the interests of enterprises frequently clash, and that the later have a tendency to maximise employment. One would expect that in a decentralised system managers would be given the right to make decisions about employment according to their own considerations in the hope that market forces would induce them to behave rationally. To expect such behaviour is realistic only if the financial position of enterprises is fully dependent on their performance. No socialist country, not even Czechoslovakia and Hungary, has ever reached such a stage of decentralisation. And this is the reason why a decentralised system also tries to regulate employment.

The two systems differ, however, in the methods they apply in their attempts to regulate employment in general and demand for labour in particular. In a centralised system the emphasis is on direct methods whereas a decentralised system stresses indirect methods. Under certain conditions the centralised system may resort to indirect methods and the decentralised to direct ones. Yet the application of direct methods in a decentralised system (mainly assignments of employment limits) would sooner or later become an obstacle to the functioning of the system. It is therefore no accident that the Czechoslovak and Hungarian reforms in the second half of the 60s brought to an end to the assignment of employment limits to enterprises. Even the Polish reform of 1973, which brought about some elements of decentralisation, resorted to such a measure, and the same is true of the reform of 1982.

(a)   *Regulation of labour demand in a centralised system*

In a centralised system enterprises are assigned a labour plan which traditionally has been composed at least of the following four targets: number of employed, growth of labour productivity, of average wage and of wage-bill. The number of employed has been broken down into at least three groups – wage-earners, engineering technical personnel (ETP) and administrative and clerical personnel (ACP).

This does not mean that a centralised system must necessarily be combined with all four targets. Nowadays average wage is no longer a target assigned from the centre; it is, however, still a component of the enterprises' plan which must be approved by supervisory authorities. In the USSR, in the aftermath of the economic reform of 1965, enterprises were for some time assigned only one of the mentioned four targets, namely the wage-bill. The Soviet planners believed they could control employment indirectly through the regulation of the wage-bill. As soon as the labour market became tight, employment limits were reintroduced (Adam 1973).

The planned wage-bill of enterprises is a product of the planned number of employed and the planned average wage. The planning of both factors has essentially been a planning of the rate of change over the previous year, which means a consideration of all the factors that have an influence on the number of employed and the average wage of workers in an enterprise. In the case of the former, and confining the discussion to production workers, this meant – to put it generally – calculating the impact of the changes in the output target on the required labour input including requisite changes in skill mix, at the same time giving proper consideration to the expected changes in labour productivity.

At first glance it seems that establishing the amount of labour required for the production of a certain product mix is a simple process, and, therefore, so must be the setting of employment limits. In reality this is not so. In the case of production workers their number depends on output targets, the labour intensity of the product mix and their work-time fund. The crux of the problem is to calculate correct norms for labour intensity of different products. For lack of information this job cannot be done properly by central planners. What the central planners can do and did is to issue instructions to enterprises how to calculate norms of labour intensity and the work-time fund of workers. In addition these calculations which must be done on special forms are scrutinised by supervisory authorities (Černy and Rufert 1970, pp. 45–7).

Apart from production workers, enterprises need maintenance workers, auxiliary workers and, of course, technical-engineering and administrative personnel. To determine how many of the latter are required is, with some exceptions, even more difficult than in the case of production workers.

It is thus obvious that limits for employment assigned to enterprises must be and are based on information supplied by enterprises themselves. But for reasons already mentioned enterprises are not eager to forward correct information, and even if they wanted to do so, they would encounter difficulties. Calculation of the norms of labour intensity can be successful only if the co-operation of blue-collar workers is assured. Yet tight norms of labour intensity are contrary to the interests of workers; there is namely a close relationship between the norms of labour intensity and work (performance) norms which constitute the basis for remuneration by piece-rates. In setting the labour intensity norms for a certain product the earnings of the workers producing this product are to a large extent determined, provided the wage rates are given.

The limits for employment are set in the light of the planned product mix. In practice the product mix is frequently changed by the planners during the planning period. If one considers that enterprises have always had some leeway in determining the detailed product mix it becomes even clearer that setting adequate limits for employment is an almost unaccomplishable task.

Despite assigning employment limits to enterprises – partly because of it – employment growth frequently deviates from the objectives of the plans. In addition the socialist economies suffer from various diseases – the reasons for which have been discussed in Ch. 2 – such as labour hoarding, underutilisation of labour, imbalances in employment structures which under certain conditions culminate in labour shortages and also excessive turnover. To cope with these phenomena the socialist countries use additional direct methods as well as some indirect ones.

Among the direct methods, apart from those already indicated, mention should be made of freezes on hiring, quota systems and orders for reducing the labour force. These methods are primarily applied to white-collar workers. Compulsory placing is another direct method which is applied primarily to blue-collar workers and certain groups of white-collar workers. It may refer to both enterprises and workers which means that enterprises are allowed to hire workers only with the approval of the labour department of national councils or must hire workers who are assigned to them (this is the less frequent case).

As to indirect methods, I have in mind primarily incentives for labour economy which may be built into the wage regulation or incentive system or may be simply their by-product.

(b) *Regulation of employment in a decentralised system*

The indirect methods which are going to be discussed can be used individually or in combination. Their usage depends to an extent on the degree of decentralisation. In a decentralised system where the wage-bill of an enterprise fully depends on its performance the most suitable indirect employment regulation seems to be taxation, a method applied in Czechoslovakia in 1966–9 (Adam 1979, p. 69). Yet in a decentralised system where the size of the wage-bill is determined by normatives the planners may forgo a special regulation of employment in the hope that normatives may also have a restraining effect on employment growth.

(i) *Taxation as a regulator of employment*   Regulation of employment with the help of taxation means levying a tax on increases in employment and granting a tax credit for a reduction in employment. The aim of this method can be twofold: to discourage enterprises from excessive employment expansion (tax payment) and at the same time encourage labour-saving (tax credit). Historically this method has been used primarily for the first purpose.

Regulation by taxation may be successful if two preconditions can be met. First, tax payment or credit must palpably affect the financial situation of enterprises. If this is not the case because the tax is very small or because enterprises are not forced to watch their finances (due to the possibility of juggling prices and/or to access to government subsidies or for other reasons) the taxation method is useless. Therefore regulation of employment by taxation makes sense only in a system where the financial situation of enterprises depends more or less on their own performance and where enterprises are allowed to use after tax profit according to their own consideration. The Hungarian authorities (and more recently the Polish ones) have aspired to make enterprises self-financed, but have not yet reached their goal.

Second, a reasonable compromise between the uniform application of taxation and its adjustment to the special conditions of individual enterprises must be found. The underlying philosophy of a decentralised system is uniformity; only under conditions where all units are treated equitably it is possible to avoid bureaucratic arbitrariness from the centre. Enterprises, however, differ in many respects, including their employment situation; some have cumulated labour reserves, others, due to output stagnation, do not intend to expand employment, still others have a great demand for labour in consequence of rapid growth possibilities. Thus a uniform tax rate throughout the economy may hurt the economy. In addition it would not make great sense to apply a tax to new enterprises. Finally, a policy of a uniform tax may also run contrary to efforts to make structural changes in the economy. A differentiated tax rate or its complete elimination may be an incentive for developing backward regions and for easing employment of handicapped people. In brief, there are good reasons for differentiated taxation. Yet there are also good reasons to doubt the ability of the central planners to estimate correctly the needed differentiation. It is namely easier to apply taxation differentially for the purpose of wage regulation than for employment regulation.

Therefore taxation, though it may seem theoretically a very viable tool for employment regulation, has many problems connected with it, as its practical application in Czechoslovakia from 1966 to 1969 showed. This may be one reason why the Hungarians have shied away from it.

(ii) *Regulation of employment by wage regulation*   Another method is to design the wage-regulation and incentive systems so that they indirectly act as a stimulus to labour economy. To design wage regulation in the way mentioned requires careful consideration of what to regulate. As is known, wages at the enterprise level can be regulated by controlling average wages or the wage-bill. Generally speaking, it can be argued that wage-bill regulation is more conducive to labour economy. Average wage regulation by definition makes enterprises indifferent to the size of employment; it may be an outright stimulus to labour hoarding; hiring less-qualified or part-time workers enables greater wage raises to be granted to workers already on the payroll. On the other hand, wage-bill regulation makes managers interested in the number of employed since maximisation of *per capita* incomes can be achieved by saving labour.

Whether average wage and wage-bill regulation acts in the way mentioned depends on many factors, primarily on the nature of the system of economic management and wage growth regulator. Wage-bill regulation in a centralised system – as historical experience shows – has usually encouraged expansion of employment beyond economic rationality. (See Ch. 2.) On the other hand, average wage regulation, if tied, for example, to a labour productivity indicator whose numerator is computed from net output, may encourage labour saving under certain conditions.

Wage regulation is used not only for employment regulation, but for other purposes too. In Ch. 5 this topic is discussed in greater detail; here only mention should be made that wage regulation is used to ensure market equilibrium for consumer goods and for a desired wage differentiation. Pursuing these objectives may require provisions in the wage-regulation system which are contrary to the objective of employment regulation. And this is why it is so difficult to design a wage-regulation system which is geared to a rational employment policy.

The stimulative potentiality of wage-bill regulation lies in enterprises having the right to determine to what extent average wages can be increased as a result of labour-saving. If an increase in average wages is prevented by some provision – in Hungary this was done for some time with the help of highly progressive taxation – then wage-bill regulation becomes an ineffective instrument for economising on labour. Recently, in an effort to increase labour productivity, Czechoslovakia and Hungary introduced new incentives for labour-saving despite the fear that such incentives might upset interenterprise wage differentials and might add to inflationary pressure.

Nowadays the bonus fund in all three countries is separate from the wage-bill and its size is dependent on the amount of realised profit. If enterprises can be made interested in maximising profit through increasing economic efficiency then it can be expected that they will also be motivated to economise on labour. Yet experience shows that even a decentralised system cannot always make enterprises follow the mentioned pattern of profit maximisation.

(iii) *Regulation of employment by increasing labour cost*   It has already been stated that labour is cheap in socialist countries and for this reason enterprises are not interested in the substitution of capital for labour, but rather in hoarding labour. To reverse this situation an increase in labour cost relative to cost of capital is needed. An increase in wages would be the simplest way to raise labour cost, but this is not a viable solution. Labour cost to enterprises can also be increased by levying a tax on the wage-bill and/or by increasing the social security contribution paid by enterprises. The weight of labour cost can also be increased by reducing the cost of labour-saving equipment in relation to labour cost.

The method of regulating employment by increasing labour cost is related to the method of employment regulation by taxation (limited to tax payment). Both of them increase labour cost, though in the second case we can imagine a solution which may not be reflected in cost per unit of production (e.g. if the tax is paid from profit). The difference between the two methods is that a tax on the wage-bill and/or increase in the social security contribution refers only to labour which is already on the payroll, whereas the tax on employment increase means an increase in the cost of newly hired manpower (but indirectly affects the total labour cost). The purpose of the first method is to induce enterprises to reduce their work force, whereas the second is to discourage enterprises from expanding employment. A combination of both may have a stronger effect on labour economy.

Since labour cost in the socialist enterprises is substantially under-estimated compared to prices of machinery, increases in labour cost must be large in order to have an effect on substitution of capital for labour. One could also argue that increases in labour cost must be large because they are on the average only a small percentage of the production costs.

2   Regulation of Labour Supply

Socialist countries are also trying to influence labour supply which seems to be easier to regulate than labour demand. The latter's success depends on managers of enterprises who, in making decisions about employment, are responding to many conflicting impulses and incent-ives. Incentives pertaining to labour supply are directed to potential workers whose interests can be addressed more effectively; therefore their response is more predictable. This difference explains why in regulation of labour supply systemic distinctions make no great difference in the methods used; most methods can be used in a centralised or a decentralised system which is not the case with regard to the regulation of labour demand as has already been demonstrated.

It is necessary to distinguish between methods which may produce a relatively quick response and methods whose effect can be felt only after a long period of time. The first group includes such methods as changes in the provisions for work at pensionable age, changes in benefits during prolonged maternity leaves, retraining programmes, and, in certain sense, expansion of the private sector. The second group includes primarily pronatal provisions, training and schooling. My focus will be on the first group.

(a) *Pension payments for work at pensionable age*

Changes in the provisions for work at pensionable age are the most important tool in the first group. In Czechoslovakia and Hungary the retirement age since the 50s has been 60 for males and 55 for females. One can only speculate why the retirement age has been set so low. Probably the desire to make achievement of full employment easier – an important objective of socialist countries – has played a significant role. It is conceivable that a low retirement age has been set with the consideration in mind of having an instrument for regulating the labour supply. Whatever the reason may have been, the planners have acquired a relatively flexible method for regulating the economic activity of persons in their early sixties or mid-fifties. It is not difficult to motivate people of this age to continue to work at least part-time if appropriate incentives are used. Needless to say, they can be applied selectively; they can be directed to certain occupations, to work in certain sectors of the economy or even in certain enterprises according to the needs of the economy. If a need arises administrative provisions or incentives can be used to reduce the activity of retirees and thus alleviate a possible threat of unemployment.

In Poland the official retirement age is still 65 (for males) and 60 (for females) with some exceptions. There it is possible to regulate labour supply in particular by dropping the retirement age for certain groups of workers or in certain periods.

In the desire to influence the economic activity of pensionable-age persons two factors are decisive: the level of pensions and the extent of the cut in pensions if persons of pensionable age continue to work.

By level of pensions is meant their ratio to net wages including income from the second economy. This ratio has an important impact on retirees' willingness to continue working, the smaller the ratio the greater the willingness to work. People are used to a certain standard of living and are not inclined to give it up easily. Conversely, if the ratio increases and reaches a level that ensures an acceptable standard of living compared to the pre-retirement age, the incentive to continue working may decline dramatically. Of course, this is true only generally; in the retiree's deliberations about work, considerations other than purely pecuniary ones play a role: penchant for the job performed, possible substitute jobs at home, hobbies, the effect on family life, etc.

Pension increases for employment reasons alone have not been very frequent; instead two groups of incentives have been used: supplements to pensions for continuing to work without collecting a pension and a variety of incentives which revolve around permission to retirees who continue to work full-time or part-time to collect the whole or part of the pension.

Supplements have not turned out to be a powerful incentive. Despite their introduction in Hungary in 1972, the number of economically active pensioners declined there (J. Timár 1981, p. 65). In Czechoslovakia, despite the increase in the level of the supplement (in 1975 from 4 per cent of the pension for one year of work to 7 per cent), the number of persons continuing to work without collecting pensions declined too (Seidl 1979). There are primarily two reasons for this phenomenon: first, average pensions in Hungary increased dramatically in the 70s and in Czechoslovakia after 1975, and second, what is no less important, there is an increasing opportunity to work part-time under relatively good terms.

Originally social reasons may have played the most important role in allowing pensioners to continue to work part-time and, in some limited cases full-time, without affecting their pensions. With increasing tightness in the labour market and with rising structural imbalances in employment, the central planners started to regulate more and more the economic activity of pensioners from the viewpoint of employment considerations. In all three countries retirees are nowadays allowed to work a certain period of time without any cut in pensions. (Statistical data show that the majority of pensioners prefer part-time work combined with full pension. Such an arrangement allows them a greater choice in the combination of work and leisure according to their desires.) In addition retirees up to a certain level of pensions are allowed to collect the whole pension on top of earnings. Finally, in sectors and occupations where there are labour shortages, pensioners can work full-time and collect both pensions and earnings or work more than the normal limit without having a cut in pension (Burdová 1976; Abonyi 1979; pp. 620–1; Brojewski 1980).

Hungary and Poland several times used pension provisions to influence labour supply. As will be shown in Ch. 10, Poland recently used quite successfully reductions in the retirement age for a certain period combined with other incentives to avert unemployment.

Since labour shortages are primarily in manual occupations, all three countries try to make pensioners work primarily in manual jobs. Figures available for the 70s show that the governments were quite successful in their endeavour (Rózsa 1978, p. 108; Piątek 1980; Seidl 1979).

(b) *Maternity leave*

All three countries nowadays apply a prolonged maternity leave programme which allows an employed mother to stay at home with her new-born child for a certain length of time without losing claim to her job. The programme was first introduced in Hungary (1967), then in Poland (1968) and finally in the CSSR (1970). In Hungary and Czechoslovakia women on leave have been entitled to an allowance from the beginning whereas in Poland it was introduced in 1981.[2]

The reasons for the introduction of prolonged maternity leave were several, mostly the same for all three countries. Governments wanted to ease the pressure for expansion of nursery facilities and thus save investment funds and outlays on nursery employees' salaries, all the more because it turned out that mothers of small children are not a great asset to the labour force since absenteeism has been high in their ranks (Takács 1967). In addition, this provision was intended, primarily in Czechoslovakia, as a way to boost birth-rates. Finally, in Hungary and Poland, it was motivated by employment considerations; in the second half of the 60s the post-war baby boom started to swell the ranks of job-seekers. In Hungary this happened at a time when the country was on the brink of an economic reform. The central planners were afraid that the New Economic Mechanism (NEM) would generate unemployment; that is, managers would respond instantly to the new profit motive by intensifying labour economy. Therefore they decided in 1967 to undertake several provisions against possible unemployment, and the introduction of a prolonged maternity leave programme was one of them. Most of the jobs vacated by mothers with small children were filled by female job-seekers (Vida Horváth 1971).

Regardless of what the reasons for the introduction of the prolonged maternity leave may have been, once introduced it can serve to some extent as an instrument for the regulation of the female labour supply. The expansion and contraction of the length of the leave itself may have quite a great effect on labour supply, considering that the number of women taking advantage of this programme is quite large and rose substantially in the last decade. In Poland in 1970 50 000 women were on prolonged leave and in 1980 487 185 (which was 9.6 per cent of the total active female labour force in the national economy). In Hungary the figures were 65 000 in 1968 and 263 000 in 1980 (11.6 per cent).[3]

To make the prolonged maternity leave an effective instrument for regulating the female labour supply would require adjusting the level of the allowance to the labour market situation, especially to the structure of demand for female labour. There are several difficulties in the implementation of such a policy, the most important being that the countries discussed cannot afford to spend excessive sums on this programme. The most effective way to attract women into the programme according to labour market needs is, of course, a differential increase in the allowance. Also to use reductions in the allowance as an instrument to make the programme less attractive to some women would be politically unpopular. In addition the programme is permeated with social considerations.

No doubt the prolonged maternity leave programme in its first years of existence fulfilled many of the hopes which were pinned on it. It helped, *inter alia*, to reduce female unemployment to the point that it is possible nowadays to talk of female full employment (Vértes 1981). As will be shown later it also helped recently in Poland to avert unemployment. Yet the programme has not turned out to be as flexible an instrument as was hoped; it contributed to labour shortages even in some sectors in Poland which is going through a serious economic crisis (*TL 1982*, no. 190).

(c) *Expansion of the private sector*

In contrast to the previously discussed tools, the private sector can play a twofold role. It can be used for influencing labour demand and for helping to regulate labour supply for the state sector. If the private sector is allowed to expand and an expansion comes into being, a new demand for labour is generated. Regardless of the character of the workers who fill the additional jobs, the expansion of the private sector has an effect on the labour supply. It may reduce the labour supply to the state sector or may even force it to compete with the private sector for available labour. The expansion may also help to absorb unemployed workers and ease the pressure on the state sector to create new job opportunities. It may even provide jobs for redundant and/or not fully utilised workers in the state sector and thus contribute to an improvement in the economic efficiency there. The expansion of the private sector also favourably affects the state of market equilibrium. What is, however, the most important for our purposes is that it can help avert the threat of unemployment.

It is obvious from the foregoing that the planners can consciously use the private sector to create new jobs and influence the labour supply to the state sector. The creation of jobs by the private sector has the advantage that it can be achieved without involving state funds for investment. Not only this, it produces revenues for the state coffers.

To what extent have the central planners used the private sector for the purposes mentioned? It is possible generally to argue that political crises and their aftermath, major economic reforms geared to enhancing

economic efficiency and periods of unemployment or threat of unemployment are conducive to the expansion of the private sector. (For
more see Adam, 1984.)

Already in 1953–4 there was a slight change in policy with regard to
the private sector. A real change occurred in 1956–8 in Hungary and
Poland. In both countries the political events of 1956 (the uprising in
Hungary and the riots in Poland) created a favourable political
atmosphere for an extension of the private sector which economic
considerations called for. Poland as well as Hungary namely suffered
from unemployment and the extension of the private sector was one of
the cures for it.

Statistical figures unmistakably confirm that after the decline in the
number of workers in the private sector reached its nadir (in 1953 in
Hungary and in 1954 in Poland) a reversal though not a dramatic one
started in 1956. In Czechoslovakia the decline continued to 1956–8
(Lengyel 1958; Rajkiewicz 1965, pp. 106 and 164; *SRC 1959*, p. 93).
However, the changes in 1956–8 did not open the way to a steady
expansion of the private sector. In Hungary in 1959 a recollectivisation
of agriculture started and in the 60s there was even a shrinking of the
private sector.

The economic reforms of the second half of the 60s (in Poland in 1973)
again brought about changes in the policy towards the private sector. In
the deliberations of the Czechoslovak reformers the revival of the small-
scale private sector was included among the provisions regarded as
requisite for an improvement in economic efficiency.[4] However, no
great change did occur. The private sector was allowed to expand
primarily where the socialist sector was absent (in small towns and
villages). It seems that one of the reasons for such a government
approach was that in its consideration about the private-sector employment did not play an important role.

Neither Hungarian nor Polish materials on the economic reform
devoted any attention to the private sector. Nevertheless NEM which
brought about a political relaxation had an important impact on the private
sector. The official statistics published by the Hungarian Yearbooks do
not give a complete picture of the state of the private sector. The figures
include only persons who report their engagement in the private sector
as the main activity. With the introduction of NEM the private sector
expanded, primarily with part-time workers, made up on the one hand
of persons outside the active labour force and on the other hand of
persons employed in the state sector who, in their spare time, acted as
self-employed artisans. Furthermore, pensioners joined the private

sector. Two Hungarian authors of a book on the second economy (Gábor and Galasi 1981, pp. 52–3) indicate that in 1978 almost 250 000 people were active in the legal private sector; of this number approximately 40 per cent were active in agriculture. According to another source, three-quarters of households share to varying extents in incomes derived from the private sector (apparently legal and illegal) (Markó 1980). The expansion of the private sector resulted among other things from the fear of unemployment.

Recently, in connection with increasing difficulties in the economy, the government has come up with new initiatives to boost the private sector which went into effect on 1 January 1982 (for more Adam 1984). Considering the Hungarian provisions historically one must admit that they represent an important milestone in the development of legislation regarding the Hungarian private sector. Their purpose is threefold: to enhance economic efficiency by reducing the cost of administering small businesses, to improve the supply of goods and services in areas where the state-sector is cumbersome and, finally, what is important for this study, to find employment for workers who might be dismissed from industry and construction. In recent years these two sectors have reduced their labour force and it is expected that this process will continue.

The Hungarian leaders neither expect nor want a dramatic expansion of the private sector (Popper 1981). They would – no doubt – like the advantages of an expansion, but at the same time are anxious to avoid the political risks involved. Incomes in the private sector are much higher than in the state sector and this not only generates dissatisfaction in the state sector, primarily among those people who do not benefit from the private sector, but adds to the pressure for wage increases and unfavourably impacts on productivity in the state sector (Gábor 1979). And this is one of the main reasons why the terms for entering the private sector have until recently not been favourable (Herner 1982).

The Polish reform of 1973 created a better political atmosphere for the private sector which was reflected in a modest expansion. An important change occurred in the second half of the 70s when the failure of the new strategy of economic growth generated disequilibria in the economy, and unemployment loomed on the horizon. To cope with this new situation the government decided among other things to speed up the expansion of the private sector. Though the expansion fell behind expectations, it nevertheless helped to stave off unemployment. It seems that the slow growth of the non-agricultural private sector was due to the tax system which discriminated against private businesses employing workers (Skarzynski 1981). It can be assumed that the new economic reform which went into force in 1982 and new legislation on the operation and management of private handicrafts will create new incentives for the expansion of the private sector (GP 1982, no. 4; TL 1982, 17 Sep).

The authorities are torn between the desire to expand the private sector and the fear of the political and social consequences of such an action. The expansion of the private sector is, no doubt, important for the economic reasons mentioned. Viewed from a political standpoint it is quite controversial: on the one hand it is a sign of the regime's increasing tolerance and may contribute to political stability, and on the other it presents the danger of increased dissatisfaction with the distribution of income and thus weakens socialist ideology. Only the future will show how willing the Hungarian and Polish governments will be to take risks. It is clear that the Czechoslovak government does not intend to deviate from the traditional path (Kontra 1982).

* * *

The discussed methods of regulation of demand for and supply of labour were not introduced with the start of central planning. Most of them are of later date. Originally the central planners tried to harmonise demand for and supply of labour primarily by direct methods: employment limits, organised recruitment, quotas for admission to schools, placement of school graduates in certain jobs, compulsory placement of adults, legal restrictions on job changes and penalties for violation of labour discipline. It soon turned out that direct methods were not an effective way to distribute labour; also, because being a restriction on the freedom of choice of jobs, they were deeply resented by the population. With the rise of economic reforms indirect methods for the regulation of employment were gradually introduced. Direct methods have not been abandoned entirely; some have survived in a modified form, and some were even reintroduced for some periods.

D   WAGE DIFFERENTIALS AND ALLOCATION OF LABOUR

In this section the role of wage differentials in matching demand for and supply of labour is discussed, more precisely the effect of wage differentials and their changes on workers' decisions about choice of occupation and workplace and the extent to which they can bring about the mobility of labour desired by the central planners due to ongoing and/or planned structural changes in the economy.

In considering the role of wage differentials in people's decision-making about choice of occupation and workplace, one must distinguish between the initial choice at an age when decisions about future occupation are made, and choices made once occupation and workplace have been selected or allocated.

1 Choice of Occupation by Teenagers

Teenagers' freedom of choice of their future occupation is not without limits. This is true even if the class criteria long applied in admission policy, primarily to universities, and administrative methods for allocation to vocational schools (applied mainly in the 50s) are disregarded. (For more see Chs 7–10.) The school system and job opportunities impose quite a constraint on the choice process. Education and training institutions are guided in their admission policy by quotas set by central planners on the basis of demand forecasted for different professions and trades in the economy. There is competition among would-be students for the quota 'openings' in the institutions. The extent of the competition is influenced by wage differentials; schooling for well-paid occupations is in greater demand. But wage differentials are not the only factor which determines the choice of occupation. Social status and working conditions in individual professions and trades (more so for girls than boys) play an important role; in some cases they eclipse pecuniary interests.

The effect of wage differentials is, to some extent, distorted by the feminisation of certain professions. For example, in Czechoslovakia lawyers are the worst-paid professionals. Nevertheless the number of applicants to law faculties is high due to the great number of female applicants.

2 Redistribution of the Active Labour Force

As far as I know, W. Galenson and A. Fox (1967) were the first Western scholars who tried to determine the role of wage differentials in labour mobility in individual industrial branches as a whole. From an analysis of statistical figures for Bulgaria, the CSSR, Hungary, Poland and Yugoslavia, they concluded that there was no consistent correlation between earnings changes and changes in employment in industrial branches in the period 1957–63. Because some studies about the West have come to the same conclusion (cf. Phelps Brown 1977, p. 51) despite the fact that the number of factors which hamper the working of wage differentials is much lower and less intensive in the West, one is inclined to take Galenson's and Fox's study at face value.

Their conclusions have, however, the disadvantage that they are made on the basis of large aggregates, and therefore cannot capture the impact of wage movements on job changes (which may mean changes in occupations or not), occurring among enterprises within the aggregates.

The findings of the two authors are in substance in line with the views of most East European economists who agree that wage differentials are only one of the factors contributing to labour mobility (e.g. Morecka 1965; Révész 1983, p. 42). To make wage differentials an instrument of labour mobility requires them to be subjected to changes according to the needs of the labour market and/or objectives of the central planners. (It is important to mention both since they need not be in harmony. To change wage differentials according to the needs of the market means to respond to the demand of enterprises for labour. As has been shown, enterprises have an almost insatiable demand for labour which need not be in line with the interest of the economy.) It is doubtful whether the central authorities can always acquire the needed information for such decision-making, but even if such information were available, it is questionable whether they could make adequate changes in wage differentials with the needed speed. There are also political reasons why the central planners prefer not to be much involved. To adjust wages according to changes in the demand for labour runs the risk that the newly established relative wages cannot be easily changed again once the conditions for the preferential treatment cease to exist. On the other hand, the effort to make changes in established wage differentials is usually resisted by those groups which are adversely affected by them (cf. Szikra 1979, p. 133).

Knowing best the situation in their enterprises, managers seem to be the natural authorities for decisions on differentials; though there is no lack of eagerness on their part to be involved, they do not have great leeway with regard to wage differentials (this is less true of Hungary). Wage differentials are a politically sensitive issue, and the central authorities are reluctant to allow managers to interfere with them much. And this may also be why the countries introduced incentives (in the form of various allowances) to encourage labour mobility, warranted from an economic point of view. Incentives are used mainly to make displaced workers undergo retraining and accept jobs where their newly acquired skills are in demand. (For more see Part II.)

Other factors preventing wage differentials from playing a decisive role can be classified in two groups, though the dividing-line is to a certain extent blurred. One is connected more with government policies and the second with the personal interests and preferences of workers. Among government policies affecting adults, employment policy deserves to be mentioned first. In different periods in the past the government placed administrative obstacles to the free movement of workers, which necessarily reduced the impact of wage differentials. Housing policy is another factor, in that it has led to housing shortages, especially in industrial centres. Changes in jobs are frequently hampered by housing shortages in locations where ample job opportunities exist.

Wage differentials have the greatest effect if they can be combined with other material, social and educational advantages (Ołędzki 1978, p. 207). To mention the most important in case of families: adequate housing, job opportunities for wives, educational facilities for children. If these needs cannot be met to the satisfaction of workers thinking of moving, higher earnings alone in the new workplace cannot be a sufficient stimulus. In considering the potential new incomes, long-term prospects including promotion and career prospects play an important role. These also affect the extent to which people are eager to take new jobs which involve a change of occupation and retraining.

That both personal preferences and wage differentials can play an important role is enabled by the circumstance that in socialist countries the initiative to move to another workplace rests mostly with the workers. A Hungarian study shows that at the end of the 60s and beginning of the 70s 86 per cent of job changes among workers with middle and higher qualifications resulted from workers' decisions. It can be assumed that in the case of manual workers the percentage was even higher (*Képzettség . . .* 1971, vol. II, p. 63). This is due, on the one hand, to the political and legal difficulties connected with the dismissal of workers in declining industries in the East and, on the other hand, to the labour shortages these countries are plagued with.

4 Appendix I
Full Employment and
Rational Employment

Though all the three countries have been committed to full employment (FE) from the start of central planning, it was some time before economists commenced to analyse its meaning, the preconditions for its achievement and its relationship to rational employment (RE). Polish economists were in a sense pioneers in this sphere: already in the second half of the 50s they had started to deal with these problems on a theoretical level. No doubt the employment situation in Poland was an impetus to such contemplations, particularly the fact that at a time when the economy suffered from unemployment in some sectors labour shortages showed up. Yet, if not for the political events of 1956 which created a fertile soil for research, the economic impetus would not have had much effect. Only later were Polish economists joined by their colleagues in Hungary and Czechoslovakia.

1 WHAT IS FULL EMPLOYMENT?

There is no agreement among East European economists about the definition of FE. It would exceed the framework of this study to record all the views in detail. Therefore the disussion will be confined to the most important views and start with the views of M. Kabaj, who had undoubtedly contributed a great deal to the elucidation of employment problems in socialist countries. He (1962, pp. 153–4) defines FE as an economic situation in which 'every ablebodied person willing to work can obtain a job in accordance with his qualifications under terms set by laws or by a special contract'. However FE does not mean to him that everyone who is willing to work must necessarily obtain a job instantly. FE includes some unemployment of people who are seeking and waiting

60

for jobs; thus frictional unemployment is a part of FE. In a paper published earlier M. Kabaj (1960) maintains that FE is achieved if no more than 2–3 per cent of the active labour force are seeking jobs.

M. Kabaj's views are not shared by all economists. In the guidelines for long-term employment policy in Hungary, worked out in connection with the drawing up of the FYP for 1976–80, FE is defined (Kovács 1974) as a situation where 'everyone performs a job according to his ability and qualifications (képzettség)'. FE presupposes not only a quantitative equilibrium (i.e. between the number of job-seekers and the number of available jobs), but also a qualitative one (i.e. between the skill mix of the workers and the required qualifications in workplaces) (Kovács 1974; Kovács 1977; J. Timár 1981, p. 198). Such a definition of FE assumes that the goal of FE can be achieved only gradually, if at all. As has been shown in Ch. 2, great incongruencies exist between the skill mix of the workers and qualifications required by the economy.

B. Fick introduced new elements into the definition of FE. To him (1970, pp. 34–5) FE is linked to the well-being of families as a whole, more precisely to the incomes of families derived from the work of their members. 'The state of FE can be regarded as fully achieved if real earnings of the working members of the families cover the costs of living at a proper level, though some of their members are without work. . . . The achievement of FE is not determined by the number of employed, but by the level of income of the family obtained from the work of its members.'

Considering his definition it is not surprising that B. Fick does not regard as decisive for the achievement of FE the question whether the economy can absorb all who want to work. From the vantage-point of employment he distinguishes two groups of people: those who need to work in order to make ends meet (this group includes people who want to work in their own professions and trades) and, secondly, those without skills but wanting to work in order to increase their standard of living, though the breadwinner alone, or in combination with other members of the family, is able to ensure an adequate livelihood. To him (1970, p. 33) FE can be taken as accomplished even if the second group has not managed to find jobs. B. Fick (1966) expounded these views in a shortened version earlier, and the reaction was mostly negative.

R. Kocanda (1966) views FE rather as a concept than as a precise variable; to him it is a quasi-commitment of society to create conditions which will enable members of society to participate in work. The extent of economic activity of the working-age population is not without relevance to him, but he does not view it as strictly as other economists do. In substance his view resembles B. Fick's. FE means employment at least at a level which will enable all breadwinners and single persons to work. 'In our situation', he writes, 'it is necessary to take for granted almost full participation of the male labour force. The extent of FE refers primarily to women.'

L. Kalinová (1979, p. 13) underscored this view by maintaining that in no socialist country was FE achieved for all able-bodied people. What was achieved was FE for men of working age.

I have presented a spectrum of views on FE representing all the three countries. In analysing these views one must remember primarily that they are (1) a product of the time written, i.e. influenced by the existing economic situation understood in a broad sense, including trends in the system of management, and (2) a reflection of certain concepts on how to solve employment problems. The two circumstances are to a great extent intertwined.

What is common to all these views is the expression of dissatisfaction, though formulated in different ways, with an employment policy which put great stress on maximisation of employment. No doubt this was one of the reasons for the strange views of B. Fick. A second reason was the desire to indirectly protest against a standard-of-living policy which was based on the assumption that if everyone obtains a job, regardless of its remuneration, an adequate standard of living is achieved.

2 FULL EMPLOYMENT AND RATIONAL EMPLOYMENT

As has been already mentioned, all three countries were engaged for a long time in maximising employment, the reason being that they hoped in this way to maximise output and at the same time achieve FE. It soon became clear that maximisation of employment unfavourably affects the economy, particularly labour productivity, technological advancement, labour discipline, average wages, etc. Therefore they started to put stress on RE.

What is the relation between FE and RE? There is no agreement among economists. With some simplification the existing views can be divided into two groups: the authors in the first group perceive FE and RE, in substance, as two interrelated non-conflicting phenomena. This does not, however, mean that they entirely exclude any possible conflicts between the two. The second group of authors perceives the two as two different phenomena which are often in conflict. What is no less important, RE is measured in terms of returns on the microeconomic level, whereas the adherents of the first view have in mind rationality on a macroeconomic level.

Some economists see in FE and RE two stages in the development of the economy. K. Secomski (1977, p. 182), a defender of this view, perhaps developed it best. In the beginning there are huge, idle human resources; their utilisation at low wages enables not only the growth of the economy to be accelerated, but at the same time an important social problem, FE, to be solved. After some time extensive economic growth starts to provide diminishing returns and it becomes clear that, in order to optimise output, employment must be rationalised. A transition to a higher stage, RE, begins; this stage is characterised by an optimal distribution and utilisation of labour. RE does not mean an abandonment of FE, rather its perfection.

The authors of a book on national planning in Poland (Baka *et al.* 1975, pp. 326–8) express a somewhat different view which, however, is in a sense more consistent with the underlying philosophy of the first group than the preceding view. To them FE is already a realisation of RE; they believe that failure to fully utilise all labour resources violates the principle of rationality. Employment policy under socialism has two aspects: one is FE, geared to ensuring everyone the right to a job, and the second is FE and RE, an instrument for achieving a fast pace of development. The two aspects are interrelated; in the initial phase of development the stress was on the first, and the present effort to implement an intensive type of growth requires the application of the second aspect. RE is a situation in which the skill mix of the labour force corresponds to the needs of the economy, and regional disparities between demand for and supply of labour are eliminated.

As representatives of the second group of views Czechoslovak economists in the period of the economic reform can be mentioned. To R. Kocanda FE and efficient employment (Czechoslovak economists use rather the term 'efektivni') are two separate problems because their solution is on two different planes. The first is a macroeconomic and the second a microeconomic problem. FE can be regarded as efficient when both requirements can be brought into harmony, i.e. when employment expands 'to the maximum limit while sustaining higher marginal contribution by the work of workers than the total costs involved with their employment' (Kocanda 1966). A similar view is taken by P. Hoffman (1966).

This line of thinking by R. Kocanda is fully in accordance with his view, expressed in his book (1965, pp. 29–30), that the development of productive forces is a more important task than FE.

Some Polish economists, apparently as a result of the economic crisis and the efforts to reform the management system, are more specific than Kocanda. A. Świątkowski (1982) argues that there should be a division of labour between the government and enterprises, the former taking care of FE and the latter, following the principle of self-financing, adhering to the criteria of RE in a microeconomic sense. The authorities should see to it that people who lose their jobs because of the enterprises' new behaviour are placed, or provided with unemployment benefits till they find new jobs. Recently, similar views have emerged in Hungary.

It is doubtful whether the second (minority) view, though attractive, could prevail in the real socialist system. As mentioned, in no country have enterprises achieved full financial independence and it is unlikely that governments will take them in this direction. A consistent realisation of A. Świątkowski's views would mean an end to the resource-constrained system though a compromise is imaginable.

3   FULL EMPLOYMENT AND LOW WAGES

Some Western economists maintain that FE in the East (in the sense that everyone who wants a job can find one) has been made possible by the existing low wages. In other words, had the socialist countries followed a policy of high wages, East European countries would have been plagued by unemployment as capitalist countries are.

It has already been shown that socialist countries followed a policy of low wages. In this connection the question is warranted: was there a cause–effect relationship between FE and low wages and, if so, which was the cause and which the effect? In Ch. 2 it was explained that FE is a necessary consequence of the working of the socialist resource constrained system, that historically the strategy of economic development and the accompanying system of management of the economy were geared to a maximisation of employment, and that the policy of low wages was to a large extent the result of the process of employment maximisation. On the other hand, the policy of low wages contributed to FE. Hence there is no clear-cut cause–effect relationship between the two: it seems more correct to talk of an interrelationship in which low wages played a more passive role.

Still the question may be asked: must FE in a socialist country be necessarily combined with low wages? First it must be made clear what is meant by low and high wages. Naturally these are relative terms; they obtain an informative value if they are related to some quantifiable variable. Above the policy of low wages was related to national income *per capita*. Figures[1] confirm that in the three countries under review average nominal wages as a percentage of *per capita* national income were and still are lower than in capitalist countries.

In answering the question, one must return to an examination of the reasons for low wages. It has already been mentioned that employment policy has not been the only reason for low wages. They are also a result of tremendous waste, high military expenditures and an efficiency-impeding distribution of labour.

Waste is a general term for various phenomena in the economy which reduce the potential amount of usable goods for consumption (productive or non-productive). Such are the production of goods for which no demand exists because of their poor quality and/or their obsolete nature, excessive use of materials and energy, unjustified losses of working time caused to a great extent by low labour discipline.

All three countries contribute to the arms race between the USSR and the USA. This is also a kind of waste since weapons cannot be used for consumption. They are singled out here because they are rarely mentioned in the East in such a context. Reliable figures about the extent of military expenditures of the three countries are not available; yet it is safe to say that they are quite high. Funds spent for military purposes could be used for creating conditions for increased wages through modernising and expanding consumer goods industries.

Some sectors of the economy, mainly heavy industry, for a long time received preferential treatment in the allocation of labour to the point that overemployment arose in some branches. At the same time the service sector (paid and unpaid) suffered and still suffers from labour shortages, a circumstance which affected the economy unfavourably in many respects. A more even distribution of labour would increase productivity in the overemployed sectors of the economy and help satisfy the increasing demand for paid services. The latter in itself may also become a stimulus to higher productivity; workers would be willing to work harder if they knew that they could use the additional purchasing power as they wished. The expansion of the private sector may have the same effect as has been shown. What is also important is that the state and the private service sector can produce their own wage-bill which cannot be said for all other sectors of the economy.

The chances of eliminating waste are not good. It would not be realistic to expect great reductions in military expenditures, and the same is true about other sources of waste which are, to a large extent, a product of the management system of the economy and the political system.

Without great changes in both, no real remedy to waste can be envisioned. Yet some changes in the distribution of labour have occurred in the last decade and can be expected to continue.

On balance it is obvious that the chances for socialist countries to achieve high average wages similar to capitalist countries with the same *per capita* national income are slim. Yet in the last twenty-five years the three countries have managed to increase real wages substantially and, at the same time, to create new jobs to the point that labour shortages exist, combined, of course, with overemployment.

Let us assume that the socialist countries managed to eliminate waste, and therefore the gap in wages as a ratio of national income *per capita* between the East and West could be at least substantially closed. This would not necessarily mean that unemployment would follow. If labour and other resources are available in a socialist system, which is supply-constrained, the planners will see to it that they are put to work, which is not necessarily the case in a capitalist economy (a demand-constrained system) as recent experience has again demonstrated.

5 Wage Policy in the Real Socialist System

A OBJECTIVES OF WAGE POLICY

To understand the objectives of wage policy it is necessary first to define the functions of wages. Usually four functions are attributed to wages. (1) Income – wages are a determinant of consumption of the population,[1] approximately 70 per cent of which is financed from wages. (2) Motivational – this function stems from the first; because wages are a factor of consumption they can serve as an instrument of motivation. (3) Cost – wages as workers' incomes are at the same time a cost to enterprises. (4) Allocative – wages help to distribute and redistribute labour.

Wages also fulfil a non-economic function – they have an effect on human relations. People have certain ideas about income distribution, more precisely about the wage differentials affecting them, their colleagues and their superiors. If they think that their ideas have been grossly violated, they may react with resentment. Wage differentials may thus be a source of conflict. A. Melich (1978) calls this function 'social'.

Wages fulfil all these four economic functions regardless of the economic system. The difference between capitalism and socialism is that in the later the objectives of wage policy are translated into a conscious endeavour on the part of government to utilise the economic functions for the sake of improving the performance of the economy and the material situation of the population. (Of course in this endeavour the government must also take into consideration the social function.) This does not mean that wages and wage differentials can be planned in every detail throughout the economy. Detailed planning is possible in administration, but not in goods producing sectors. If incentives have to play a role in the management of the economy, productive enterprises must be given some room to manœuvre with wages. Even in a strictly centralised system – as experience shows – enterprises are allowed to exceed the planned amounts of the wage-bill and incentive funds, provided they overfulfil the targets. Therefore the term 'planning' does not really reflect precisely the government's activity pertaining to wages. The term 'regulation', which includes planning as well as other methods, is more suitable.[2]

Regulation has two aspects: regulative and stimulative. The first is concerned with the growth of wages within the limits of the plan in order to avert an emergence of market disequilibrium for consumer goods. As is known, equilibrium is achieved if total incomes[3] minus savings correspond to the value of goods and services available for sales. Here equilibrium is thus a macroeconomic category. However the struggle to attain it is determined on the microeconomic level; in the final analysis the size of the global wage-fund as the greatest part of the total incomes of the population is determined in enterprises.

To regulate the wage-bill at the level of enterprises means to be concerned with the wage as income and as a factor of costs. In theory the two need not be in conflict; it is possible to reduce labour costs per unit of production and at the same time increase wages, provided labour productivity grows adequately. This, in other words, means that if the output of enterprises remains the same employment must decline.

Emphasising the wage-bill does not mean that the growth of average wages is not of importance for equilibrium. The size of the wage-bill in enterprises is determined by average wages and the number employed. If average wages grow faster than labour productivity, cost-push inflation will probably arise. The same may be true if no proper consideration is given to the 'social function' of wages. A fast increase in the average wages of certain groups may generate demands for increases from other groups in the name of historical comparability.

The stimulative aspect of regulation is very broad and affects many areas. To put it generally its main purpose is to encourage productivity growth. In more concrete terms this means encouraging workers to produce more during a time unit, also to lower costs per unit of production by saving material, equipment and energy, to improve the quality of goods, in brief, to use most effectively the productive apparatus as well as labour.

For the stimulative aspect of wage-regulation differentials are more important than levels. Wages act as a stimulus if workers feel that their effort is remunerated properly in terms of the earnings of other workers whose jobs can be related to theirs. There is a direct connection between the stimulative aspect and employment in that wage differentials are one of the important instruments for allocating labour according to the needs of the economy.

The stimulative aspect of wage regulation was developed before the regulative. There were several reasons for this: first it is more difficult to develop a regulative system since it requires the build-up of a complicated linkage with various activities of the economy. But what was perhaps more important was that in the initial planning period the authorities did not feel so strongly the need for a regulative system, since they were obsessed with maximisation of output without due regard to costs. And finally the need to have some system in place for individual remuneration is, of course, of greater importance.

It is obvious from the foregoing that the two aspects of wage regulation are intended to direct and co-ordinate the mentioned functions of wages; the regulative aspect the income function, and the stimulative aspect the motivational, allocative and the cost functions. Hence it can be argued that in the final analysis the objective of wage policy is to steer and harmonise the two aspects of wage regulation which need not necessarily be in harmony – a frequent case in practice.

The extent of the harmonious use of the two aspects of wage regulation depends, of course, on the level of wages (nominal as well as real) and their dynamics. Generally it can be said that the higher the level of wages the greater the possible compatibility of the two aspects. The faster average wages can grow without conflicting with the regulative function the greater their stimulative potential. A widening of wage differentials applied for stimulative reasons is under such conditions more acceptable to the workers whose relative wage position is to be worsened.

The methods applied in wage regulation also have an impact on the extent of congruity between the two aspects. Without going into detail it is possible to say that congruity is easier to achieve in a decentralised than in a centralised system.[4]

B　FACTORS INFLUENCING WAGE POLICY

In Ch. 2 it was mentioned how wage policy was affected by the strategy of economic development and the system of management of the economy. Therefore these factors can be omitted here; instead focus will be on factors which complement or compete with wages as determinants of the level of consumption and real incomes, and therefore have an effect on wage policy.

1 Social Benefits

Wages (including bonuses) are only part, though the main part, of workers' incomes. As is known, workers also receive transfer payments (which in Hungary are called social benefits in cash – a term used in further discussions – e.g. pensions, family allowances). In addition people receive social services (social benefits in kind – health care, education).

Since the global wage-fund and the global fund for social benefits are parts of the global consumption fund, it is clear that wage policy must be co-ordinated with the social benefits policy. In making decisions about the share of both parts in the consumption fund and the rates of their increases, the central planners are guided by the problem they want to address, taking into consideration, of course, the role that wages and social benefits can play in production and distribution.

In contrast to wages social benefits cannot be used directly for stimulative purposes in the production process. They can, however, if they are used properly, contribute indirectly to the expansion of production and to an increase in the efficiency of the economy, particularly in the long run. Yet social benefits can be and are used for mitigating differences in *per capita* household incomes resulting from wage differentials and demographic factors (varying numbers of children and, as a result, different numbers of employed in the household).

Depending on the objectives which the central planners follow in the political and ideological sphere and on the problems the economy is confronted with, one mode of distribution takes precedence over the other. Usually when the economy is faltering and there is a desire to improve its performance by intensifying incentives, greater stress is put on wage increases and the widening of wage differentials. When dissatisfaction builds up with the state of wage differentials, or when lower income groups press for a betterment of their material situation, the planners may provide redress by expanding social benefits.

Giving priority to social benefits may also result from ideological considerations. In the early 60s Khrushchev launched a propaganda barrage about the forthcoming transition to communism, which prompted a debate about the possible transition to communist distribution according to needs. Of course this had a partly favourable effect on the growth of social benefits.

After the Second World War great stress was put on social benefits. One of the tenets of the Marxist labour movement is that the state is obliged to care for the needy, the sick and the old. For this reason and also for political reasons the communist leaders, even before seizing monopoly power, pushed for the expansion of social programmes. So, at the end of the 40s and the beginning of the 50s, social benefits grew relatively rapidly, primarily in Czechoslovakia, and this mitigated to a certain degree the impact of declining real wages on the standard of living.

After 1953 wage increases got greater priority, and the expansion of social benefits was halted for a short time. The approach to the two modes of distribution has been changed several times in the last three decades. On the whole social benefits grew rapidly in the 70s and have been gradually extended to all social groups (including persons working in the private sector).

2 Employment

Especially in the first phase of central planning planners relied heavily on the expansion of employment as a method for ensuring a certain standard of living. Though such an expansion or wage increases may bring about the same *per capita* family income they differ in their economic and social effects. Wage increases strengthen the incentive function of wages, motivating workers to improve performance and acquire new skills. Employment has often expanded at the expense of wage increases, mainly when the planned limit for employment is exceeded, and therefore it has dampened the incentive potentiality of wages. Employment expansion can also have an unfavourable effect on wage differentials. If it means that less funds are available for wage increases, adjustment in wage differentials in order to make them more responsive to the need for incentives becomes politically more difficult. And this is one of the reasons why the central planners in different periods have hesitated to honour their pledges to enact greater wage differentiation. In addition fast employment expansion usually hampers increases in labour productivity and becomes an important factor of low labour discipline with all its consequences.

Increases in the standard of living by expanding employment also have a social dimension; more people must work in order to achieve the same *per capita* income. On the household level this means that the wife must often take a job simply for financial reasons and perhaps at the expense of the proper care of children, and a second shift in the household. In addition such an increase in the standard of living introduces inequalities in income. Households differ in the number of able-bodied members capable of engaging in economic activity, and those with many small children are at a disadvantage.

3 Prices

Because of their role in determining real incomes and real wages, prices can be used for redistributive purposes (this means setting relative prices differently than in a free market or in deviation from relative cost, in order to affect the real income of different social and income groups). Considering this function of prices, what crosses one's mind are price increases. However the level of real incomes can also be affected by price decreases, and hence increases in real incomes can be achieved by price-cutting instead of by nominal wage increases.

In all the socialist countries prices, including consumer prices, are under the control of central authorities. There is, however, a difference in the control between different systems of management. In a centralised system most consumer prices cannot be changed without the explicit approval of central authorities. Generally authorities follow a policy of rigid prices even at the expense of market disequilibria for consumer goods; the desire to prevent open inflation is stronger than equilibrium considerations. In such a system growth of real incomes is more or less equal to the growth of nominal incomes.

In the beginning of the 50s all three countries (particularly Czechoslovakia) followed the Soviet pattern of increasing real incomes by cutting retail prices, a pattern which at that time was labelled by many as socialist. After some time this policy was abandoned for various reasons, one being that the planners recognized that it was an obstacle to wages being used as an incentive. Wage growth can be adjusted according to the needs of the economy, whereas price cutting benefits only people who purchase the cheapened goods.

In a decentralised system prices are more flexible and more responsive to changes in the relationship between supply and demand. Planners give precedence to market equilibrium for consumer goods over price rigidity, mainly if the price increases are not high. In this system consumer prices grow, and therefore nominal incomes must grow faster than consumer prices if real incomes are to increase.

In both systems, particularly the centralised one, planners believe that prices should have a redistributive role, also because it enables them to let wages play a greater stimulative role. The widening of wage differentials for stimulative reasons can be mitigated by setting price relativities which favour low wage groups. Indeed, in the early 50s, when the new 'socialist' price system was introduced, relative prices were set according to the Soviet pattern in a way that benefited low income groups and the urban population at the expense of the agricultural population. A highly differentiated turnover tax was used for this purpose. Low tax rates were set on foodstuffs, high rates on clothing and footwear, and very high rates on articles which were regarded as non-essential. Within individual groups of goods there were great differences in rates; generally luxury and high-quality goods were taxed more heavily than low- and medium-cost goods. With some exceptions no turnover tax was imposed on services. Since economically active people in agriculture do not buy food to the same extent as the urban population and do not use services to any great extent (as they do not use urban transportation and they live in private houses) the tax system burdened them more than the rest of the population.

In the thirty years which have elapsed since the introduction of the new price system, many changes have occurred in price relativities. Several price reforms which were instituted in the interim have changed, or may even have eroded the redistributive role of retail prices. The turnover tax was reduced substantially; prices of many foodstuffs no longer contain a turnover tax; on the contrary they are subsidised. (For more see Adam 1979, pp. 21–32.)

In planning wage changes the planners take into consideration their objectives in consumer price policy and the chances of achieving them and vice versa. Therefore, for a better understanding of wage policy, one must also study price policy.

C   WAGE DIFFERENTIAL POLICY

In Ch. 3 the allocative role of wage differentials has been discussed; I feel that it is the proper place to do so in context with employment regulation. Here primarily factors which influence the policy of the real social state with regard to wage differentials and the criteria used for wage differentiation are discussed. In Ch. 11 an analysis of the evolution of wage differentials is given.

It is known that the communists, when they seized political power, committed themselves to what could be called a more equal distribution of income. Some Western publications give the impression that the communist leaders promised an egalitarian distribution of income (e.g. Triska 1980, p. 268). It must be stated that this is a mistaken assumption.

From the beginning the communist leaders maintained that distribution of income would be governed by the principle of distribution according to work, as expounded by Marx in his *Critique of the Gotha Programme*, and this is by no means egalitarian distribution (for more Ch. 6). Historically it could not have been otherwise; it should not be forgotten that in the first half of the 50s all the East European countries slavishly imitated the Soviet pattern. At that time the system of wage differentials instituted in the 30s by Stalin was still in operation, and this system allowed quite wide differentials in some spheres. This is not to say that the three countries introduced the same wage differentials as the Soviets. Practically it was not possible to imitate the USSR in every detail since, as will be shown, wage differentials developed to some degree spontaneously; they were influenced by forces which could not be entirely controlled from the centre. In addition, for various reasons, the countries under review, especially the CSSR, made far-reaching changes in wage differentials, which put them ahead of the USSR in equality. Some of the changes were made in the period when the struggle of the communists for power culminated, and they were used as an instrument for gaining support, particularly from production workers.

Besides political and ideological considerations, wage-differential policy is influenced by the functions wage differentials fulfil in the economy. According to H. Phelps Brown (1977, p. 49) they fulfil three functions, provided they are kept within certain limits.

'First, differentials must not be inconsistent with the required numbers of people deciding to complete training courses and acquire occupational qualifications. Second, given a labour force with certain qualifications, differentials must not be inconsistent with the required numbers of people deciding to move into and remain in particular places of work, industries and localities. The first two functions can be summed up as the matching of the supply of labour to the demand. The third function appears when the first two have been performed: people with given qualifications being occupied in given jobs, their pay must be so arranged, individually and one with another, as to stimulate to work hard.'

The functions mentioned certainly also have relevance in a socialist system and therefore they cannot be ignored in policy-making without damaging the economy.

Considering the political and ideological commitments of the socialist regimes and the mentioned functions, it is clear that the communist leaders must follow two objectives: on the one hand they must aim as much as possible at economic equality in order to strengthen their political base, that is, to gain and retain the support of manual workers who are the mainstay of the regime, and, on the other, they must ensure a certain inequality in order to be in a position to utilise the stimulative power of wage differentials in the economy. Communist leaders are not so naïve as to believe that appeals to class consciousness, communist morale or patriotism will trigger the initiative, qualifications and effort needed to achieve a healthy economy. They know that inequalities in wages are required to make the economy work. Needless to say, the two objectives are in conflict; the consistent pursuit of one objective can only be achieved at the expense of the other.

From the foregoing it does not follow that the central planners of the three countries have usually had a well-thought-out long-term policy for wage differentials (cf. Jacukowicz 1974, p. 51). The policy has been, rather, marked by many *ad hoc* interventions in the wage structure in response to political or economic considerations. There is no way to track down all or even most of the plans; nevertheless it is safe to say that only a few of them were implemented.

It should be remembered that governments' ability to fully control wage growth is limited to non-profit-making enterprises and organisations, which receive their wage-bill from state-budget allocations. Basic wages of employees in these enterprises and organisations (here disregarding wage adjustments due to promotion) are adjusted not on an annual basis but at intervals of several years, always as a result of an explicit decision of the authorities. On the other hand, for incentive reasons and also because piecework plays an important role in the remuneration of manual workers, profit-making enterprises have a certain leeway in wage determination, and thus an impact on wage differentials.

After this very general exposition a more specific discussion about the criteria for wage differentiation, still on a general level, can be started. Judged on the basis of the evolution of wage differentials it can be argued that the most important criteria applied in the policy of wage differentiation have been the following: individual performance, qualifications, position in the hierarchy of management, working conditions, situation in the labour market, payment forms, priority attributed to certain sectors or industrial branches, performance of enterprises and historical relationship.

The criterion of individual performance is fully applied in the same jobs performed at the same places of work (e.g. a more productive operator of a nail-producing machine will earn more than his less productive colleague). The criterion is modified when the same job is performed in different industrial branches and sectors of the economy.

It is generally accepted that the higher qualification[5] one has, the higher his earnings should be. Differences in costs of qualifications and the need to stimulate acquisition of qualifications are indicated as the most important reasons for such a policy (Hudák 1978). In practice this postulate is very often not followed; qualifications alone are mostly not adequately appreciated. The best proof of this is that nowadays the difference in pay between an engineer with a university background and a skilled manual worker is small. The same is true of differentials between skilled and unskilled workers. Quantity of work, particularly if paid by piece-rates, frequently overshadows the role of qualifications.

Qualifications, combined with a position in the hierarchy of management of the economy or government administration, are highly appreciated. The higher position one has, the higher his earnings usually are. Does this mean that of the two factors, qualifications and position, the latter is more important in earnings gradations? From what has been said about qualifications themselves, one is inclined to such a view. To give a definite answer it is still necessary to explore the relationship between qualification and position. If the assumption could be made that qualification is always a prerequisite for a position then the importance attributed before to position is not clear-cut. Yet it has been shown in Ch. 2 that in the selection of top managers qualifications are not always the decisive factor. This would indicate that position after all plays a more important role, a statement which is corroborated in a Hungarian study (Berényi 1967, pp. 105–6).

Qualification as a factor of wage differentials is declining in importance. The main reasons for this phenomenon in the East are: the gap in qualifications is on the whole narrowing increasingly, the supply of unskilled workers who are willing to perform arduous jobs lags more and more behind the demand, and costs of education are increasingly borne by the state (Szikra 1979, pp. 58–62).

Working conditions play an increasing role, mainly in conditions of labour shortages. There is a general tendency to shun arduous jobs or jobs which must be performed under difficult working conditions. Hence the only way to attract labour in sufficient numbers to such jobs is by offering higher wages or other incentives. Some economists believe that the long-term trend is to give increasing weight to working conditions in wage differentials (Schmidt 1975), and this is necessarily at the expense of qualifications.

With this I have arrived at the role of the labour market. It has already been shown that it does play a role, and, it is necessary to add, it must play a role if freedom of choice of job is to be basically maintained. Of course the role of the labour market in a socialist economy is much smaller than in a capitalist economy; as shown in Ch. 3 socialist countries used in the past and to some extent use nowadays other forces than the market to influence allocation of labour.

Piece rates were for a long time higher than time rates for the same skill grade. The higher wages for piecework do not always result from greater effort; but often from workers' ability to influence the work norms.

Many economists believe that wage differentials are much influenced by the system of preferential wage treatment (introduced during the first medium-term plans) which has favoured the material sphere[6] and, within it, the fast-growing heavy industry and construction. Figures, which will be indicated later, fully confirm this. In the last three decades no great changes have occurred, with one exception – agriculture. It is possible to agree with Szikra (1979, pp. 69–70) that the rise of existing intersectoral and intraindustrial wage differentials was partly a response to the disparities between supply of and demand for labour. However her assertion that qualifications and the extent of the arduousness of the work are the most important determinants, followed by sex and age structure, of intersectoral and interbranch differentials raises doubts. Hungarian figures about wages are not broken down enough to test her statement. Since she gives the impression that her assertion refers to all socialist countries it is possible to contest it by alluding to the decline in wages in Czechoslovakia in 1948–53 in education and culture, and health and welfare. Is it possible to explain this decline (in the former by 6 per cent and latter by 3 per cent) at a time when wages in the national economy and industry grew by 32.5 per cent and 55.1 per cent respectively (cf. Adam 1974, p. 71) only by the factors mentioned by Szikra? No doubt the criterion of priorities played an important role.

In the past economists rejected the idea that the performance of enterprises should have an important effect on wages. With growing concern for economic efficiency more and more economists favour such a solution (e.g. Fick 1971; Hudák 1978). During the last twenty years year-end rewards, which are supposed to be a direct reflection of enterprise performance, have begun to play a limited role in earnings of workers, but never an important one. Only the salaries of top managers have been closely tied to the performance of enterprises. Central planners have been reluctant to thoroughly link wages to the perform-ance of enterprises for varying reasons, one being that such an arrangement would necessarily widen interenterprise differentials to an extent which might become embarrassing to the politicians. For more see Ch. 6.

Historical relationships have mainly survived in wage differentials between sexes. Though the constitutions of the countries discussed do not allow wage discrimination against women, the practice has sustained it.

It is very difficult, if not impossible, to attach value to all the mentioned factors on a scientific basis. There are no figures which would show the share of individual factors in the differentiation of wages. There are some fractionary figures indicating the role of qualifications, and some figures are available on the role of working conditions, where these are remunerated in terms of supplements.

Is there any criterion for the extent of the spread in wage differentials in a socialist country? Szikra (1979, p. 15) believes that the upper limit of wage differentials (the lower is the minimum wage) should be at a point which allows the employees' needs to be met at a high level, but one which does not exceed what is required at the existing stage of development for a reasonable personal or family consumption and investment serving this purpose.

D   WAGE SYSTEM

The regulative and stimulative aspects of wage regulation are embodied in a wage system, understood in its broadest sense. This is not to say that the wage system is a mere reflection of wage policy. Once established the wage system has a 'life' of its own and may affect wage policy. An analysis of the wage system and its functioning gives an insight into wage policy and its functioning.

By wage system is meant the arrangement of elements of remuneration in a way that is supposed to make a workable whole tending in a desired direction. The use of the term 'workable whole' does not in any way mean that it must work well. One should distinguish both a narrow and a broad sense in a wage system. 'Narrow' refers to the elements of remuneration without all the regulative and stimulative devices, whereas the wage system in its broad sense includes all these devices. In this study the wage system is understood in its broad sense, though here its narrow dimension is discussed.

The wage system has three components; one is of a macroeconomic nature and the other two are microeconomic. My interest is concentrated on the microeconomic components.

The macroeconomic component lies in the way the global wage-fund is determined and distributed among sectors of the economy and socio-economic groups. The global wage-fund includes wages paid out through the economy during one year not only in the process of the so-called primary distribution of income (in the material sphere) but also in the secondary and tertiary distribution of income (in the non-material sphere). Its size depends on the distribution of national income into accumulation and consumption; in the determination of the latter the value of the planned availability of total goods and services must be considered, if shortages and inflationary pressures are to be avoided (cf. Morecka 1960, pp. 486–99).

The microeconomic components consist of the determination of the wage-bill of enterprises and the regulation of its use, and the determination of wages of individual workers. This author has already explained in some detail in another book (1979) wage-bill determination and regulation in various countries and at different periods depending on the system of management of the economy. In addition wage-bill regulation is discussed in connection with employment regulation, since the planners have indirectly used the former for the regulation of the latter. Therefore only a brief discussion of the determination of the wage-bill on the enterprise level is given here, and the focus is mainly on the determination of wages of individual workers. Both are described primarily as they were introduced in the first stage of planning; their further evolution is discussed in Part II.

1 The Determination of the Wage-bill

In Ch. 3 it was indicated how the level of the planned wage-bill of enterprises is determined. In the traditional Soviet system the actual wage-bill usually deviates from the planned, since the former depends on the extent of fulfilment of planned output targets. In the first years of central planning the overfulfilment of targets, as already mentioned, was rewarded by an additional, proportional (the adjustment coefficient was unity) allocation of funds to the wage-bill. In the second half of the 50s the coefficient was reduced below unity.

Due to its shortcomings (see Ch. 2) wage-bill assignment in a centralised system has gone through some changes, discussed later in connection with employment regulation. Here it need only be mentioned that the linkage of wage-bill growth to plan targets has been retained.

Only countries which have embarked on major reforms have dropped this linkage.

2   Determination of Wages of Individual Workers

In its underlying principles the system of wage determination for individual workers, which was taken over from the Soviet Union, is more or less identical for the whole material sphere. In the following analysis the system as applied in industry is discussed. It consists of three components: tariff system, payment forms and norm setting for pieceworkers.

(a) *Tariff system*

The tariff system determines one side of the 'equation' of distribution according to labour, that is, the wage-rates (basic salaries) to be paid for a certain job. They are established for all employees, manual and non-manual, more or less according to the same principles. Yet, due to the different function of manual and non-manual workers in the production process, the practical application of the principles is different. First the tariff system for manual workers is discussed, then that for non-manual workers.

The tariff system consists of three elements:

Skill grades, in which jobs to be performed are classified on the basis of job evaluation manuals. Since the number of jobs is enormous and since their nature and the conditions under which they are performed vary greatly, the evaluation clearly cannot be done from one centre. The central job evaluation manuals usually set out only the rules for the classification of jobs, indicate the allocation of typical jobs to grades in individual industrial branches and serve as a basis for drafting job evaluation manuals for individual industrial branches. Enterprises adapt these to their own needs.

Naturally jobs are assigned skill grades indicated in the manuals on the basis of criteria which vary from country to country, mainly in the weight attributed to them. The main criteria are the following: sophistication of the job, qualifications needed for its performance, its importance or the material risk involved, and, in some branches, the working conditions as well.

In the 50s in all three countries the number of grades used ranged from 7 to 10. Usually mining and metallurgy had more skill grades.

Workers are assigned so-called personal grades for which qualifications and experience are the decisive criteria. Yet the workers are remunerated mostly on the basis of the jobs they perform and not according to personal grades, though in principle workers should – if possible – get jobs with the same classification as their personal grade (cf. *Incomes* . . . 1967, ch. 8, p. 8, and Jacukowicz 1974, p. 6).

Wage-rate for the lowest skill grade. Supposing working conditions are equal in all sectors of the material sphere, then it could be argued theoretically on the basis of the principle of distribution according to work that the rate for the first skill grade should be identical everywhere. In practice the rates for the first grade varied (and still vary) substantially by sectors and branches of industry, not only within one country, but also betweeen countries. The main criterion for differentiation was the social importance attached to individual sectors and branches, though working conditions also had an influence. And these were also the reason why, in the first phase of planning, every industrial branch and many sub-branches had their own wage-rate scale. Usually mining and metallurgy had the highest rate for the first grade, and the food industry the lowest.

Wage coefficients determine the rate of progression within the wage-rate scale in terms of the percentage difference between the rate for the lowest grade and the rates for successive grades. If the wage-rate for the first grade is given, the wage coefficients determine the wage-rates for individual skill grades and thus the spread between them, including that between the lowest and the highest rate within the wage-rate scale. The spread in wage coefficients, and thus in rates, is supposed primarily to reflect differences in the skills required for performing jobs of varying complexity.

The ratio of the highest to the lowest rate in the wage-rate scale was fixed in industry on the order of 2–3, depending on the branch. In the 50s the overall spread across the wage-rate scales (i.e. the ratio between the highest rate in the best-paid branch and the lowest rate in the worst-paid branch) was higher than within the wage-rate scale. However it would be fallacious to draw conclusions about wage differentiation from this fact alone; as will be shown later, many other factors determine employment income. In addition few jobs in practice are allocated to the lowest grades.

For a long time wage-rates for piecework were (as mentioned) higher than for timework; it was argued that time-rate workers were exposed to a smaller intensity of labour since their remuneration does not depend on work norms.

(b) *Payment forms*

The second part of the 'equation' of distribution according to work is the measurement of the work (or operation) to be remunerated. The problem is not only to ensure that the work performed corresponds to the remuneration received, but also to encourage the worker to improve his performance. With this philosophy as a point of departure, the ideal payment form seems to be payment by results. And, in fact, immediately after the seizure of power by the communist parties and in some countries even earlier, there was a massive campaign for and a rush towards a rapid spread of piecework. Some even went so far as to present piecework as the socialist payment form (cf. Buda 1965 B; Pudlik 1953) what surely contributed to its rise to predominance. It is worth mentioning that the communist leaders were not afraid that a campaign to introduce piecework might cause a backlash, after all in the past their party had bitterly attacked piecework as an instrument of capitalist exploitation of workers. They knew very well that the workers would not really resist the spread of piecework; in fact, in many instances, they pushed for its introduction, for they soon realised that piecework was a good way to achieve higher wages.

In some branches, particularly mining, progressive piece-rates were used. However this payment form has no significance nowadays.

(c) *Work norms*

Piece-rates as a payment form by result imply work norms which set the amount of work to be done for a certain remuneration. In practice three types of work norms were gradually introduced; the simplest, the so-called 'statistical norms' (a result of averaging past performance), 'progressive average norms' (in substance statistical norms adjusted to the performance of outstanding workers) and 'technically based norms' (norms resulting from detailed work studies) (cf. 'Productivity in . . .', 1956). Naturally the central authorities tried hard to expand the third type of norms where possible, at the expense of the first two. The revision of norms and their tightening, carried out relatively often mainly in the first phase, served this purpose.

* * *

Wage-rates are a reward for work performed per hour at normal labour intensity. Earnings (wages) are higher, because piece-rate workers get additional payments for overfulfilling work norms, and time-rate workers usually get supplementary payments. In addition workers get bonuses and are eligible for an additional payment if they work overtime.

Since the norm setting was far from ideal (in many cases the norms set were too slack, in some other too taut), and there was a fear that norms might be overfulfilled excessively, limits were set for the overfulfilment of norms, and an informal ceiling was usually put on the earnings of individual workers. The ceiling was flexible and was usually a compromise between what the individual worker felt that he was entitled to, based on his performance and the earnings of his colleagues, and what the supervisor regarded as just, taking into account the average wage set for the workshop and the actual earnings of other workers. Workers who did not want to respect these rules of the game were sure to encounter revisions of norms or work with taut norms.

(d) *Tariff system of non-manual workers*

Most of the jobs performed by non-manual workers cannot be characterised with as much detail as manual jobs, simply because some elements of the jobs and their weight cannot be predicted. For this reason non-manual jobs are not classified into skill grades directly; this is done through the functions which non-manual workers perform (e.g. workshop planner, enterprise planner, procurement clerk, foreman). The concrete assignment of the grade to individual functions depends on the qualifications and experience required for performance of the job. The responsibility involved, measured mainly by the position in the hierarchy of command, plays a very important role.

Since non-manual work (functions) requires a greater skill variety than manual work, the number of skill grades was and is much higher for non-manual workers than for manual workers. Salary-rate scales were differentiated in individual countries according to the social importance attached to industrial branches and working conditions, and according to the size of enterprises. Separate rate scales were set for managerial technical staff and separate (lower) scales for administrative staff.

6 Appendix II
Distribution of Income
According to Work

1 MARX'S VIEWS ON DISTRIBUTION OF INCOME

Few economic topics have received as much attention in the East, particularly in the past, as the principles governing income distribution. In a sense this is not surprising, since it is one of the central problems of a theory of economic systems. Yet this is not the only reason for the great interest in the topic; many economists feel that analyses given hitherto are simplistic, or at best open-ended; they therefore regard it as a challenge to make a contribution to the topic. Like many other theoretical theses this too has gone through important changes.

In all the socialist countries it is an accepted quasi axiom that income under socialism is distributed according to work. (Here I disregard so-called non-equivalent distribution.) In the past East European economists, following Soviet economists' patterns, regarded this concept of distribution as a law of socialism. By this they intended to emphasise that this is a regularity which asserts itself in certain socioeconomic conditions, more precisely, under socialism. Many books and papers appeared under this title. Even as late as 1970 L. Borcz titled his book *The Law of Distribution According to Work* (translation from Polish). More and more economists have for some time been talking about principle instead of law, or simply about distribution according to work.

The principle of distribution according to work relies heavily on Marx's conclusions about distribution in the *Critique of the Gotha Programme*. According to him, in the first phase of communism (i.e. socialism) distribution is carried out on the same principle as the exchange of commodities, 'as far as this is exchange of equal values'. More precisely 'the individual producer receives back from society – after the deductions have been made – exactly what he gives to it. What

84

he has given to it is his individual quantum of labour. . . . The same amount of labour which he has given to society in one form he receives back in another.' Thus Marx made it clear that the communist ideal of distribution 'from each according to his ability, to each according to his needs' is not feasible under socialism. Communist distribution presupposes a new approach to labour – which will manifest itself by viewing labour 'as life's prime' want – and an abundance of consumer goods and a new division of labour. All these preconditions are lacking in a society 'just as it emerges from capitalist society'.

Does Marx's position not contravene the socialist demand for equality in distribution? For Marx it emphatically did not. 'Equality consists in the fact that measurment is made with an equal standard, labour.' Due to the fact that people differ physically and mentally, 'this equal right is an unequal right for unequal labour' (Feuer 1959, pp. 117–18). From these quotations it is perhaps clear that Marx unequivocally rejected the idea of egalitarianism, as far as it means equal incomes.

Marx was not, however, specific in formulating his ideas about income distribution under socialism. He did not suggest how labour should be measured, and whether other factors should be considered at all. Marx's *Critique of the Gotha Programme* was intended rather as a programmatic statement (a response to the Gotha Programme) than as a profound analysis of a distribution system in a future society. He was apparently interested primarily in showing how income distribution would be brought into harmony with his concept of socialism in contrast to capitalism, and, of course, in making clear that in a future society distribution would be carried out differently than in a capitalist system; under socialism the only source of income would be work, with incomes from other sources than work (such as capital) being eliminated.

2 INTERPRETATION OF MARX'S VIEWS

Marx's views on distribution were interpreted in the USSR as distribution according to quantity and quality of labour input. More precisely this meant that differentiation of wages should be determined by these two criteria. It has been implicitly understood that distribution according to work has little to do with the level of wages. Marx's statement 'the individual producer receives back from society – after the deductions have been made – exactly what he gives to it' has been discussed little apart from various general statements on this topic. This has been no accident. The authorities have tried to prevent a discussion of this problem for fear that this might result in a criticism of the macroeconomic distribution of national income. Some attempts to back up the principle of distribution according to work by including labour replacement costs as its determinant may have been intended as a response to Marx's statement.

To turn this very general interpretation of distribution into a guide for setting wages in a way that would make them best fulfil their functions, many questions must be answered. To mention the most important: what does quantity and quality of labour mean? To what extent can they be quantified? How should working conditions be treated? What should the role of responsibility in setting wages be? To what extent should demand for and supply of labour be taken into account in fixing wages? Should wages be independent of the performance of enterprises or should they reflect it? The nature of the questions is such that it is logical to pose a further question: can the questions raised be solved in a way that does not contradict the principle of distribution according to work? Does not consideration of the questions raised necessarily lead to a violation of the principle of equal wage for equal value of work which is a logical deduction from the principle of distribution according to quantity and quality of work? Without going into any detail now, it is already possible to assert that distribution according to work, as experience shows, is full of contradictions. This is also the reason why some economists try to supplement the principle of distribution according to work with other principles, or to loosen its framework.

There is no agreement among East European economists on the questions raised. Let me start with the concept of quantity and quality of labour. Most economists understand by the term 'quantity' not only the duration of the work performed, but also its intensity; some economists even include working conditions. Even more controversial is the term 'quality'. It is usually accepted that quality of labour means the degree of the job's complexity, reflected in the need for certain skills in order for the workers to be able to perform it. Some authors conceive quality very broadly; they include in it working conditions and, what is more important, social importance of labour (e.g. Průša 1969, pp. 56–7; Maier 1963).

Again social importance of labour is not understood by all economists in the same way. Generally it can be said that the application of this criterion in practice means that in fixing wages the importance of individual sectors, branches of industry and enterprises to the objectives of the national plan is taken into consideration. Furthermore the importance of various occupations to society and the degree of responsibility connected with them are also considered. Finally the criterion of social importance also takes care of the scarcity aspect in that, in the process of determining wages, the relation between demand for and supply of labour is taken into account.

The main reason for including social importance of labour in quality of work seems to be the desire to reconcile this criterion with the principle of distribution according to work. Some economists try to reconcile theory with practice by simply extending the term 'distribution according to work' by including social importance as a third criterion (e.g. Gerloch 1962, p. 30).

Other economists see in the application of the criterion of social importance a deviation from the principle of distribution according to work and feel that this should be terminated as soon as economic conditions allow (e.g. Borcz 1970, p. 98). Some go even further and regard the application of social importance às damaging to the economy (e.g. Kordaszewski 1960, pp. 185–6). One economist (Jacukowicz 1974, pp. 23–4) suggests that the criterion of social importance should be applied in a way that makes clear that it presents a deviation from the distribution principle mentioned.

3   IS INPUT OR OUTPUT RELEVANT FOR THE DISTRIBUTION PRINCIPLE?

Should 'quantity' and 'quality' be understood in terms of input or output and how should they be quantified? In the beginning of central planning the view prevailed that labour input should be the decisive criterion. Wage was regarded as the respective worker's share in the total national income and not as a share in the value of output produced and sold by the enterprise in which the worker was employed. Behind such an interpretation was the idea that wages represent remuneration for work regardless of an enterprise's economic performance. This idea was supported by a completely unjustified dogmatic thesis that under socialism all labour input has a social character; that is, everything that is produced in accordance with the plan is also socially necessary.

The economic reforms of the 60s, which put great stress on economic efficiency, also brought about a change in the perception of wages. In all the reforms the principle was adopted that remuneration should to a certain degree depend on the performance of enterprises, thus on output. The words 'to a certain degree' should be underlined since in none of the three countries was the principle adopted that wages should fully depend on the performance of enterprises. The Yugoslav interpretation of distribution according to work, where the level of wages depends more or less fully on the performance of enterprises (as is the case in collective farms in the Soviet bloc countries), has been rejected. Some economists regarded it as a violation of distribution according to work (e.g. Borcz 1970, p. 86). Under conditions in which workers have no influence, or at best only a little, on the product mix, the choice of technology and other factors which, in the end result, have a decisive impact on performance, it is only just that they should not be responsible for performance. In the socialist countries, as has already been mentioned, only the top managers' salaries are to a great degree dependent on the performance of enterprises.

In order to reconcile the partial linkage of wages to performance with the principle of distribution according to work, some economists (e.g. Brčák 1974) started to coin a so-called theory of a dual principle of distribution. It was argued that distribution according to work was limited to the sphere of basic wages (wage-rates topped by earnings from piecework) whereas bonuses tied to the performance of enterprises were determined by the law of value.

K. Szikra (1979, pp. 19–25) uses an argument similar to that of the Yugoslav economist A. Vacic to reject his idea that output is the criterion for distribution according to work. A. Vacic (1978) argues namely that in a socialist country with commodity production (market relations) only products which obtain recognition of their social usefulness in the market can be considered for distribution. And such recognition is not tied to the work of individuals – simply because it cannot be determined – but to the products of enterprises. K. Szikra believes that just because it is impossible to find out the precise share of individual groups in the product, labour input, not output, can give the answer to the whereabouts of the wage centre around which – in her opinion – wages of different categories oscillate. (Wages of individual workers are, however, differentiated according to their performance.) She takes the position (1979, pp. 25–8) that the wage centre is, like the price centre, determined by the reproduction costs, in this case, of labour. In her opinion these costs have two components: the costs of acquiring qualifications and the input of labour during the work process in terms of mental, physical and emotional involvement. In the second component she includes responsibility and working conditions connected with the work; that is, factors which are accounted for when setting wage-rates. The weight of the two components changes with economic development. In the recent past a shift has become observable in favour of physical work and working conditions at the expense of qualifications and responsibility.

Z. Morecka (1960, pp. 494–502) also regards labour input as decisive for distribution according to work, and holds the view that costs incurred in acquiring different kinds of qualifications should determine to a great extent the qualification differentials. To her, production costs of labour consist of two parts: a general part, which reflects the reproduction costs of simple labour and which should be recovered by minimum wages paid to unskilled workers; and a second, specific part, whose size depends on the extent of heterogeneity of labour as reflected in qualifications, labour intensity and working conditions, and which should enable the output of different use values according to the needs of the economy.

To what extent is the principle that reproduction costs of labour should to a great degree determine wage differentiation followed in practice? One Hungarian economist (Kovács 1977) maintains on the basis of computations that wage differentials for qualifications in Hungary reflect well the differences in the average cost of acquiring qualifications, whereas a Polish economist (Krajewska 1974, p. 177) argues that no proper methods have yet been worked out to enable the costs of acquiring qualifications to be included in differentials.

It is worth while mentioning that some economists believe that the policy of FE and the need to provide every employed person with a wage corresponding at least to minimum subsistence puts limits on distribution of income according to work (cf. Borcz 1970, p. 267).

4 THE PRINCIPLE AND PRACTICE OF DISTRIBUTION OF INCOME

Now that all these various views have been presented, the question is warranted: to what extent does the practice of income distribution correspond to the 'theory'? It is very difficult, if not impossible, to give a precise answer based on quantitative calculations to this question, one reason being that there is no single theory of distribution. Nevertheless it is safe to use common sense in arguing that the practice deviates from what could be regarded as the minimum criterion for distribution according to work. How can one otherwise explain that an average university-educated engineer with several years' experience earns hardly any more than a skilled worker, and that many unskilled and semi-skilled workers earn more than skilled, though their working conditions are hardly different at all. Or, to take another example, the same work performed in different sectors of the economy and industrial branches is rewarded substantially differently. Every objective East European economist with some knowledge of wage differentials in his country will agree that they are marked by many distortions in different directions. The frequent statements of politicians about the need of bringing wage differentials into line with distribution according to work confirms this.

One could argue that differentiation of average earnings in the material sphere, where the central authorities do not have full control over wages, is not a good indication of the relationship between practice, as determined by the central authorities, and theory. Yet wage-rate differentiation, which is under the strict control of the central authorities, did not seem to be much better in the past. In this connection the comments made by W. Krencik (1972, pp. 85–6), Polish expert, about the state of wage-rates in 1970 are of interest. He found that in some branches of industry wage-rates for the highest skill grades were only a little higher than the lowest rates in some other branches. What is even more important, wage-rates for jobs involving the same qualifications, arduousness and responsibility varied substantially. W. Krencik maintains that these great differences cannot be explained only by the different importance for the economy of individual branches.

In the 70s (even earlier in Hungary) – as will be shown later – the three countries reduced the differences in wage-rates for the same jobs in different sectors and industrial branches. This policy was perhaps carried the farthest in Hungary. Provisions were also undertaken to make the wage-rate differentials for skill more pronounced between manual workers. Therefore it is possible to argue that in setting wage-rates which are fully controlled by the authorities, the principle of distribution according to work is increasingly used as a guide, though a very crude one for the determination of wage-rates. But the role of the principle is much, much smaller in the determination of average earnings, primarily in profit-making enterprises where, many other factors, especially the relationship between demand for and supply of labour, are considered.

Part II

7 Employment and Wage Policies 1950–55

A INTRODUCTION

After the seizure of political power by the communists all three countries embarked on medium-term plans: Czechoslovakia and Hungary on five-year plans (the former for the period 1949–53 and the latter for 1950–4) and Poland on a six-year plan for 1950–5. The medium-term plans were preceded by short-term plans, a two-year plan in Czechoslovakia (1947–8) and three-year plans in Hungary and Poland (for 1947–9). The main goal of the short-term plans, known as reconstruction plans, was to bring the economy to a level higher than the pre-war one, with a simultaneous start to a restructuring of the economy (industrialisation), which was followed with great vigour in the medium-term plans. Naturally this goal was more demanding in Poland, where the economy suffered greatly from war events, than in the other two countries, particularly Czechoslovakia, where war destruction was minimal.

The reconstruction plans proceeded amid profound social changes in the ownership of the means of production which started soon after the war. In agriculture this meant agrarian reform, and in the non-agricultural sectors nationalisation of means of production. The latter was carried out in several stages and was completed after the communists took over political power entirely (Průcha et al. 1977, pp. 105–18).

The reconstruction plans were in many respects different from the medium-term plans introduced later. They were partial plans covering only some sectors of the economy, and wages and prices were not part of the planning process. Plan targets were binding on government and planned sectors, but by no means on enterprises. The Soviet system of management of the economy was not yet applied. It was expected that rational behaviour by enterprises would be achieved by making them responsive to market signals (for more see Berend 1974, p. 65; Olšovský and Průcha 1969, p. 347; Kosta 1978, pp. 37–41). The main purpose of

93

planning was to concentrate investments on projects which the governments regarded as specially important and to eliminate bottlenecks which might hamper the development of the economy.

The reconstruction plans envisaged a relatively even distribution of investment funds among sectors of the economy (Jędruszczak 1972, p. 38). Even the needs of agriculture and the non-productive sectors (including housing) were properly taken into consideration. What was perhaps most important was that the reconstruction plans were designed to bring about a higher standard of living. At the start of the reconstruction plans the communists were still far from being in control of political power, especially in Czechoslovakia, and therefore had to pay great attention to the standard of living. By the end of the three-year plan real wages in Hungary had increased by 10 to 20 per cent over the level of 1938 (Berend 1974, p. 68).

In their final version the medium-term plans were drafted according to Soviet pattern. Domestic planners were under increasing pressure from Soviet experts and authorities to slavishly follow Soviet practices.

In all three countries the objective of the medium-term plans was, according to the political leaders, to build the foundations of socialism by rapid industrialisation, in which the greatest stress was put on the development of heavy industry, a policy motivated largely by military considerations (cf. Berend 1979, p. 99; Kuziński 1956). The Soviet Union was preparing for a hot war, and the East European countries were supposed to contribute to the armament build-up. Nevertheless all three medium-term plans envisaged a substantial increase in the standard of living.

International tension generated by the outbreak of the Korean War brought about an acceleration of the industrialisation drive in Czechoslovakia and Hungary.[1] In Czechoslovakia the modified FYP envisaged an increase in industrial production of 98 per cent instead of 57 per cent, and in heavy industry of 133 per cent instead of 66 per cent (Lukeš and Rybnikář 1968). The Hungarian planners pledged even higher increases; the national income was supposed to increase by 130 per cent against the original 63 per cent, and in industrial production the corresponding figures were 210 per cent against 86 per cent, with heavy industry having to grow the fastest (Berend 1979, p. 98; Balogh and Jakab 1978, p. 174). Naturally investment outlays increased dramatically too; the greatest part of investment was channelled primarily into heavy industry.

The industrialisation drive generated great imbalances in all spheres of the economy. Shortages of raw materials as well as of consumer goods emerged; the latter resulted not only from neglect of consumer goods industries, but also from the imposed collectivisation of agriculture. Social and political tensions arose and spread due to the great burden the population was forced to bear and to the limitations imposed on human rights.

Stalin's death in 1953 and the ensuing modifications in foreign and domestic policies (rearrangement of priorities) created an atmosphere for change. The biggest changes took place in Hungary; there the strategy of economic development was modified for a short time. I. Nagy, who in May 1953 became the new prime minister, and his associates saw to it that the role of heavy industry was reduced, and agriculture and the consumer goods industry became the focal point of government policy (Balogh and Jakab 1978, pp. 217–24). In Czechoslovakia and Poland changes also occurred. In 1954–5 the plan targets were reduced, and with them investment outlays, and more attention was devoted to agriculture and the consumer goods industries in an effort to improve the standard of living (Golębiowski 1977, p. 122).

The changes in the three countries were only temporary (in Hungary I. Nagy was forced to resign in 1955) without really affecting permanently the adopted Soviet strategy of economic development.

B   EMPLOYMENT POLICIES

1   Employment Plans

One of the objectives of the reconstruction plans in Poland and Hungary was to cope with unemployment. In the Polish reconstruction plan the objective of full employment was explicitly stated.[2] The Hungarian planners were more cautious; the plan envisaged only an ever-increasing number of workers and the elimination of latent unemployment in agriculture (*Hungarian* . . . 1947, p. 42). Yet both reconstruction plans were permeated with the idea that the objective was not to increase employment for the sake of employment. The Polish (*Polish* . . . 1946, p. 23) stressed optimum employment in the sense that labour would be directed to enterprises which, due to their conditions and technical equipment, showed the greatest productive possibilities. The Hungarian plan was even more specific; it stressed the need for rationalisation of production and set as an objective optimum output. 'In other words – the plan [*Hungarian* . . . 1947, p. 43] reads – the utilisation of manpower in a way that does not result in an increased demand for workers, on the contrary. . . .'

Czechoslovakia was in a different situation. Due to the evacuation of most of the German nationals to occupied Germany, labour shortages, mainly of skilled workers, were felt in many branches of industry in the Czech lands, particularly in Sudetenland. In Slovakia labour reserves still existed, and many Slovaks therefore moved to work in the CSR (*Průběh plnění* . . . 1948, pp. 241–4).

The reconstruction plans brought about a rapid improvement in employment. In 1949 only 5 per cent of job-seekers in Poland could not find job (Jędruszczak 1972, p. 150). A similar situation came about in Hungary.

The ambitious medium-term plans generated a dramatic increase in the demand for labour; the countries were short of capital, and labour was to serve partly as a substitute for capital. What was also important was that concerns for a rational utilisation of labour were put on the back-burner. According to the final version of the six-year plan employment in the Polish socialist sector (outside agriculture) was to increase by 58 per cent (from 3 600 000 in 1949 to 5 700 000 in 1955, of that female employment was to increase by 1 230 000) and industry by 65 per cent. At the same time the plan envisaged a substantial increase in labour productivity, 66 per cent in large- and medium-scale industry and 85 per cent in construction (Minc 1950, pp. 53, 60). In Hungary the FYP was supposed to increase industrial employment by 480 000 and labour productivity by 50 per cent (*Hungary's* . . . pp. 3–4).

In Czechoslovakia during the FYP the number of economically active in the economy was to increase by 5.6 per cent, by 18.5 per cent in industry and by 50 per cent in construction, and was to decline by 4.2 per cent in agriculture. At the same time productivity was expected to increase by 32 per cent in industry, 53 per cent in construction and 35 per cent in transportation (Kocanda 1965, p. 118; Voborník 1952). The Czechoslovak targets were, for understandable reasons, the most modest.

The increased output targets in 1950–1 brought about a further substantial increase in demand for labour. The revised Czechoslovak plan assumed an additional increase in the number of economically active outside agriculture of 354 000 (Voborník 1952) and in Hungary an additional 650 000 workers were needed in order to meet the new targets (Balogh and Jakab 1978, p. 179).

In 1954–5 economic growth was decelerated in order to take care of the imbalances which had arisen during the previous period. Therefore the targets for employment increases also became more modest; however no exact figures are available.

2   Employment Growth and its Sources

Incomes in Post-war Europe: . . . (1967, Ch. 7, p. 11) quotes planned and actual figures on employment for the whole economy (without cooperatives and private agriculture) and industry. Though the actual figures do not always square with the official, they nevertheless give some idea about employment plan fulfilment. It seems that in Czechoslovakia the 1950–1 increased employment plan – not to mention the original one – was exceeded. In Poland the increase in industrial employment remained below the plan (similarly in Hungary), whereas the increase in employment in the economy (outside co-operatives and private agriculture) exceeded it (see Table A.1, p. 234).

Table 7.1 reveals that the growth in the number of economically active in 1950–5 was not as dramatic as one would expect from a first glance at planned figures; in Poland, where the growth rate was the highest, it was 12.6 per cent, in Hungary only 7.3 per cent (for 1951–6) and in Czechoslovakia 7 per cent. Dramatic changes occurred in total employment outside agriculture, primarily as a result of a very fast increase in industrial and constructional employment. In Hungary in 1949–55 industrial employment increased by 48.6 per cent and in Poland by 34.4 per cent. Even in Czechoslovakia, which had a respectable industry even before the Second World War, it increased by 19.3 per cent.

The evolution in employment meant great changes in the structure of employment, as Table 7.2 shows. The changes would, of course, be much greater if the period starting from the beginning of the reconstruction plans was considered. Unfortunately I have not come across such comparative figures. In all three countries the share of industrial employment increased at the expense of agriculture. In Czechoslovakia in 1955 employment in industry surpassed agriculture slightly, whereas in Hungary, despite progress in industry, agriculture had still (in 1956) 77 per cent more economically active than industry.

(a)   *Evolution of the working-age population*

The growth in the working-age population as a factor of the mentioned employment increases did not play the same role in all three countries. As Table 7.1 and other statistical figures reveal, the growth of the working-age population in Czechoslovakia stagnated in the period 1950–5. In 1955 it was 0.8 per cent smaller than in 1948 and 0.7 per cent higher than in 1950. The level of 1948 was not achieved until 1958.[3] Due to this

TABLE 7.1 *Growth of the population, working-age population and economically active population 1950–55*[a]

	Poland			CSSR			Hungary		
	A		B	A		B	A		B
	1950	1955	1951–5	1950	1955	1951–5	1951	1956	1951–5
1. Population	25 000	27 600	2.0	12 389	13 093	1.1	9 383	9 883	1.0
Index 1950 = 100[b]		110.4			105.7			105.3	
2. Working-age population	14 500	15 600	1.5	7 428	7 483	0.1	5 905	6 052	0.5
Index 1950 = 100[b]		107.6			100.7			102.5	
3. Economically active population[c]	10 186	11 467	2.4	5 529	5 915	1.4	4 254	4 563	1.4
Index 1950 = 100[b]		112.6			107.0			107.3	
4. Participation rates									
(a) 3:1	40.7	41.5		44.6	45.2		44.2	45.8	
(b) 3:2	70.2	73.5		74.4	79.0		69.9	74.2	

A – In absolute numbers (in thousands).
B – Compounded annual growth rates.

[a] In Poland the figures for population and working-age population refer to the end of the year, and figures for the economically active are annual averages, as is the case for all figures in the CSSR. All Hungarian figures refer to one year later than other countries' figures since they pertain to the very beginning of the year. Polish figures on participation rates result from data referring to different times of the year.
[b] In Hungary 1951 = 100.
[c] Working-age population means in Poland men 18–64 years, women 16–59 years, in CSSR 15–59 and 15–54 and in Hungary 14–59 and 14–54.

SOURCES Poland – *RS 1981*, p. xxxii; Czechoslovakia – *SRC 1981*, p. 20, and *SRC 1982*, p. 24; Hungary – *SE 1980*, pp. 3–4, and Lengyel 1958.

TABLE 7.2 *Growth of the labour force 1950–55*[a]

	Poland			CSSR[b]			Hungary[c]		
	A		B	A		B	A		B
	1950	1955	1951–5	1950	1955	1951–5	1951	1955	1951–5
1. National economy	10 186	11 467	2.4	5 529	5 915	1.4	4 254	4 563	1.2
Index 1950 = 100		112.6			107.0			107.3	
2. Socialist sector[d]	4 832	6 790	7.0		4,267				
Index 1950 = 100		140.5							
3. Material sphere	9 273			4 815	5 062	1.0	3 545	3 851	1.7
Index 1950 = 100					105.1			108.6	
4. Non-material sphere	913			714	853	3.6	709	712	0.1
Index 1950 = 100					119.5			100.4	
5. Industry	2 107	2 795	5.8	1 667	1 942	3.1	817	1 123	6.6
Index 1950 = 100		132.6			116.5			137.4	
6. Construction	510	734	7.6	316	363	2.8	195	211	1.6
Index 1950 = 100		143.9			114.9			108.2	
7. Agriculture inclusive of forestry[e]	5 553			2 056	1 932	−1.2	2 112	1 990	−1.2
Index 1950 = 100					94.0			94.2	
8. Transport and communications	460	565	4.2	294[f]	336	3.4[f]	184	252	6.5
Index 1950 = 100		122.8			114.3			137.0	
9. Trade	535	662	4.3	391	410	1.0	236	275	3.1
Index 1950 = 100		123.7			104.9			116.5	
10. Health and social care[g]	138[h]	226[h]	10.4	106	153	7.6			
Index 1950 = 100		163.8			144.3				
11. Education, culture, physical education[i]	228[h]	344[h]	8.6	184[f]	237	6.5[f]			
Index 1950 = 100		150.3			128.8				

TABLE 7.2 (Contd.)

	Poland			CSSR[b]			Hungary[c]		
	A	B		A	B		A		B
	1950	1955	1951–5	1950	1955	1951–5	1951	1956	1951–5
12. Communal and housing services	108	151	6.9						
Index 1950 = 100		139.8							
13. Collectivised agriculture	420								

A – In absolute numbers (in thousands). B – Compounded annual growth rates, in percent.

[a] Polish and Czechoslovak data refer to annual averages, Hungarian to the beginning of the year. In Poland data include full-time as well as part-time employees, the latter being recalculated into full-time employees. Data for items 3 and 4 in Poland are estimates.
[b] In CSSR women on maternity leave are not included (except in items 8–11 up to 1965 inclusive); the same is probably true for Poland and Hungary.
[c] The base year for indexes in Hungary is 1951.
[d] In the CSSR without collective farms.
[e] In the CSSR forestry is not included; in Poland only socialist forestry is included.
[f] A refers to 1951; B refers to 1955/1952.
[g] In Poland physical education is included.
[h] Socialist sector only.
[i] In Poland physical education is left out; instead arts are included.

SOURCES Poland – RS 1981, p. xxxii; Rocznik Statystyczny Przemysłu 1981, p. xl; RS 1975, p. 51; RS 1972, p. 109; RS 1960, p. 60.
        CSSR – SRC 1982, p. 24; SRC 1981, p. 22; SRC 1967, p. 22.
        Hungary – SE 1980, p. 4.

stagnation, increments to the number of economically active persons came necessarily from other sources, primarily from the increase in the participation rate of women which was anyhow the highest among the three countries. The high employment increases in industry, construction and other sectors were also made possible by the high exodus from agriculture.

Hungary was not much better off regarding the growth rate of the working-age population; it was 2.5 per cent for the period 1951–6. As in Czechoslovakia, the increase in the number of economically active was achieved by a fast increase in female economic activity.

Only in Poland was the increase in the working-age population high, 7.6 per cent for the period 1950–5. Largely due to this fact the growth rates of the economically active population could be higher than in the other two countries. Yet the participation rate (computed as a ratio of the working-age population) lagged behind in Poland; in 1955 it was still 73.5 per cent against 79.0 per cent in Czechoslovakia and 74.2 per cent in Hungary (see Table 7.1).

(b) *Housewives*

Housewives played an important role in the employment plans. In Poland the government undertook special provisions to ease the increase in female employment. Economic ministries were ordered to make sure that in enterprises under their jurisdiction the percentage of women in the work force reached a certain target. In addition, men had to vacate service sector jobs which could be filled by women (Jędruszczak 1972, pp. 158–9).

The Czechoslovak and Hungarian planners used methods similar to the Polish. The Czechoslovak ministry of labour set targets for the percentage of women in employment in individual enterprises. In Hungary a government decree stipulated that in 1951 females were supposed to make up 50 per cent of the newly hired workers in manufacturing (Čech 1959, p. 91; Schönwald 1980, p. 124).

(c) *Workers of pensionable age*

In all three countries pensions were at a low level in the period discussed; therefore many persons of pensionable age continued to work. This author has only come across figures for Hungary dealing with the number of people working beyond retirement age; they show that their number grew from 1949–53 and then started to decline. In 1949 36.8 per cent of all persons beyond retirement age worked, making up 11.4 per cent of the economically active population. In 1955 the corresponding figures were 34.5 per cent and 10.4 per cent (Lengyel 1958).

(d) *Agriculture*

The exodus from agriculture which started with the introduction of the reconstruction plans was substantially accelerated by the start of collectivisation of agriculture, which followed the inception of the medium-term plans. In some areas of the countries it took on the form of a flight. There are no precise figures on the number of people who left agriculture. What are available are figures on the evolution of the numbers of economically active in agriculture. According to these figures the number declined in Czechoslovakia in 1948–53 by 17 and in Hungary in 1949–53 by 11.7 percentage points. The exodus from agriculture was probably greater than the figures indicate. They do not include, for example, all the young people who in the meantime had reached working age and had gone to work outside agriculture. As indicated, there are no proper figures for Poland; what exist are figures about migration from the rural areas, which is not equal to an exodus from agriculture. According to these figures 552 000 people left rural areas in 1951–4 (inclusive) (Rajkiewicz 1965, p. 126).

In 1953–4 pressure for collectivisation abated; mainly in Hungary there was even an opposite trend. Consequently the flight from agriculture came to a halt; many peasants even returned to work on the land. In addition, the appropriate authorities in Czechoslovakia undertook great efforts to attract school-leavers to agriculture (Kocanda 1965, p. 121). The number of economically active in agriculture started to grow again.

(e) *Institutional changes*

Provisions aiming at changes in ownership relations also helped to direct manpower to fast-expanding sectors. The vast majority of small businesses, handicrafts and services was simply shut down, and their owners and employees were 'advised' to take jobs in nationalised sectors. The central planners believed (this soon turned out to be in many respects a fallacy) that it would be possible in the new system to produce many of the products provided by small-scale plants in large plants with a smaller number of workers and greater efficiency.

Many plants with similar output were merged into larger units. The banking system was drastically reorganised and concentrated; a monobank system with many branches scattered throughout the country came into being. A comprehensive social insurance system was introduced; other insurance services were cut drastically. All these measures displaced a great number of people. In addition activities which were labelled as typically capitalist (brokers, real estate agents, sales agents) were abolished, and workers were advised to take jobs in the socialist sector.

At the same time, when the authorities mobilised workers for the industrialisation effort, an oppressive apparatus and bureaucracy created for the oversight and control of the population and the economy mushroomed.

4 Problems in the Implementation of the Employment Policy

The most formidable problem planners were confronted with was to match demand for and supply of labour at all levels of the economy and to match qualifications of would-be jobholders with the requirements of the economy. There is only enough information about the first problem, to which I will confine myself. The planners were not successful in their efforts; they were forced to witness labour shortages developing in some sectors and industrial branches at a time when overmanning was taking roots in some others. Labour shortages were strongly felt in coal production (Rajkiewicz 1965, p. 124; Fonal 1956) and in Czechoslovakia and Hungary in construction. Despite recruitment efforts and the preferential wage treatment of labour in these two sectors the authorities did not manage to create a permanent labour force there; in the beginning of the 50s the job openings there were filled to a great degree by prisoners, including political detainees (Fonal 1956). After 1953 the governments, primarily in Hungary, moderated their repressive policies, and consequently many political prisoners were released or at least freed from arduous forced labour. In addition, due to declining real wages and to the lull in forced collectivisation, many peasants, mainly in Hungary, left the coal industry and construction.

Agriculture was another sector where labour shortages were felt (particularly in Poland and Czechoslovakia), due to a higher exodus from there than was planned. Forced collectivisation induced young people particularly to look for jobs outside agriculture. This began a worsening of the age structure of farmers, a process which, in the course of time, has been aggravated.

Starting with 1953 when investment outlays were reduced, overmanning in some sectors became worse (Daskiewicz 1955). White-collar overstaffing was found especially burdensome at a time when planners were starting to give more consideration to efficiency aspects (Sedlák 1961).

All the countries started to be plagued by a decline in the level of labour discipline, which was reflected in absenteeism, excessive underutilisation of working time, indifference to quality resulting in excessive spoilages and excessive labour turnover, to mention the most important phenomena. The individual elements of this behaviour have taken on different intensity in different periods, but on the whole they persist.

The general reasons for low labour discipline have been discussed above. Here only the reasons which directly resulted from conditions in the period discussed will be briefly mentioned. Many persons were forced to join the labour force against their will or were assigned to jobs which they did not like (*Pracovní sily* 1954, no. 2). Their behaviour was a protest against the treatment they were exposed to. The situation was compounded by the fact that the pecuniary motivation was undermined by declining real wages and consumer goods shortages. Indifference to quality was to a great degree the result of the imposition of piecework. Low labour discipline was also fuelled by the inability of the planners to master the tremendous organisational problems which were connected with the great influx of people to the labour force.

Of course the governments tried to cope with the problems. The main thrust of the provisions was in two directions: to tighten labour discipline and to cope with the growing number of administrative workers. Already in 1950 Poland had enacted, according to Soviet pattern, a law for the securement of the 'socialist discipline of labour'. Absenteeism over a certain number of days could result in jail terms and reduction in wages, both meted out by the courts. In addition the law curtailed the right of workers to change jobs according to their choice (Jędruszczak 1972, pp. 166–7). A similar law was adopted in Hungary (Schönwald 1980, pp. 129–31). The Czechoslovak leaders hesitated for some time to follow the draconian Soviet measures. Finally, in the beginning of 1953, they decided to act; if not for Stalin's death the law would have been put into force.[4] However the right to leave jobs was curtailed in Czechoslovakia too.

All three countries tried to reduce the number of administrative workers and to transfer them to manual work. The provisions applied were not very successful; their main effect was to halt the growth of administrative workers for some time (Balogh and Jakab 1978, p. 239; Daskiewicz 1955).

5   Methods of Labour Recruitment and Labour Allocation

State authorities reserved the right to monitor labour mobility and to intervene in the labour market according to the requirements of the planning process and political considerations.[5] In the following three areas the authorities were involved to different degrees. First, they recruited or helped to recruit labour for enterprises which could not find enough workers. Second, they helped place job-seekers: those wanting to enter the labour force for the first time (housewives, youth) or those looking for new jobs. Third, they placed people in jobs; this in substance referred to two groups: one, those with newly acquired skills (from vocational schools, high schools and university) whose distribution according to certain criteria, the central planners believed, was warranted from an economic and social viewpoint, and, second, disabled people who, without the help of authorities, had a small chance of finding and maintaining a proper position.

I will concentrate on the first and third areas. In the explanation of how the authorities coped with the first task, it will also become clear how job-seekers were helped to find jobs.

(a) *Free and organised recruitment*

'Free' recruitment meant that enterprises had the right to hire people according to their own criteria. Yet enterprises' rights were limited by the numerical limits set for employment and by the geographical area in which they were allowed to look for workers. Free recruitment had two forms. Enterprises were allowed to find appropriate workers, and the employment contract was submitted to the labour department of the national council[6] for formal approval. Labour departments, which also served as labour exchange offices, had the right to suggest candidates to enterprises from among the job-seekers who approached them for help; the final decision was, however, in the hands of enterprises (Kocanda 1965, p. 137).

'Organized' recruitment, a method taken over from the USSR and used in Czechoslovakia, Hungary and probably also in Poland, had the following features: the planners drew up a national plan for recruitment, which contained the sectors and industrial branches (in some cases even the enterprises) for which recruitment was required and the number of workers. Administration of recruitment was implemented by a central body in the form of quotas handed down through the chains of local governments. Recruitment for priority sectors (where regular hiring practices were not successful) was carried out in the non-priority sectors (e.g. light industry) among discharged conscripts, the agricultural population, people who often changed jobs and job-seekers.

The recruitment was supposed to be based on persuasion and incentives. Persons who agreed to work in priority sectors were entitled to an allowance and a wage supplement (equalisation supplement) for some time, if the earnings in the new position were lower than in the previous one (Kocanda 1965, p. 37; Schönwald 1980, pp. 122–3). However enterprises and national councils used administrative pressure on would-be recruits in order to fulfil the quota. Enterprises often improved upon the allowance in order to make the recruitment more acceptable.

Data available for Czechoslovakia show that organised recruitment made up only a small percentage of total recruitment. In 1953, when it reached its highest figure (41 000), it made up 8.4 per cent. In addition organised recruitment did not prove effective in providing permanent workers for sectors which suffered from chronic shortages. In 1953, of the total number of recruits in coal-mining, only 12.7 per cent renewed the one year contract (Kocanda 1965, p. 134).

Though organised recruitment was only introduced in 1951, administrative coercion had earlier been used to get people into priority enterprises. By administrative coercion I mean cases where people were literally forced to take a certain job and cases – which occurred probably much more frequently – where people were given the option to find a manual job in a certain sector (or production) or be assigned to a certain job. Such treatment was applied primarily to many businessmen, who were forced to shut down their businesses, to employees in jobs which were regarded as typically capitalist, to political opponents of the regime or even to workers who performed jobs which were no longer in demand.

It is interesting that, of the three countries, Czechoslovakia applied the harshest administrative methods against some white-collar workers. It was the only country which carried out the so-called Action 'A' which meant an organised transfer of 77 000 administrative workers (from state and local administration) to manual jobs. This action was largely motivated by political considerations, namely by the desire to get rid of elements which seemed unreliable to the authorities and at the same time to create job openings for reliable 'cadres'.

Apart from administrative coercion the authorities used full-fledged forced labour. People incarcerated for political reasons, interned 'class enemies' (as kulaks) – at the end of the 40s and the beginning of the 50s their number was high – and criminals were used for work for which government incentives could not attract enough workers (as in mining, construction). Needless to say, this was cheap labour, an aspect which surely played an important role.

Military conscripts who, due to their class origin or expressed views, were regarded as unreliable were also used for unpopular jobs. In the ex-enemy countries, where the armed forces in the initial period were small, some of the conscripts were also used for work.

(b) *Placement of graduates*

In this area the objectives of the plan were implemented by administrative methods above all. They were applied to youths once they completed compulsory school attendance; they could not freely choose between vocational training and high school. Their freedom was even more limited with regard to the kind of training or high school. In an attempt to match the demand for skilled labour with the supply, quotas were set for each trade. In admissions to the more popular trades, not only the preferences and the ability of the applicants were decisive; class origin and other factors entered into the decision too (Kocanda 1965, p. 128).

In the beginning of the 50s vocational training was concentrated, according to the Soviet pattern, in Labour Reserve Schools under the auspices of a central agency. Graduates of Labour Reserve Schools were allocated to certain jobs, which they could not leave for three years without approval.

The same system was applied to graduates of professional high schools and most university graduates. Let me dwell for a moment on the procedure for allocating university graduates in Czechoslovakia. The Planning Commission balanced the ministry of education's plan for the expected number of graduates from different specialisations with the demand for graduates structured according to sectors and regions. As a result of this balancing, branch ministries were assigned graduates for enterprises and organisations under their jurisdiction. The concrete allocation of individual students to jobs was made by the deans of faculties in co-operation with advisory committees, composed of representatives of the Party, trade unions and youth organisations. The wishes of graduates were registered, but not always respected; the so-called national interest was decisive. Graduates could appeal the resolution to the president of the university, whose decision was final (Čech 1959, pp. 82–7). A similar system was applied in Poland (Olędzki 1974, pp. 226–7).

National councils played an important role in placing disabled people. In co-operation with enterprises local governments drew up a list of jobs for disabled people and handed down binding quotas for individual enterprises (Čech 1959, pp. 90–9).

6   Regulation of Employment

From the start of central planning the planners were determined to apply Soviet administrative methods, i.e. setting limits for employment at the enterprise level. Yet they could do so only by stages; first the needed statistical data had to be acquired, mainly data about the norms of labour intensity of products, work norms, manpower balances and expected labour productivity growth. I have already mentioned the problems involved in arriving at correct data on the labour intensity of products and work norms. Here it should be mentioned that planning the number of workers needed for individual enterprises also caused much difficulty. Even if all the data mentioned above are available, the solution is not easy. It must be remembered that enterprises are not evenly equipped technically, and the output mix was often changed for various reasons (Frankowski 1952). Furthermore the planning of the wage-bill could not be instituted at the start of the FYPs.

In the first phase the authorities relied on enterprises to voluntarily follow a reasonable employment policy and to set the number of workers on the basis of output and productivity plan targets. In the next stage (in Czechoslovakia this was in 1952) the central planners assigned annual binding limits for employment, according to Soviet patterns, in the form of the so-called 'registered number of employees'.[7] It was hoped that the control over enterprises' manpower management would be increased by the central assignment of the wage-bill to enterprises and the banks' right to control the drawing of funds for wages (Voborník 1952).

C WAGE POLICIES

The period must be divided into two phases: the first up to some time in 1953, and the second up to 1955 inclusive. The first phase is characterised by a full subordination of standard-of-living considerations, including wage policy, to the strategy of economic development. The second period is sometimes called in the literature the 'consumption period', in which the governments tried to make up partially for the material hardships they imposed on their countries in the previous phase, thus attempting to improve the relationship with the working population which was rapidly nearing the breaking point.

During the reconstruction plan period the economy recovered, and with it the standard of living increased. Real wages increased not only statistically, but also in terms of increasing availability of consumer goods. In Poland the gradual abolition of the rationing system was completed by January 1949. In Hungary the rationing system was in substance abolished with the application of a currency reform in 1946. Only Czechoslovakia stuck to the rationing system without interruption up to 1953, but even there the supply of consumer goods was improving.

The start of the medium-term plans, and particularly the increase in output targets in 1950–1, necessarily brought about a radical change in wage policy. All three countries envisaged in their plans remarkable increases in the standard of living, though not in specific terms. The Hungarian FYP projected a 35 per cent increase in the standard of living (*Hungary's* . . . , pp. 4, 6) and the Czechoslovak a 35 per cent increase in total consumption (personal and collective) *per capita* (*First Czechoslovak* . . . 1949, p. 57); neither specified what this would mean in terms of real wages. Only the Polish six-year plan promised a 40 per cent rise in real wages as well as a 50–60 per cent increase in the standard of living (Minc 1950, p. 53). To any central planner worth the name, it must have been clear that the standard-of-living targets were out of reach. This may also have been the reason why the targets were formulated so vaguely. The ambitious industrialisation plans, the obsession with maximum growth and the feverish armament combined with the methods used to achieve the objectives made the standard-of-living targets unattainable. In addition employment increased substantially and with it the demand for consumer goods. However the output of consumer goods industries lagged behind the demand, and in agriculture forced collectivisation hampered growth of agricultural output. On top of all this the economy was very inefficient.

Under such conditions personal consumption, and particularly real wages, could not grow much. As Table 7.3 shows, real wages in all three countries declined in 1951–3 (in Poland in 1952–3). The most dramatic decline was in Hungary; according to the table, which is based on official figures, real wages dropped by 19 per cent in 1950–2. Yet , if one considers what happened in the 1951 quasi-currency reform, one cannot but speculate that the decline must have been much bigger. The same is true of the other two countries.

The figures on the drop in real wages do not give a complete picture of the extent to which the workers' pay fell; they do not reflect the great shortages in consumer goods, which made it difficult to realise the existing purchasing power.

The drop in real wages was brought about by several instruments, the most important being the currency and quasi-currency reforms, which were combined with wage and price adjustments. The currency reforms

TABLE 7.3   *Evolution of nominal wages (A),[a] consumer prices (B) and real wages (C)[b] 1948–55*

		1948	1949	1950	1951	1952	1953	1954	1955
Czechoslovakia[c]	A	100	106	115	122	128	134		
				100	106	111	116	124	127
	B	100	132	146	167	179	191		
							100	97	94
	C	100	80	79	73	71	70		
				100	96	94	95	104	110
Poland[d]	A		100	121	132	144	204	216	225
	B		100	107	118	135	192	180	176
	C		100	112	112	107	106	119	124
Hungary[e]	A		100	107	114	147	155	174	178
	B		100	106	128	179	178	170	168
	C		100	101	90	82	87	102	106

[a] Inclusive bonuses.
[b] Refers to the state sector.
[c] The upper line of nominal wages – *Stručný statistický přehled 1945–1960* (Prague, 1960) p. 176. The upper line of prices (which represent a weighted average of both rationed and non-rationed prices) – Kožušník 1964, p. 96. The upper line of real wages is a computation of both. The rest is computed from figures taken from *Incomes . . . 1967*, table 7.13. Real-wage figures for 1950–2 are only estimates. The two sets of figures on real wages differ considerably; the true figures were probably somewhere in between.
[d] Prices are computed from data in *RS 1957*, p. 238. The rest – Morecka 1965. Money wages refer to net wages.
[e] *Statisticheskii sbornik, Po voprosam truda i zarabotnoi platy v evropeiskikh sotsialisticheskikh stranakh* (Moscow, 1959) p. 121. Prices refer to cost of living.

aimed at solving several problems: providing funds for increasing investment outlays by depriving people of a great part of their savings, mitigating imbalances in the markets for consumer goods and creating conditions for new policies (Polish and Czechoslovak reforms in 1953).

Poland had two currency reforms, but the first in 1950 did not bring about the market equilibrium sought; in 1951 the rationing system was reintroduced. In January 1953 the authorities carried out a price reform which was in a sense a currency reform with no change of bank notes. Prices were increased by 40 per cent and nominal wages by 30 per cent (Kucharski 1972, p. 320).

In 1951 Hungary carried out a quasi-currency reform which brought about a drastic increase in prices; most consumer goods prices were increased by 50–100 per cent, whereas nominal wages rose by only 20 per cent (Berend 1974, pp. 42–3, 84).

In Czechoslovakia there was a currency reform in June 1953 combined with a price reform and wage adjustments. The new price level was about 15 per cent higher than the weighted average of rationed and free market prices which had existed before the reform (Adam 1974, pp. 107–8).

The decline in real wages was mitigated by the rapid expansion of employment which was viewed as the main instrument of standard-of-living improvement (in the Polish six-year plan this was specifically stated (Minc 1950, p. 53). Rapidly growing employment opportunities increased the number of wage-earners in most families, thus increasing the *per capita* earnings of a family, even if real wages per worker declined. As a result of employment expansion personal consumption grew slightly.

Needless to say, in families where the number of earners could not be increased for whatever reason (say because of illness or small children), the decline in real wages was quite palpable. These disadvantages were to some extent mitigated by the extension of social programmes, old-age insurance, sickness insurance, family allowances, etc.

The period of vast social changes, which marked the medium-term plans, created opportunities for vertical mobility, reflected in higher earnings, for many families, but also for downward mobility and lower earnings for other families.

Using employment as an instrument for increasing the standard of living affected wage increases in two ways: it was a reason for planning lower average wage increases, but it also hampered the achievement of planned targets in average wages if expansion of employment surpassed the limits. Part of the increases in the global wage-fund was namely used for wages for newly hired workers at the expense of wage increases. This is also one of the factors of the low-wage policy which has been discussed before.

The governments trusted that the stimulative aspect of wage policy which was weakened by declining real wages would be furthered by pushing the spread of piece rates. It will be shown later that this policy had unfavourable effects on the economy.

The stimulative aspect of wages was also used to attract labour to sectors and branches which were regarded as paramount for the objective of the plans. Where the rationing system was still in operation, as in Czechoslovakia and Poland, it also served this purpose. In heavy industry rations for production workers were much higher than in other sectors.

The events of 1953 brought about a change in government policies with regard to the standard-of-living and wage increases, after the highest communist bodies pledged to improve the standard of living (*Rudé právo* 1953, 16 Sep; *TSz 1953*, Oct–Nov). All three countries managed to bring price increases to a halt by releasing more resources for consumption and, in Czechoslovakia and Poland, by carrying out in 1953 a currency and quasi-currency reform respectively. Following the Soviet pattern the three countries, primarily Czechoslovakia, adopted price-cutting as a method of increasing real wages. This had necessarily an effect on the growth of money wages and on the stimulative aspect of wages. If the rate of growth of real wages is set, then the more consumer prices decline, the more money wages must lag behind real wages, thus reducing the stimulative effect of wages.

In 1954–5 real wages grew relatively fast. According to figures in Table 7.3, real wages in the CSSR in 1955 exceeded the level of 1950 by 10 per cent. In Poland, though real wages grew fast in 1954–5, even official figures show that the target for the six-year plan was reached only partially; in 1955 real wages exceeded the level of 1949 by 24.2 per cent. Computations made in the 70s reveal that real wages increased by only 9 per cent (Meller 1977, p. 55).

8 Employment and Wage Policies 1956–65

A INTRODUCTION

The beginning of the period was rich in events; uprising in Hungary and riots in Poland, both directed against the USSR and against the local communist regime. Therefore for both there was a lesson to learn. For the USSR there was a clear indication that the domination of East European countries by the crude old methods could not continue. For the East European countries the 1956 events were a clear message that the vast majority of the population yearned for more freedom and was fed up with an economic policy that neglected its material interests. People particularly resented the permanent call for sacrifices for the sake of the future which they viewed as uncertain at best. They were demanding an implementation of the original promises pertaining to the standard of living. It became clear that in order to achieve both objectives: the ambitious economic goals and increases in the standard of living, improvements in economic efficiency must be achieved. And this could not be accomplished without reforming the system of economic management. Yet the communist governments were not willing to institute economic reforms which went beyond the framework of the traditional centralised system (Brus 1981 p. 11, 18). This was true even for Poland, where the expectations were high due to the change in leadership. Some minor changes in the system of management were, however, introduced, first in Poland (1956), followed by Hungary (1957), then Czechoslovakia (1958). In addition some changes in economic policy were implemented, one being in agricultural policy. Some of the changes were more or less cosmetic or of a psychological nature at best, such as the abolition of compulsory agricultural deliveries and their replacement by contractual deliveries; some were, however, substantive, such as the reduction of required deliveries combined with higher prices for agricultural produce. Of the three countries only Poland

113

compromised so-called socialist principles by reconciling with the collapse of collectivisation.

Poland, and Hungary too, also made concessions to small businesses. The policy of issuing licences was eased and taxation reduced. This contributed not only to a restoration of market equilibrium, but also to the creation of jobs (Kochanowicz and Obodowski 1958).

The phase under consideration includes two planning periods (up to 1960 and 1961–5) which were distinctive in many respects. The first period was marked by quite a good economic performance with respect to quantitative as well as qualitative indicators. The second was a disappointment for all three countries, particularly Czechoslovakia. In 1958 the first long investment cycle came to an end; many investment projects begun in the first half of the 50s were completed and put into operation, and this boosted output. A new investment drive started immediately, spurred to some extent by Khrushchev's ambitious plan to overtake the USA in output *per capita* (Ungvárszki 1976, pp. 96–7). The failure to learn a lesson from pursuing maximum growth rates, thus overcommitting investment funds necessarily brought about imbalances in the economy, with a consequent slowdown in investment activities as well as output in the second period (cf. Goldman 1964).

In the first period Poland and Hungary were extended foreign loans, which helped to overcome internal disequilibria, whereas in the second period the obligation to repay these loans aggravated balance-of-payment problems.

In the beginning of the first period Poland and Hungary suffered from unemployment. Yet, through the whole period but mainly at the end of the second planning period, the countries were plagued by overemployment combined with labour shortages in some sectors. The fast growth of the administrative apparatus was primarily blamed for this situation.

The working-age population grew on the whole according to the needs of the economy. In Poland, where the growth rate had been the highest in 1950–5, it substantially declined, and thus easing the pressure for job opportunities through most of the period. In Czechoslovakia, which already suffered from labour shortages, there was an increase in the working-age population. In Hungary there was no change.

The growth of the population was a cause for concern. In all three countries there was a decline in the population growth rate as a result of lower birth-rates, a development brought about to a great extent by the abolition of anti-abortion laws. This development foreshadowed trouble for the 70s in the job market, mainly in Hungary where the decline in the growth rate was the biggest.

TABLE 8.1 *Growth of the population, working-age population and economically active population 1956–65*[a]

	Poland				CSSR				Hungary			
	A		B		A		B		A		B	
	1960	1965	1956 –60	1961 –5	1960	1965	1956 –60	1961 –5	1961	1966	1956 –60	1961 –5
1. Population	29 800	31 600	1.5	1.2	13 654	14 159	0.8	0.7	10 007	10 166	0.2	0.3
Index 1955 = 100[b]	108.0	114.9			104.3	108.1			101.2	102.9		
2. Working-age population	16 300	17 100	0.9	1.0	7 634	7 960	0.4	0.8	5 906	6 055	0.4	0.5
Index 1955 = 100	104.5	109.6			102.1	106.4			101.8	104.4		
3. Economically active population	12 401	13 521	1.6	1.7	6 005	6 370	0.3	1.2	4 626	4 666	0.3	0.2
Index 1955 = 100[b]	108.1	118.0			101.5	107.7			101.4	102.3		
4. Participation rates												
(a) 3:1	41.6	42.8			44.3	45.0			46.2	45.9		
(b) 3:2	76.1	79.1			78.7	80.0			78.3	77.1		

A – In absolute numbers (in thousands).
B – Compounded annual growth rates.

a Notes in Table 7.1 except b refer to this table too.
b Index for Hungary refers to 1956 = 100.

SOURCES   Poland – *MRS 1983*, pp. xxiv, xxv.
CSSR   – *SRC 1982*, p. 24; *SRC 1975*, p. 42.
Hungary – *SE 1980*, p. 3, 4; *SE 1966*, p. 51.

In the first period real wages grew fast, primarily in Hungary and Poland, while in the second a substantial slowdown occurred. In Czechoslovakia and Poland this slowdown was also the result of fast-growing employment and the desire to prevent inflationary pressures.

B   EMPLOYMENT POLICIES

1   Poland

Unemployment in Poland affected primarily women and youths, but in many small towns and some regions also affected men. At the same time other regions, mainly those newly acquired from Germany and the highly industrialised areas suffered from labour shortages. There are no figures for the rate of unemployment. A very crude idea can be obtained from published figures on the number of job-seekers compared to the number of openings. Another indication about unemployment was the projection of the Planning Commission for 1956–60 according to which 235 000 workers were redundant (Rajkiewicz 1965, p. 137).

One of the reasons for unemployment was a direct result of the policy *vis-à-vis* the small-scale private sector; it was liquidated without enough substitute jobs being available to all the people working there (Jędruszczak 1972, p. 192).

A substantial slowdown in the growth rate of investment outlays in 1956–7 was a contributing factor to unemployment in that the demand for labour diminished relatively. Since the first years of the FYP for 1956–60 were intended to be used for removal of imbalances built up during the previous planning period by completing projects started before 1956, no great increases in investment were needed. In addition, huge wage increases in 1956 restrained investment increases (Obodowski 1966). Had it not been for the modest increment in the working-age population (in 1956–60 0.9 per cent annually) the unemployment situation would have been even worse.

The FYP envisaged dealing with unemployment in two ways: first, by increasing pensions, thus making people of pensionable age more willing to retire and vacate positions for job-seekers, and, second, by releasing funds for creating 135 000 new jobs (Rajkiewicz 1965, pp. 137–8). In 1958 old-age pensions were increased by 47.5 per cent on the average (Krogulski 1959) and as a result in 1959–60 the number of pensioners increased by 170 000, whereas in the period 1955–8 only small changes took place.

The new policy on agriculture and the private sector had also contributed to an easing of unemployment. Not only did the exodus from agriculture decline, and thus the pressure for jobs outside agriculture, but many persons returned to work on the land. The private sector underwent a substantial expansion which brought employment with it (Rajkiewicz 1965, p. 108).

Simultaneously huge gains in real wages in 1956–7, which, thanks to a relatively good performance of the economy (national income in 1956–60 increased by 6.6 per cent annually), did not erode in the following years, reduced pressure for jobs by women and youths.

With the gradual liquidation of unemployment more and more attention was devoted to overemployment and labour shortages in some sectors, mainly construction, and the communal economy. Persisting overemployment at a time when wages were growing fast and when the supply of goods, despite the good performance of the economy, lagged behind demand contributed to imbalances in the market. This was all the more a cause for concern since the planners were readying for a new investment wave, which started in 1958 (and peaked in 1959, to decline substantially in 1964–5). For all these reasons the government decided to embark on a policy of employment rationalisation which aimed at achieving higher productivity (as a result of the improvement in the quality of the labour force and organisation) and at ensuring at the same time labour for sectors plagued by shortages. In 1958 this policy was primarily directed against administration (it was supposed to drastically reduce the staff of ministries), but in 1959 it was extended to the material sphere (Jędruszczak 1972, pp. 193–4).

On the whole this policy was successful. Employment grew much less than the plan envisaged. In 1956–60 employment in the socialist sector was to increase by 1 273 000 (19.6 per cent), but it increased by only 605 000 (9.4 per cent);[1] in socialist industry the corresponding figures were 626 000 (23.2 per cent) and 295 000 (10.9 per cent) (Rajkiewicz 1965, pp. 136, 143). (See also Table 8.2.) The number of economically active increased by 8.1 per cent. The target for labour productivity in industry was greatly overfulfilled (44 per cent against 27 per cent) (Meller 1977, p. 82).

The Polish economy also grew relatively fast in the period 1961–5. (National income increased by 6.2 per cent annually against the target of 7.1 per cent.) What disturbed the planners was that qualitative indicators as well as factors which determine market equilibrium, remained much behind the target. The increase in productivity in industry fell well below the target (28.3 per cent against 40.0 per cent) (Meller 1977, p. 102). And

TABLE 8.2 Growth of the labour force 1956–65[a]

	Poland				CSSR				Hungary[b]			
	A		B		A		B		A		B	
	1960	1965	1956–60	1961–65	1960	1965	1956–60	1961–65	1961	1966	1956–60	1961–65
1. National economy	12 401	13 521	1.6	1.7	6 005	6 370	0.3	1.2	4 626	4 666	0.3	0.2
Index 1955 = 100	108.1	117.9			101.5	107.7			101.4	102.3		
2. Socialist sector	7 194	8 531	1.2	3.5	4 829	5 382	2.5	2.2				
Index 1955 = 100	105.9	125.6			113.2	126.1						
3. Material sphere	11 233	12 099	1.9[c]	1.5	5 033	5 122	−0.1	0.3	3 937		0.4	−0.0
Index 1955 = 100	121.1[c]	130.5[c]			99.4	101.2			102.2	102.0		
4. Non-material sphere	1 168	1 422	2.5[c]	4.0	972	1 248	2.6	5.1	689	736	−0.7	1.3
Index 1955 = 100	127.9[c]	155.7[c]			113.9	146.3			96.8	103.4		
5. Industry	3 158	3 728	2.5	3.4	2 253	2 449	3.0	1.7	1 386	1 606	4.3	3.0
Index 1955 = 100	113.0	133.4			116.0	126.1			123.4	143.0		
6. Construction	811	901	2.0	2.1	458	478	4.8	0.9	261	316	4.4	3.9
Index 1955 = 100	110.5	122.7			126.2	131.7			123.7	149.8		
7. Agriculture inclusive of forestry	5 517	5 462	−0.1[c]	−0.2	1 446	1 259	−5.6	−2.7	1 630	1 299	−3.9	−4.4
Index 1955 = 100	99.3[c]	98.4[c]			74.8	65.2			82.0	65.3		
8. Transport and communications	692	795	4.1	2.8	367	418	1.8	2.6	298	319	3.4	1.4
Index 1955 = 100	122.5	140.7			109.2	124.4			118.2	126.6		

9. Trade	741	812	2.3	1.8	416	460	0.3	2.0	329	340	3.6	0.7
Index 1955 = 100	111.9	122.7			101.5	112.2			119.6	123.6		
10. Health and social care	308	381	6.4	4.3	178	215	3.0	3.9				
Index 1955 = 100	136.3	168.6			116.3	140.5						
11. Education, culture, physical education	435	548	4.8	4.7	286	380	3.8	5.9				
Index 1955 = 100	126.5	159.3			120.7	160.3						
12. Communal and housing services	242	314	9.9	5.3								
Index 1955 = 100	160.3	207.9										
13. Collectivised agriculture	496	650	1.7[c]	5.6								
Index 1955 = 100	118.1[c]	154.8[c]										

A – In absolute numbers (in thousands). B – Compounded annual growth rates.

[a] All notes in Table 7.2 except [c] and [f] refer to this table too.
[b] The base year for indexes in Hungary is 1956.
[c] 1950 has been used as the base year.

SOURCES Poland – *RS 1977*, pp. 41, 42.
CSSR – *SRC 1982*, pp. 24, 25; *SRC 1981*, pp. 22, 23; *SRC 1967*, p. 23.
Hungary – *SE 1980*, p. 4.

this in turn led to the limit for employment being already achieved by 1963. At the end of the FYP employment in the socialist sector was 18.6 per cent higher instead of the planned 10.6 per cent, and in industry 18 per cent against the planned 8.7 per cent. According to S. Jędrychowski (1966) this was caused by the failure to put into operation capacities with higher productivity, and to carry out the plan of mechanisation of labour-intensive work, and by an increase in job-seekers of 150 000 more than was assumed in the plan due to a lack of statistical figures! The unfavourable evolution of productivity in industry was also due to the increase in costs per unit of production which resulted from a worsening of the labour–output ratio (in 1955–60 1 per cent increase in industrial output required 0.18 per cent increase in employment; in 1961–5 it was 0.35 per cent) (Karpiński 1967).

The rapid increase in employment combined with a failure to meet targets for consumer goods, primarily due to a crop failure aggravated the market disequilibrium for consumer goods and thwarted the achievement of the plans for nominal and real wages. More about this later.

In 1963 the central authorities embarked on a rationalisation of employment, which included the following provisions: the planned employment limit for 1964 was reduced, the amount of overtime was limited and a stricter control of the wage-bill was instituted (Bajszczak and Obodowski 1964 a). In addition, growth of investment was reduced. As a result of these provisions employment increased in 1964 by only 125 000, the lowest increment in the FYP. But in 1965 employment accelerated again; it reached 320 000 (Obodowski 1966). One reason for the difficulty in restraining employment was the start of a rapid increase in the working-age population due to the post-war baby boom. In 1965 the increment in the working-age population was 258 000 against 44 000 in 1960.

2   Hungary

Almost at the same time as Poland, Hungary (in 1957) was overtaken by unemployment. This was the direct result of a long general strike – a protest against the Soviet occupation of Hungary and restoration of the communist regime – which paralysed economic life. Since energy and raw materials were in short supply, the government initiated dismissal of workers, primarily administrative (Lengyel 1958). One can speculate that the dismissals were also aimed at easing the pressure on the market for consumer goods, thus avoiding greater inflationary pressure, which threatened the economy due to high wage increases in 1956 and even higher in 1957.

There are no exact figures about the extent of unemployment. It seems that it was less than 100 000 at the beginning of 1957 and steadily declined during the year (*Népszabadság* 1957, 14 Mar). It would have been much higher had Hungary not received quick help from its neighbours in the form of shipments of consumer goods, raw materials and long-term credits (*Rudé právo* 1957, 19 Mar). The government tried to ease the problem of unemployment by introducing unemployment compensation and partial obligatory placement (Rózsa and Farkasinszky, 1970).

For some time it was not clear what kind of employment policy Hungary would follow. Task forces, entrusted with the conceptualisation of the next three-year plan, differed substantially in their views on employment. Some believed that job-creation was not the most important task of socialism and that employment should be subordinated to socialist industrialisation and to economic efficiency considerations, a view opposed by others (Ungvárszki 1976, p. 102). The original three-year plan for 1958–60 was rather designed in the spirit of the first view. It envisaged a modest rate of economic growth. Investment funds were to be used for the extension and modernisation of existing capacities and for the completion of non-finished investment projects. This cautious approach resulted from a realistic estimate of the possibilities of the domestic economy as well as of the balance-of-payments difficulties. As soon as it was discovered that employment would be affected more heavily than had been assumed, the politicians got cold feet. In the second half of 1958 investment was increased (and peaked in 1959 as in the other two countries, to decline in 1962 absolutely) and unemployment was dealt with (Ungvárszki 1976, p. 102; Goldman 1964).

Despite the increase in investment Hungary was again exposed to unemployment. This time it was caused by a 1959 government decision to rapidly and completely collectivise agriculture which was largely privatised during the 1956 events. This put into motion a new exodus from agriculture and increased the number of job-seekers in the cities (Berend 1979, pp. 134–6; Rózsa and Farkasinszky 1970).

The number of the economically active population grew only modestly in the quinquennium 1956–60, by 0.3 per cent annually on the average. However great structural changes occurred; the number of economically active in industry increased substantially due to the expansion of large-scale state industry (by 23.4 per cent, 263 000 persons), and greatly surpassed the plan 'target'; this was made possible by a large transfer of workers from agriculture, where the number of economically active declined by 360 000 (19.1 per cent). Surprisingly employment in the non-material sphere declined at the same time.

On the whole the Hungarian plan for 1961–5 was more demanding than the preceding three-year plan. The planners' expectations were dashed in many respects; national income for the quinquennium increased by 25 per cent instead of the planned 36 per cent (M. Timár, 1973, p. 23). Industrial output targets were almost met (47 per cent against 50 per cent), but agricultural output achieved only 45 per cent of the planned increment (10 per cent against 22 per cent). Fast collectivisation had an unfavourable effect on output, mainly in the first years of the FYP, and on the balance of payments, which was in deficit during the whole period. Labour productivity declined compared to the previous three-year plan. All these factors contributed to the large underfulfilment of the target for real wages (9 per cent against 16 per cent) (Berend 1979, p. 131).

The size of the economically active in 1961–6 increased only modestly, by 40 000 (0.9 per cent). Employment in industry and construction continued to grow fast (15.8 per cent and 21.0 per cent respectively), but the number of economically active in agriculture declined by 20.2 per cent (also because of higher incidence of retirement). As a result employment in the material sphere stagnated. However, this time the non-material sphere registered an employment increase of 6.8 per cent.

Despite the relatively huge exodus from agriculture and the slightly greater increments in the working-age population (0.5 per cent annually) labour shortages started to show up in 1963 and deepened in 1964. There were shortages, primarily of skilled manual workers in some important trades as well as of unskilled labour for physically strenuous work; a shortage of engineers and technicians was also felt. The shortages were caused primarily by the fact that in 1961–5 there were 120 000 less school-leavers than job vacancies. The situation was compounded by the failure to correctly forecast the future skill-mix requirements and education and training (J. Timár 1966). With regard to engineers, the capacity of the universities to train technicians lagged behind the economy's requirements. The shortages were particularly severe in Budapest, the industrial centre of Hungary (Buda and J. Timár 1963). Simultaneously with the labour shortages some pockets of female unemployment existed in some areas.

The government tried to cope with these problems in two ways. Enterprises were pressured to release redundant labour and not to fill jobs which became vacant due to attrition unless there were good economic reasons for doing so. So in the beginning of 1965 some 8 000 people were dismissed in the hope that they would find jobs in sectors plagued by shortages (Buda 1965 A). In addition, placement procedures were tightened up (*Népszabadság* 1965, 21 Jan).

3 Czechoslovakia

Of the three countries Czechoslovakia was the only one where the year 1956 passed without great turmoil, one reason being that in 1956 Czechoslovakia was still going through what can be called a 'consumption period'. Nevertheless the Czechoslovak leadership undertook several provisions which were supposed to heighten the immunity of the population against the anti-communist manifestations in neighbouring countries; in 1956 the workweek was shortened by two hours and the social insurance system was improved (Pick 1959; *Sociální* . . . 1975, p. 122) and in 1957 the decision was taken to institute an economic reform.

Because of the political situation in the country the government could afford to continue in substance its economic policy; the second FYP for 1956–60 was ambitious and envisaged primarily a rapid development of heavy industry. For this purpose most of the investment funds were channelled into the extracting industry, metallurgy and heavy machinery (Průcha 1974, p. 313). In addition, the plan aimed at completing the socialist transformation of the state and society, and this meant a speeding up of the completion of collectivisation. The performance of the economy was relatively good (national income grew on the average by 7 per cent annually and social labour productivity by 7.2 per cent) and the same was true of the standard of living, particularly up to 1959.

Czechoslovakia did not suffer from unemployment; on the contrary it suffered from labour shortages, caused partially by small increments in the working-age population and the shortening of the workweek. Of course these shortages were accompanied by overemployment in certain sectors. Coal-extraction, metallurgy and construction belonged to the sectors traditionally affected by labour shortages.[2] Several of the special reasons for labour shortages in the coal industry and in metallurgy have a general relevance for the whole period under review. The work is arduous, usually these industries are located in areas short of labour, and finally they render few job opportunities for women. In the second half of the 50s an additional factor was in play: increases in wages in other sectors eroded the wage advantages coal and metallurgy workers had enjoyed (Čech 1959, p. 122).

There was also a labour shortage in agriculture in some areas, primarily in the border areas in Bohemia. On the other hand collectivisation released a lot of labour in Slovakia, where productivity was much lower than in the Czech Lands.

In 1956–60 the total number of economically active people increased by only 1.5 per cent (90 000). The material sphere even suffered a slight decline (0.1 per cent) in the number of economically active; yet the non-material sphere registered an increase of 14 per cent (120 000). Employment in industry continued to grow fast (3.0 per cent annually) whereas agriculture experienced a decline of 25 per cent (486 000), the highest in a five-year period. The rapid but uneven decline in the number of economically active in agriculture, part of which was due to retirement, caused great fluctuations in the total number of economically active (in 1959 there was even a decline of 55 000).

For several reasons the CSSR had to pay the most for the obsession with economic growth. First, the obsession was stronger there than in the other two countries; second, it proceeded under conditions of labour shortages, and, third, exogenous factors compounded the economic crisis. In 1958 many investment projects begun during the early 50s were put into operation, and it was thus possible to achieve high growth rates, mainly in heavy industry in the period 1958–60 (Goldman and Kouba 1967, p. 45). In 1959 the CSSR, like the other two countries, embarked on a new investment wave and an ambitious third FYP; national income was to increase by 42 per cent, industrial output by 56 per cent and agricultural production by 22 per cent (*PH 1960*, no. 12). It soon turned out that the plans were beyond the reach of the Czechoslovak economy and the FYP was scrapped. The CSSR's economic performance in 1961–5 turned out to be – disregarding the current performance – the worst in post-war history. National income increased by 10 per cent (in 1963 it even declined absolutely) and industrial production by 29 per cent. Agricultural production even registered an absolute decline (−2 per cent). Needless to say, productivity growth was low.

The great stress on heavy industry avenged itself. To maintain the increasing capacity of heavy industry, the CSSR was forced to import more and more raw materials, paid for by increasing exports of machines and equipment. This in itself should not have been of concern, provided the returns from trade were good, which was not the case in Czechoslovakia. Channelling a great share of investment into heavy industry deprived the consumer goods industry of funds for modernisation, and this in turn tied down an excessive labour force (for more see Adam 1974, pp. 36–8; Vachel 1965). The sudden collapse of trade with China, combined with a poor performance in agriculture in 1961, aggravated the situation. As a consequence Czechoslovakia was forced on the one hand to increase imports of food from capitalist states (which worsened the balance of trade) and on the other hand to reduce the intended imports of raw materials which resulted in a contraction of output (Bernášek 1969).

The ambitious FYP meant increased demand for further labour at a time when the labour market was tight anyhow. The situation was compounded by the fact that the government could not continue ignoring the service sector. In 1956–60 real wages and incomes grew relatively fast; therefore there was popular pressure for channelling more labour into the service sector, which had become an obstacle to the exercise of choice by consumers in the use of their growing purchasing power. The expansion of social programmes, to which the government committed itself, also required more labour. Though the number of working-age people increased in 1960–5, this increase was a far cry from the needs of the economy. In addition, the exodus from agriculture slowed down substantially (in 1960–5 the number of economically active in agriculture including forestry declined by 187 000 only (13 per cent)).

Despite the poor showing of the economy the period 1961–5 could boast of a high increment in the number of economically active, 6.1 per cent (365 000). Most of the increase was in the non-material sphere; employment there accelerated to 5.1 per cent annually (for the whole period the number increased by 276 000)[3] while in the material sphere employment grew, but at a modest rate, 0.3 per cent annually. In industry employment continued to grow at a relatively high rate, 1.7 per cent. This growth in employment, which surpassed the plan limit could only be achieved under existing conditions by an increase in the participation rate of women.

Despite labour shortages not a small percentage of labour was tied down in obsolete and inefficient enterprises (with low productivity or producing goods for which no demand existed) which the authorities for lack of productive capacity could not afford to shut down or did not dare do so. A strange situation came into existence; there was, on the one hand, a shortage of skilled labour in highly productive plants and, on the other hand, a waste of labour in obsolete and inefficient factories (Vachel 1965; Sokol 1965). This is not to say that no effort was undertaken to bring about a change. Statistics show that in the post-war period concentration of production in modern plants asserted itself, and many small plants were liquidated (Sýkora 1964). However this undertaking proceeded slowly for political reasons and lacked consistency and sometimes rationality. Often small, potentially efficient plants were shut down for the sake of 'gigantomania'.

Authorities also tried to counteract the tendency to a growing number of administrative employees. In 1964 they decided to reduce the administrative apparatus. This provision slowed down for a while the growth of white-collar workers (Shaffer 1965).

4   Employment Regulation

In employment regulation at the enterprise level no substantial changes occurred in the period under review. Enterprises were still assigned limits for employment. True, according to one author in Hungary, the assignment of binding limits for employment ceased as a general rule in 1957 (Palotai 1962). This does not mean that enterprises were free to hire workers as they pleased. Ministries could assign limits in their jurisdiction, if they felt they had good reasons for doing so and they apparently took advantage of this.

In the preparation stage of the 1958 Czechoslovak reform the planners assumed that the directive 'targets' for employment would be eliminated in the course of the reform. But during the whole existence of the reform (1958–63) maximum limits for employment were assigned to enterprises (Kocanda 1965, p. 148).

Up to 1964 no attempts were made in any of the countries under review, except the CSSR, to design special indirect methods for the regulation of employment. One can only speculate on the reasons for this phenomenon, one probably being that at that time employment regulation was not yet in the forefront of the planners' interest. In Hungary and Poland in certain years there was an oversupply of labour. In addition the planners still believed in the effectiveness of direct methods. When indirect methods came into play they were simply a by-product of the incentive and wage-regulation systems, which underwent some changes as a result of greater stress on economic efficiency and the desire to restore and maintain market equilibrium, a justifiable concern, primarily in Hungary and Poland, in the wake of huge wage increases in 1956–7. The first objective – greater stress on economic efficiency – was to be achieved by creating incentives that would stimulate enterprises to accept more demanding targets and thus reveal concealed reserves. For this purpose all the countries decided to link bonuses closely to performance and use profit as a success indicator for the size of the bonus fund.

Suggestions by economists to measure performance in comparison with the previous year and thus to discontinue the link with plan targets were not acceptable to the planners. Yet profit as a success indicator combined with a new method of measuring performance would have stimulated enterprises to give more consideration to market demand in making decisions about output mix, instead of concentrating on the easiest way to meet plan targets. Several years were needed before this idea asserted itself in the reforms of the second half of the 60s.

The second goal – maintenance of market equilibrium – was handled much less uniformly than the first. In Czechoslovakia and Poland the rule that the wage-bill should grow proportionally to fulfilment of targets, a rule which led to frequent overdrafts of the wage-bill and to the generation of inflationary pressures, was eliminated. In addition in 1959 the CSSR embarked on a new wage-regulation system, in which wage increases were linked to productivity growth through normatives. In Hungary in 1957 a very strict control of average wages was introduced.

The best example for the development of the incentive system was in Poland. The *Polish Theses* (a collective work of the Economic Council established in 1956), which were approved in 1957, called for 'linking incentives to changes in enterprises' results rather than to the fulfilment of plan targets and replacement of global output by profit as the chief indicator of success and the source of premia funds' (*ESE 1963*, ch. VI, p. 40). This idea was implemented for a short time in some enterprises during the reform of the 'enterprise fund' which became the focus of incentives (Fick 1967, pp. 116, 123). However, in 1960, both the 'enterprise fund'[4] and bonus fund for salaried workers were designed in a way to reconcile two different concepts – on the one hand both were based on the increment in profit over the previous year and, on the other hand, both were linked to the plan target for financial results.

The 'enterprise fund', which was supposed to act as an incentive to improved economic efficiency and thus a stimulus to labour economy, could not fulfil the role assigned to it for two reasons. First, even after its substantial increase, it was too small to have an effect on enterprises' decision-making (Fick 1970, p. 152). Second, the old wage-regulation system was in substance maintained.

Only in 1963, after economic growth slowed down, after employment grew faster than envisaged in the plan and when overexpenditure of the global wage-fund was not matched by corresponding increases in output of consumer goods, did the government decide to act. It abolished the automatic allocation of funds to the wage-bill for overfulfilment of targets in approximately 50 per cent of all industrial enterprises. Instead overfulfilment of targets was financed from the special reserve funds of associations and ministries, provided it was considered to be economically justifiable (Fick 1964; Weber 1964).

It is not known whether this new provision had any effect on labour economy. At any rate it did not last long. In addition, the incentive system for salaried workers again underwent a change in 1964. The fight between those who argued for synthetic indicators and those in favour of special indicators ended with victory for the latter. Profit as a success indicator was dropped, and bonuses were again linked to the fulfilment of the annual plan targets (among others, output mix, exports, savings of materials and labour (Krencik 1972, pp. 109–11; Fick 1967, pp. 223–4). As a result of this change the incentive system for salaried workers was based on different principles from the 'enterprise fund'.

In 1957 Hungary introduced a new element in the incentive system – profit sharing; it assured all workers in an enterprise of a year-end reward, a maximum of one month's pay. The size of the fund depended on the level of profitability achieved in relation to the minimal rate assigned by the centre. Since, in the following years, many enterprises found themselves in a disadvantageous position because of low increases in profitability, the amount of produced profit was instituted for them as a new indicator in 1964 (Bokor 1965; Wilcsek 1970). Profit also played a role in the determination of bonuses for top managers of enterprises (Bánki 1973).

Two circumstances weakened the possible favourable effect of the incentive system on labour economy; the steady decline in year-end rewards (in 1963 only 9.2 days) and the shift in 1964 to produced profit. While linkage of the size of the profit-sharing fund to the increment in profitability pushes enterprises to reduce costs per unit of production and thus to practise labour economy, a shift to profit may motivate enterprises primarily to expand output (Bokor 1965).

Worst of all was the impact of the wage-regulation system, introduced in 1957 for the purpose of restoring wage discipline, which had collapsed in 1956. Enterprises were assigned growth rates in average wages without any linkage to their performance including productivity. An exception was allowed in industrial branches where productivity can be reliably measured in physical units (coal-mining) (Hegedüs 1960; Buda 1965B).

Understandably such a system cannot affect productivity and labour economy favourably; regulation of average wages is an incentive for labour hoarding, since the easiest way to circumvent the system is to hire workers who can be paid below average wages. An inquiry into the reasons for exceeding employment limits in industry indirectly confirmed the statement above (Buda 1965B).

Czechoslovakia was the first country to link wage increases to productivity growth combined with long-term normatives, whose purpose was to instil into managers a feeling of long-term certainty about the rules of the game. The centre assigned enterprises a minimal growth rate for productivity and a long-term normative for wage growth for a 1 per cent rise in productivity. For productivity growth over the plan average wages could grow at a higher rate than given by the normative (Bajcura 1969, pp. 42–3; Sokol 1969).

It seems that the system itself was not wrong; its failure to stimulate productivity growth was primarily caused by the planners' inability to design genuine long-term normatives. Such normatives can be designed if economic growth proceeds according to the plan targets; otherwise there is a need to change the normatives frequently, which understandably reduces their effectiveness. And this was what happened in Czechoslovakia. In addition, when it turned out that the FYP for 1961–5 had to be scrapped, the whole reform was soon scrapped too (1962) and the old incentive system and wage regulation were in substance restored.

In 1964, for the first time, both Hungary and the CSSR introduced a stimulus to labour-saving by allowing enterprises to use 50 per cent of their savings due to labour economy for wage increases (in the CSSR the reward was earmarked for collectives who were credited with labour-saving) (Rózsa 1965; Shaffer 1965).

5 Placement Policies, Unemployment Benefits and Retraining

Changes in the political climate and the trend to economic reforms brought about a substantial decline in the use of administrative methods. Placement activities were decentralised and the national councils took on more of the traditional role of labour exchange (advisory activities, dissemination of information about available jobs, etc.).

Already in 1954 in Hungary – probably in connection with the more liberal atmosphere which marked I. Nagy's advent to power – the 'organized recruitment' had been decentralised and liberalised. Compulsory allocation of labour was limited to persons who quit their jobs without legal approval or who were fired for violation of labour discipline. After the political crisis, in January 1957, compulsory placement was restored (Schönwald 1980, p. 126), to be later abolished and reintroduced from time to time. Its purpose was to cope with labour shortages and the great turnover, and also to help women and the disabled to find jobs.

In Czechoslovakia in 1957 the reduced functions of 'organized recruitment' were mostly delegated to national county committees. The central authorities' role was limited to intercounty shifts of labour for mining and some important construction projects, whereas organised recruitment for priority enterprises in the territory of individual counties was transferred to county committees and district committees (Kocanda 1965, pp. 133–4).

The 1958 law pertaining to the role of national committees set forth the principle that the recruitment of the needed number of workers should be primarily the concern of enterprises, and that the national committees should see that the hiring of workers was in harmony with the needs of the economy. The new law did not mean the abolition of organized recruitment, rather its limitation to important cases (Plichta 1959).

The 1962 Polish regulations regarding labour exchange distinguished two systems: (1) for categories of workers who had difficulty finding jobs (housewives, youths, administrative workers) and (2) for categories of workers who were in great demand. In the first case the labour departments helped people find jobs, while in the second they limited themselves to posting lists of vacant jobs. Apart from this regular labour-exchange activity labour departments also fulfilled so-called active labour exchange, which in practice meant finding jobs for people who, for some special reasons, urgently needed them. This category included discharged conscripts, released convicts and people in a serious economic situation. All these people had priority claims to jobs, if other candidates had no better qualifications (Olędzki 1974, pp. 224–5).

In all the three countries labour exchange did not cover employees of the state apparatus, justice, universities, research institutes, etc. All these institutions recruit labour by their own means.

Changes in the allocation of graduates of different schools also occurred. In Czechoslovakia the three-year obligation to work in an assigned job was abolished in 1959 (Kocanda 1965, p. 131). However, pressure was still exercised on graduates to work at suggested jobs (Kačmarik 1959).

In Poland the compulsory allocation of graduates to jobs was abolished gradually in 1957–8. In 1964 the government reintroduced placing of university graduates, arguing that the previous system led to a concentration of professionals in big agglomerations at the expense of small industrial centres, and thus violated the principle of rational employment. The rule of staying three years in the assigned job was renewed; failure to obey resulted in penalties. According to the law, students were supposed to repay 50 per cent of the costs of education financed by the state. In addition, students who drew a stipend during their studies were obliged to repay it (Olędzki 1974, pp. 227–8).

What did the Hungarian and Polish governments do to ease the plight of the unemployed? In Hungary unemployment compensation could be granted for a period of six months. In the middle of 1957 it was limited to applicants who could not find jobs appropriate to their qualifications and physical and mental ability. For control purposes they had to report twice monthly to the placement agencies for job offers (*Esti Hirlap* 1957, 16 June).

The Polish government was reluctant to introduce unemployment benefits; even some economists argued against it (Rajkiewicz 1957). Instead the government introduced severance payments for those administrative workers who returned to agricultural work, became self-employed or became domestic workers (*Głos Pracy* 1957, 4 Apr).

In all three countries costs connected with the retraining of workers for new jobs and wages paid to the workers during their retraining were and are borne by the government and/or employers.

In the recruitment of workers for the hard-pressed branches the three countries also used incentives; yet little is known about their concrete form except in Czechoslovakia. There hiring bonuses, for example, were used in the recruitment of workers for coal-mining (Shaffer 1965).

C WAGE POLICIES

1 Policy of Wage Increases

The period under review is marked by a faster increase in money wages than in real wages in all three countries, a development which had already started in 1954. The pace in nominal and real-wage increases was not uniform throughout the period and the countries. On the whole the countries stuck to the known rule that growth of wages should lag behind the growth rate in productivity. The concrete relationship was influenced by two factors especially: internal political development and fluctuations in economic growth.

The first played the most important role in the beginning of the period in Hungary and Poland which went through deep political crises. It also had an echo in the Czechoslovak wage policy. In Hungary the authorities painstakingly tried to reduce workers' resistance to Kádár's new regime by various means, and wage increases no doubt played an important role. In Hungary nominal and real wages increased in 1956–7 on the average annually by 15.7 per cent and 14.6 per cent respectively, and in Poland by 12.6 per cent and 9.9 per cent respectively. In Czechoslovakia the wage increases were not so dramatic, but still respectable (2.9 per cent and 5.2 per cent) (see Table 8.3). The events of 1956 also contriuted to an improvement in social legislation.

Wage increases in 1956–7 could be regarded to a certain degree as the aftermath of the consumption period, which was characterised by lower investment ratios than before. In 1959 all three countries embarked on a new investment wave, and this had, of course, an effect on wage increases, discernible in Hungary and Poland more than in Czechoslovakia. In the first two countries the growth rates in real wages declined substantially; in Poland in 1960 there was even a moderate absolute decline.

Considering 1956–60 as a whole, real wages grew fast; but only in Hungary did they exceed the planned rate. In Poland real wages fell behind the plan only moderately (see Table A. 1, p. 234); however nominal wages grew twice as fast. Of the three countries, Poland experienced the fastest increases in prices.

Wage policy in 1956–60 was also influenced by several other factors. Growth of employment compared to the previous quinquennium slowed down considerably (this is true, even if we consider that in Hungary and Czechoslovakia the plan limits were exceeded) and this enabled the planners to use the growing global wage-fund more for wage increases. In Poland, for example, during the six-year plan, the global wage-fund grew 24 per cent annually; on the average increases in employment accounted for 20 per cent of the total increase in the wage-fund. The corresponding figures for 1956–60 were 11 per cent and 13 per cent (Morecka 1974).

Changes in price policy also had an impact on nominal wage increases and, indirectly, on the evolution of real wages too. Poland and Hungary abandoned the policy of price-cutting in 1956, whereas Czechoslovakia continued it up to 1960, but at a much smaller rate. The price reductions did not bring about the hoped for market stability; on the contrary they became a factor of disequilibrium (Csikós-Nagy 1974; Vlach 1968). The selection of goods for price decreases was not always governed by market considerations; political aspects played an important role. Goods, which

TABLE 8.3 Evolution of nominal wages (A), consumer prices (B) and real wages (C) 1956–65[a]
(annual growth rates)

		1956	1957	1958	1959	1960	1961	1962	1963	1964	1965	1956–60	1961–5
Poland	A	11.0	14.3	5.4	7.8	3.2	4.4	3.6	4.8	3.1	2.6	8.3	3.7
	B	−0.6	5.6	2.1	2.6	4.8	1.7	3.2	2.3	1.0	2.6	2.9	2.2
	C	11.5	8.3	3.3	5.0	−1.5	2.6	0.4	2.5	2.0	0.0	5.2	1.5
CSSR	A	3.9	1.8	2.2	2.0	3.1	2.5	0.7	0.0	3.3	2.6	2.6	1.8
	B	−2.6	−2.0	−0.1	−2.4	−2.0	−0.5	1.2	0.5	0.4	1.2	−1.8	0.6
	C	6.6	3.9	2.3	4.6	5.2	3.0	−0.6	−0.4	2.9	1.3	4.5	1.2
Hungary	A	10.2	21.2	4.0	4.3	2.5	1.2	2.0	3.9	3.0	1.1	8.2	2.2
	B	−0.6	1.9	0.6	−1.2	0.6	0.6	0.6	−0.6	0.6	1.2	0.2	0.5
	C	11.4	17.9	4.3	4.9	2.0	0.0	1.9	4.4	2.4	0.0	8.0	1.7

[a] Nominal wage figures – which are net figures in Poland and Hungary, and gross in Czechoslovakia – refer to the socialist sector in Poland and the state sector in Czechoslovakia and Hungary.

SOURCES Poland – RS 1981, pp. xxxiv–xxxv.
CSSR – Kazimour 1980, p. 159.
Hungary – SE 1980, p. 19; SE 1982, p. 17.

the economy was not able to ensure in a sufficient supply even at existing prices, were often offered at lower prices. In addition the policy of price reductions, which resulted in a slowdown of average wage growth, became an obstacle to the use of wages as an incentive. All three countries (Poland and Hungary as early as the second half of the 50s) gradually adopted the principle that prices should be more responsive to the state of the market; in practice this meant that prices slowly crept upwards; however, compared to Western increases, these were slight. The abandonment of the previous price policy boosted nominal wage increases.

The reform of the wage system, mainly the changes implemented in the wage-rates, affected average wages too. To make the reforms acceptable to the workers, Czechoslovakia in particular allowed some wage increases on this account.

All three countries planned for 1961–5 lower increases in real wages in the light of the planned acceleration in economic growth, but none achieved even this reduced goal. They witnessed a slowdown in economic growth combined with some strong fluctuations, primarily in the CSSR, and this had an impact on the evolution of wages. In Czechoslovakia real wages increased annually by 1.2 per cent against the planned target of 4.6 per cent (in 1962–3 there was even a small absolute decline). Nominal wages grew a bit faster (1.8 per cent) than real wages; the difference was eaten up by price increases; the government tried in this way to reduce the impact of consumer goods shortages. (For this purpose it even cut old-age pensions by introducing a progressive tax in the range of 1 per cent to 12.5 per cent (Adam 1983).) The large overrun of employment limits also contributed to the slowdown in the growth of nominal wages

Poland went through a similar development. Real-wage increases also fell behind the target (1.5 per cent against 4.2 per cent); what was worse in Poland was that this small rate became a standard for all of the 60s. Available figures for planned targets for average nominal wages and global wage-funds in Poland show that both were overfulfilled. Average nominal wages increased by 3.6 per cent annually against the targeted 3.3 per cent and the global wage-fund by 7.3 per cent against 5.4 per cent. A larger increase in the global wage-fund than in nominal wages was necessary to accommodate the high exceeding of employment limits. Despite the overfulfilment of the target for the global wage-fund employment's share in its increase rose to 46 per cent from 13 per cent in 1956–60 (Morecka 1974).

Hungary fared the best with regard to fulfilment of the real-wage target. It planned a much smaller rate than the other two countries, being more realistic than they were in its assessment of the growth potential of wages under conditions of increased accumulation. Real wages grew on the average by 1.7 per cent annually – though very unevenly through the years – against the targeted 3 per cent. The results achieved in real wages were also due to the fact that employment in the national economy (outside agriculture) grew at a slower rate than envisaged in the plan.

2   Wage Determination for Individual Workers

The methods of wage determination for individual workers were from the beginning marked with shortcomings which, in the course of time, became worse. The assignment of wage-rates from the centre and their rigidity were two of the main shortcomings of the system. They left almost no leeway for enterprises to take initiative in determining wage-rates. Managers were not allowed to fix wage-rates even within certain limits. They could develop some initiative in the classification of workers, mainly non-manual workers, into skill groups, but even this possibility was greatly limited, due to the strict control of average wages and the wage-bill.

The petrification of wage-rates over a long period of time was an even worse shortcoming. Even if prices do not change, the continued inflexibility of wage-rates may cause trouble. Due to productivity increases, average wages increase too, and this means that the percentage share of wage-rates in average wages declines. The more this share declines the smaller the role wage-rates can play in stimulating the acquisition of skills. If average wages depend greatly on the overfulfilment of work norms, which is the case when the share of wage-rates in average wages declines, then the role of skill in wage differentials diminishes. In the setting of individual wage-rates skills needed for different jobs are considered, whereas the way norms are overfulfilled often conflicts with these principles.

In the beginning of the 50s the situation was compounded by high rates of inflation (open and repressed) as a result of the fast industrialisation drive. For all these reasons the share of wage-rates in average wages increasingly declined, and shrank in some industrial branches to below 50 per cent.[5] Because wage-rates remained unchanged, the only way to ensure higher wages to pieceworkers was to slacken work norms, thus letting the workers greatly exceed the norms or grant them additional bonuses. In the case of timeworkers payments additional to the wage-rates had to be extended.

This process of slackening work norms introduced new elements of disorder into the effort to base remuneration on rational grounds. It resulted in a situation in which the norm-setting became more or less a means of ensuring a certain level of wages, instead of serving as an incentive for increasing output. In addition the slackening of work norms, combined with the system of supplementary payments, contributed to distortions in planned wage differentials.

The massive spread of piecework proved to be a mistake, as could be expected. Moral considerations aside, piecework can no doubt be advantageous for productivity gains compared to timework in the following cases: where quality is not at stake, where it is easy to estimate in advance the work to be done (and thus to set reasonable norms) and to control its results, and, furthermore, where costly side-effects do not threaten and where it is possible to ensure simple and inexpensive administration of the piecework. In the drive for quantitative results these aspects were not taken into proper consideration; piecework could be partly blamed for the fact that workers' efforts were primarily directed to quantity at the expense of quality. It also encouraged a huge waste of materials and instruments and caused much spoilage. The piecework drive brought into existence a large amount of fictitious piecework, whose only purpose was to ensure higher wages for workers. Finally piecework contributed – as already mentioned – to a levelling of wage differentials for skill, and thus became a disincentive to acquiring skills. It often enabled unskilled and semi-skilled workers, who normally perform work demanding less care for quality, to achieve almost as high wages as skilled workers.

The adverse effect of piecework could have been substantially reduced if only the norm-setting had been more adequate. Apart from the disorder introduced in the norms by wage-rate rigidity, there were other factors which could be blamed for this situation. One was simply that adequate norm-setting could not keep pace with the fast spread of piecework. This was all the more true since norms could not be set from one centre; they had to be adjusted to working conditions, including the technological level of individual enterprises ('Some Aspects . . .' 1959). And finally, workers, for understandable reasons, were not very eager to cooperate in objective work studies, which would enable norms to be set on a scientific basis.

After 1956 all three countries embarked on a reform of the wage system.[6] The reforms were marked by several common features, reflecting the fact that all the countries were plagued with the same diseases. However there was no longer a uniform approach; for some problems different countries took different solutions.

The level of wage-rates, and thus also the share of wage-rates in average wages, was increased in order to strengthen their role in remuneration. The extent of the increases varied from country to country depending on how much wage-rates fell behind average wages and on what was regarded as a desirable amount of overfulfilment of work norms. In Czechoslovakia it was decided that in piecework the wage-rate should comprise 75–85 per cent of earnings, and in timework 80–90 per cent (Mihalik 1959); by contrast, in Poland and Hungary the corresponding figure for piecework was 95–100 per cent (Krencik 1972, p. 104; Buda 1965B).

Czechoslovakia used the reform to widen wage-rate differentials, and boosted the role of skill in remuneration. The newly introduced branch qualification catalogues put greater stress on the evaluation of the skills of individual wage-earners than did the old system which concentrated more on the evaluation of individual jobs. The wage-earner's basic reward was made more dependent on his personal skill grade (for more see Adam 1974, p. 54).

In all the countries the extent of piecework was restricted. The prevailing tendency was to eliminate spurious piecework whose only justification was to enable workers to earn more, and to confine it to work where it is economically warranted by the character of the work, technology and organisation of production. Despite these measures piece-rates remained the most important payment form. Where piece-rates were abolished, they are usually replaced by time-rates combined with some kind of bonus. The limiting of piece-rates affected most of all progressive piece-rates which, even before the reform, played an important role only in Poland. Hungary introduced regressive piece-rates (Buda 1965B).

In Hungary and Czechoslovakia enterprises were given the right to decide about payment forms (Hegedüs 1960; Havránek 1960) and in all three countries attempts were made to improve the norm-setting.

In Czechoslovakia and Poland one of the goals of the wage reform was to put remuneration of the same trades performed in different branches on a more equal footing (Krencik 1972, p. 70; Mihalik 1959). This was a first step in scaling down the impact of the criterion of social importance on wage-rates.

The reforms of the system of wage determination for individual workers did not mean a substantial change in the system; the decision-making power of enterprises was only slightly expanded in this sphere. The fixing of wage-rates remained in the hands of the central authorities, and the afore-mentioned rigidity of the rates was retained. There was, however, a modification in basic salaries; the centre set only limits for individual skill grades within which enterprises were allowed to manœuvre, subject to certain restrictions. Only in Hungary was the same system extended to blue-collar workers.[7] However the freedom of enterprises to manœuvre was limited by the strict control of average wages mentioned earlier.

9 Employment and Wage Policies 1966–75

A INTRODUCTION

The period as a whole can be characterised as a period of reforms and as the most successful in terms of improvements in the standard of living. All three countries – above all Czechoslovakia – tried to learn a lesson from the shocking experience of the early 60s. In addition balance-of-trade difficulties as well as gradual exhaustion of labour reserves forced governments to embark on reforms of the management system. It was also a period when labour shortages started to show up on a larger scale than before – primarily in Czechoslovakia – and became of great concern to the central planners.

In this period growth of the working-age population registered the highest rates. In Poland the average annual rate was 1.3 per cent in 1965–70 to increase to 1.8 per cent in 1970–5, a somewhat troublesome development. In Czechoslovakia in 1965–70 there was a deceleration of growth – which aggravated the tight labour market – but in 1970–5 the percentage level of 1955–60 was again reached. In Hungary the growth rate of the working-age population peaked in the first half of the period to decline again in the next half to 0.3 per cent.

The population growth in Poland and the CSSR developed in the same direction. In 1965–70 the growth rate continued to decline (in the CSSR to 0.2 per cent), to increase in the period 1971–5 (in the CSSR partially as a result of measures to promote population growth). Unlike the other two countries, Hungary did not have changes in population growth.

In all three countries the participation rates increased in 1966–70, to decline or stagnate in 1971–5 (see Table 9.1).

After preparations which lasted for some time – mainly in Hungary – the reforms were put into effect, first in Czechoslovakia (1966) and then in Hungary (1968). The Polish leaders also intended to reform the system of management starting in 1971, but were forced to scrap the reform due

139

TABLE 9.1 *Growth of the population, of working-age population and economically active population 1966–75*[a]

	Poland				CSSR				Hungary			
	A		B		A		B		A		B	
	1970	1975	1966–70	1971–5	1970	1975	1966–70	1971–5	1971	1976	1966–70	1971–5
1. Population	32 700	34 200	0.7	0.9	14 334	14 802	0.2	0.6	10 352	10 563	0.4	0.4
Index 1965 = 100[b]	103.5	108.2			101.2	104.5			101.8	103.8		
2. Working-age population	18 300	20 000	1.3	1.8	8 158	8 484	0.5	0.8	6 273	6 370	0.7	0.3
Index 1965 = 100[b]	107.0	117.0			102.5	106.5			103.6	105.2		
3. Economically active population	15 175	16 572	2.3	1.8	6 871	7 060	1.5	0.5	5 010	5 093	1.4	0.3
Index 1965 = 100[b]	112.2	122.6			107.9	110.8			107.4	109.2		
4. Participation rates												
(a) 3:1	46.4	48.4			47.9	47.7			48.4	48.2		
(b) 3:2	82.9	82.9			84.2	83.2			79.9	80.0		

A – In absolute numbers (in thousands).
B – Compounded annual growth rates.

[a] Notes in Table 7.1 except [b] refer to this table too.
[b] Index for Hungary 1966 = 100.

SOURCES Poland – *MRS 1983*, pp. xxiv, xxv.
CSSR – *SRC 1982*, pp. 24, 25, *SRC 1980*, pp. 20–4.
Hungary – *SE 1980*, pp. 3, 4, 130.

to riots which broke out in December 1970. Poland did not join the reforms until 1973.

The three reforms differed: the most far-reaching was the Czechoslovak, particularly considered in the form it took in 1968–9. In the section dealing with employment regulation I will discuss some aspects of the reforms; here only some general observations are given. The Czechoslovak and Hungarian reforms eliminated in substance the system of annual plans with output targets binding on enterprises, and thus considerably increased enterprises' autonomy. The Polish reform did not go so far. In Czechoslovakia most enterprises were given the right to determine their own wage-bill, its distribution and the number of employed. The growth of the wage-bill and employment were controlled by taxation on gross income. The Hungarian reformers were more cautious. They used and use taxation too for controlling wage growth, but this is the 'second line of defence', the first being the linkage of the growth of the wage-bill to a net indicator. The latter method was also adopted by the Polish reformers.

The period consists of two medium planning periods. Taking the experience of the first half of the 60s into consideration, the planners endeavoured to make the plans for 1966–70 more realistic. The FYPs for 1971–5 envisaged higher targets for economic growth than in the preceding period; mainly in Poland the targets were greatly overfulfilled. All three countries tried to combine economic growth with expansion of consumption; this time they succeeded, Poland particularly achieving remarkable success in real-wage increases, though only for a short period of time. This was also the period when social benefits were expanded rapidly, primarily in Hungary and Czechoslovakia.

B EMPLOYMENT POLICIES

1 Poland

In the period 1966–75 the Polish planners faced a formidable task: to cope with unprecedented increments in the working-age population. In the period 1961–5 the increment (men aged 18–64 and women 18–59) was 800 000, whereas in 1966–70 it was 1.2 m. and in 1971–5, 1.7 m. The central planners assumed from compiled manpower balances that in the period 1966–70 the creation of 1.5 m. new jobs was needed and in the period 1971–5 even more, 1.8 m., if unemployment was to be avoided.

In the FYP for 1966–70 Poland in substance continued the old strategy of economic growth; it endeavoured to speed up the process of development of heavy industry. True, greater stress was put on qualitative methods for achieving these goals: the planners aimed at high productivity, greater export specialisation and greater application of science (Karpiński 1974, pp. 107–8).

Consumption was handled, as before, as a residual (Meller 1977, p. 104). and whenever difficulties arose in meeting the targets of heavy industry consumer goods industries felt the pinch.

Of the 1.5 m. planned new jobs, 80 per cent were to be generated in the material sphere, and of these more than half were to be in industry (it was supposed to grow by 3 per cent annually). This was in harmony with the objectives of the FYP, which envisaged an increase in industrial production of 44 per cent and an increase in national income of 34 per cent. The high growth rates of industrial employment were also due to the expected increase in labour-intensive products and a desire to improve the quality of products, mainly those earmarked for exports (Bajszczak and Obodowski 1964B; Jędrychowski 1967).

The planners envisaged an expansion of employment in the service sector and small-scale production, but not to the extent that was needed and possible. The strategy of job-creation was not very different from that of the past; it still relied heavily on investment. Yet a larger expansion of employment in the service sector and small-scale production (mainly in private ownership) would not only have eased investment requirements, but would also have alleviated labour shortages there. The shock of 1970 was needed to make the planners change their strategy of job-creation.

The absorption of new job-seekers went fast, even faster than assumed in the plan. In the first three years of the FYP, industry alone exceeded the plan target by 100 000. This was made possible by an exodus from agriculture at a time when no change was planned (Jędrychowski 1967). A faster increase in investment than planned enabled the overplan absorption of labour. Despite fast increases in employment the imbalances in demand for and supply of labour were not eliminated. In some branches of industry (mainly coal-mining) and highly industrialised regions, labour shortages persisted, whereas in other region women could not find jobs (*TL* 1969, 9 Mar).

The fast increases in employment worried the government for various reasons. They hampered productivity increases and threatened even the planned small increases in wages. In addition, in the second half of the FYP, the economic situation in the country worsened. The terms of trade deteriorated and blunders in investment were committed. Bad weather conditions unfavourably affected agricultural output so that it fell far below the target, merely fulfilling 56 per cent, and disequilibria in the market for consumer goods started to show up (Karpinski 1974, p. 107; Gołębiowski 1978, pp. 77–3).

To cope with these problems the government decided in 1969 to reduce investment outlays in 1970. Furthermore the county national councils were entrusted with the task of increasing control over employment with the obvious objective of hampering its growth (*PiZS 1970*, no. 7). Due to these provisions the growth rate of employment in 1970 declined to 1.9 per cent in the socialist sector and in socialised industry to 1.6 per cent. However, to compensate for the reduced possibility of increasing employment, many enterprises resorted to an expansion of overtime work.

The target for the creation of 1.5 m. new jobs in the socialist sector as well as the target in industry were overfulfilled. Employment in the socialist sector grew by an annual 3.9 per cent and industry by 3.6 per cent. The whole material sphere grew in terms of employment much more slowly (1.8 per cent) due to agriculture, whereas the non-material sphere registered an acceleration (6.1 per cent). The number of economically active in the national economy grew by 2.3 per cent (see Table 9.2).

In 1968 the party leaders decided to introduce an economic reform (supposed to go into effect in 1971) whose main purpose was to create conditions for 'intensive and selective development'. In practice the FYP for 1971–5 and the economic reform assumed the continuation of the austerity policy for wages. An integral part of the economic reform was supposed to be a price reform which would have brought about a radical change in price relativities by making foodstuffs much more expensive (Jezierski and Petz 1980, pp. 267–9; *TL 1970*, 3 Dec). In a climate already charged with tension the price reform triggered riots, the end result of which was the fall of W. Gomulka and his associates. E. Gierek, the new communist leader, rescinded price increases, scrapped the economic reform and promised a new strategy of growth. This new strategy aimed at restructuring the economy and at the same time modernising it with the most modern technology in order to finally achieve an intensive pattern of growth. In contrast to the past when a new investment wave usually prospered at the expense of consumption, the new strategy also envisaged high increases in real wages and consumption, and improvement in housing and social conditions (cf. Fallenbuchl 1982A, p. 37). The architects of the new strategy also pledged themselves to bring about a more rational employment policy (Meller 1977, p. 126).

TABLE 9.2 Growth of the labour force 1966–75[a]

	Poland				CSSR				Hungary[b]			
	A		B		A		B		A		B	
	1970	1975	1966 –70	1971 –5	1970	1975	1966 –70	1971 –5	1971	1976	1966 –70	1971 –5
1. National economy	15 175	16 572	2.3	1.8	6 871	7 060	1.5	0.5	5 010	5 093	1.5	0.3
Index 1965 = 100	112.2	122.6			107.9	110.8			107.4	109.1		
2. Socialist sector	10 325	12 202	3.9	3.4	5 902	6 253	1.9	1.2				
Index 1965 = 100	121.0	143.0			110.0	116.2						
3. Material sphere	13 260	14 301	1.8	1.5	5 429	5 514	1.2	0.3	4 237	4 209	1.5	–0.1
Index 1965 = 100	109.6	118.2			106.0	107.6			107.8	107.1		
4. Non-material sphere	1 915	2 271	6.1	3.5	1 442	1 546	2.9	1.4	773	884	1.0	2.7
Index 1965 = 100	134.7	159.7			115.5	123.9			105.0	120.1		
5. Industry	4 453	5 150	3.6	2.9	2 632	2 712	1.5	0.6	1 776	1 789	2.0	0.1
Index 1965 = 100	119.4	138.1			107.5	110.7			110.6	111.4		
6. Construction	1 075	1 406	3.5	5.5	554	622	3.0	2.3	385	420	4.0	3.5
Index 1965 = 100	119.3	156.0			115.9	130.1			121.8	132.9		

	Poland				CSSR				Hungary			
	A	A	B	B	A	A	B	B	A	A	B	B
7. Agriculture inclusive of forestry Index 1965 = 100	5 392 98.7	5 017 91.9	−0.3	−1.4	1 178 93.6	1 024 81.3	−1.3	−2.8	1 226 94.4	1 059 81.5	−1.1	−2.9
8. Transport and communications Index 1965 = 100	940 118.2	1 057 133.0	3.4	2.4	469 112.2	469 112.2	2.3	0.0	369 115.7	402 126.0	2.9	1.7
9. Trade Index 1965 = 100	1 046 128.8	1 222 150.5	5.2	3.2	522 113.5	605 131.5	2.6	3.0	420 123.5	468 137.6	4.3	2.2
10. Health and social welfare Index 1965 = 100	452 118.6	599 157.2	3.5	5.8	251 116.7	297 138.1	3.1	3.4				
11. Education, culture, physical education Index 1965 = 100	680 124.1	781 142.5	4.4	2.8	402 105.8	435 114.5	1.1	1.6				
12. Communal and housing services Index 1965 = 100	399 127.1	497 158.3	4.9	4.5	208 106.7	211 108.2	1.3	0.3				
13. Collectivised agriculture Index 1965 = 100	802 123.4	959 147.5	4.3	3.6								

A – In absolute numbers (in thousands). B – Compounded annual growth rates.

[a] All notes in Table 7.2 except [c] and [f] refer to this table too.
[b] The base year for indexes in Hungary is 1966.

SOURCES Poland – *MRS 1983*, pp. 38–41.
CSSR – *SRC 1982*, pp. 24, 25; *SRC 1981*, p. 192.
Hungary – *SE 1980*, p. 4.

Naturally Poland could not finance a strategy which assumed high rates of investment growth and real-wage growth from its own resources, and therefore resorted to borrowing in the West, whose technology it was also interested in importing. The planners assumed the credits would be largely paid off by manufactured goods produced in the new and modernised plants.

The FYP adopted for 1971–5 soon turned out to be too modest in light of the good performance of the economy (which was favoured by a remarkable increase in agricultural output, partially due to the elimination of compulsory deliveries and increased prices) and improved terms of trade. In 1973 the FYP was modified; the target for national income growth was changed from 39 per cent to 55 per cent; for industrial production the corresponding figures were 50 per cent and 60 per cent, for agricultural output 19–21 per cent and 25.5 per cent, and real wages 18 per cent and 38 per cent (Jezierski and Petz 1980, p. 338). To help achieve these objectives in the economy investment was increased to unprecedented rates; in 1971–5 it grew on the average by 18.5 per cent annually.

The FYP for 1971–5 envisaged the creation of 1.8 m. jobs. As a result of modernisation some of the investment was labour-saving rather than job-creating. Under such conditions the strategy of job-creation could not remain the same as in the previous FYP, all the more because costs of creating one job by investment increased dramatically, by approximately 64 per cent (from Zl 580 000 to 950 000). Therefore the planners endeavoured to place at least some new job-seekers in positions which could be created without investment outlays; so 200 000 jobs in industry were to be created by expanding shift work. In addition the planners intended to expand employment in small-scale production where, due to the low level of technical equipment, it was possible to create many jobs with small investment outlays. Finally the planners decided to create job opportunities by expanding services (mainly the distribution net) (Kabaj 1972a).

The new strategy speeded up the growth of employment. In 1971 employment in the socialist sector and industry grew by 3.1 per cent, and in 1972 it reached 4.4 per cent and 4.0 per cent respectively. There was also a substantial improvement in female employment. The ratio of female job-seekers to openings for females, which in 1966–70 ranged around 4 and in 1970 reached the 8 mark, declined rapidly and was already below 1 in 1973.

Expectations that the economic reform put into effect in January 1973 would bring about an improvement in labour economy did not materialise. Therefore in the fourth year of the FYP – as if a tradition were being followed – the government introduced limits on employment. According to official explanations the aim of this provision was to make sure that there would be enough manpower for new productive capacity as it became available as well as for services and trade (*Polityka* 1974, 10 Aug). Limits on employment were also motivated by a downturn in the economy: the terms of trade started to deteriorate due to investment overstrain and rapid increases in wages, and shortages of materials and consumer goods began to show up. (The situation in consumer goods worsened, when Poland was hit by a crop failure in 1975.) Government efforts brought down employment growth in 1975 to 2.3 per cent (in the socialist sector). However employment in the socialist sector for 1971–5 surpassed slightly the 'target' and grew by 3.4 per cent annually; industry grew by 2.9 per cent. The non-material sphere registered a deceleration; it grew (including trade) by an annual 4 per cent. The number of economically active in the economy increased by only 1.8 per cent annually. The faster increase in employment in the socialist sector than in the national economy was made possible by a decline in agriculture (of 1.4 per cent annually). See Table 9.2.

2   Czechoslovakia

The CSSR entered the phase under discussion with different employment worries from its neighbours. Labour resources not engaged in the economy were more or less exhausted. The participation rate reached 80.0 per cent in 1965. If one considers that the number of young people involved in education and training was still growing relatively, the participation rate was high indeed. Huge transfers from agriculture were neither desirable nor possible; however territorial transfers were still possible, but to a very limited extent. The possibility of attracting more housewives into the labour force was believed to be limited. The situation was compounded by the relatively low increments expected in the working-age population and, in addition, by the government's intention to reduce the workweek (Kubík and Rendl, 1965). On the other hand a delayed increased influx of young people into the labour force was expected due to the extension of compulsory education to 15 years and the extension of studies in senior high schools in the early 60s (Tesařová 1972).

Considering the situation in the labour market and the experiences of the early 60s, the central planners who were already under the influence of the forthcoming economic reform came up with a relatively modest plan for 1966–70. The plan envisaged an increase of 21 per cent in national income and 31 per cent in industrial output. Increases in productivity were supposed to be by far the paramount factor in national income growth. Employment in the material sphere was supposed to stagnate (increase by 7 000 persons) and in industry it was to increase by a modest 0.8 annually. A great part of the planned increment in the number of economically active and of those leaving agriculture had to find jobs in services (Kubík and Rendl 1965).

The aim of the FYP was to carry out structural changes which would enable the economy to become more efficient and balanced. For this purpose the reformers called for a preferential development of those branches which had the potential to enhance economic efficiency and also to contract or even liquidate plants and lines of production which were unprofitable and unable to produce products with demanding parameters (Kouba *et al.* 1966). To achieve this objective in the initial period of the reform, the national committees on the county levels which were entrusted with the task of regulating employment had to see to it that priority enterprises received the needed manpower (Formánek and Pick 1965).

In the period 1966–70 the economy grew much faster than envisaged in the FYP despite the political events of 1968–9. Apparently the economic reform had a favourable effect on the economy (cf. Kosta 1978, p. 152). National income increased by 6.9 per cent annually, and social productivity by 5.6 per cent. Agriculture also performed well; gross output grew by 4.8 per cent. Important progress was achieved in the standard of living. The much higher overfulfilment of the national income target than of the productivity target contributed to the surpassing of the employment 'targets'. There were also other, probably even more important, contributing factors. In 1967 the reformers embarked on an accelerated implementation of the final aims of the reform, which *inter alia* meant abolishing employment controls where they still existed. Taxation became the instrument for controlling employment.

Employment in the material sphere outstripped the limit by a large percentage; it grew by 1.2 per cent annually (against planned zero) and in industry employment grew by 1.5 per cent (against 0.8 per cent). At the same time the planned decline in the number of economically active in agriculture fell behind the plan (it was − 1.3 per cent annually against the planned − 2.4 per cent). Employment in the non-material sphere also grew faster than envisaged in the plan (2.9 per cent annually). As a result of all these changes the total number of economically active grew by 1.5 per cent against the planned 0.4 per cent. [1]

The relatively fast growth of employment was made possible by a further absorption of housewives into the labour force. Their number increased beyond expectations by 267 000.

The central objective of the fifth FYP for 1971–5 was to improve the standard of living by expanding the economy and enhancing its economic efficiency. The government pledged itself to improve the social insurance system and provide more housing for the population, goals motivated largely by political considerations, namely by the desire to improve its shaky position. Otherwise the FYP in substance was intended to continue structural changes which were focused on the petrochemical and machine industries. The targets for 1971–5 were higher than in the previous FYP, but lower than actual performance (*HN* 1971, no 22).

The plan projected an increase in the number of economically active in 1971–5 of 2.6 per cent (180 000). Employment in the state sector was supposed to grow much less than in 1966–70, only by 300 000. The number of school-leavers who are available to fill jobs was estimated to be only 0.5 per cent higher than in the previous period. In 1968–70 the admission to schools of various levels was liberalised, and more young people were admitted than before (Tesařová 1972). It was assumed that of the mentioned 300 000 a large number would serve for replacement of employed women taking prolonged maternity leave. In industry and construction employment was supposed to increase by 123 000 (3.8 per cent) (the greatest part in Slovakia) while in agriculture it was to decline by 127 000. The service sector was again to increase fast, this time by 158 000 (Bakič 1971).

The quinquennium of 1971–5 was successful; the output targets as well as targets for improving the standard of living were mostly overfulfilled. National income increased by 30 per cent (against the planned 28 per cent), social labour productivity by 25.3 per cent, output in industry by 38.5 (against 34–6 per cent) and gross output in agriculture by 11.6 per cent (against 14 per cent) (Kynstetr 1981).

The quantitative 'targets' for employment were met despite the fact that the number of women on maternity leave increased more than assumed; yet the total number of females employed continued to grow. Employment in industry and construction increased together by 0.9 per cent and industry alone by 0.6 per cent. This was partially due to a higher decline in agriculture than was projected (− 2.8 per cent annually against planned −2.2 per cent). Growth of employment in the non-material sphere remained slightly below the target.

In the period discussed labour shortages became substantially entrenched, and as always were combined with overemployment. According to an investigation by the ministry of labour and social affairs in 1974, 21 per cent of all industrial positions in the main shift could not be filled because of a shortage of labour (Mikeš and Steinich 1976). An official of the Planning Commission estimated the labour shortage in industry at 300 000 provided a shift coefficient of 1.5 per cent and capacity utilisation of 85 per cent were assumed. Due to the labour shortage the capacity utilisation in industry was predicted to decline in 1975 to 52 per cent. One of the main reasons for the labour shortage was the stress on building new plants (instead of modernising existing ones) without simultaneously liquidating antiquated ones (Pick 1974). According to reports new machines were installed at an annual rate of 9.2 per cent, whereas old machines were liquidated at a rate of 1.6 per cent (Mikeš and Steinich 1976; Tesařová 1976). In other words labour shortages increased at a time when fixed capital in machinery and equipment grew at an unprecedented rate and, of course, further improvement in the quality of the labour force was achieved. Apparently a great part of the added machinery was not of a labour-saving nature.

3   Hungary

In the period 1966–71 the working-age population experienced the highest growth rate (3.6 per cent) in the post-war period. The baby boom of the 50s, generated partly by an abortion prohibition law, started to reach working age. Though the growth rate was approximately 50 per cent of the Polish rate, the Hungarian economists labelled it as a demographic wave (Vida Horváth 1971), and were worried that the country might not be able to provide enough jobs. This worry was compounded by the projected number of school-leavers. (See later for more.)

The threat of possible unemployment was also fuelled by the expected consequences of the introduction of the New Economic Mechanism (NEM) in 1968. The planners namely overestimated the impact of NEM on managers' attitudes to economic efficiency; they believed that enterprise managers would respond instantly to the profit motive, and that, in their effort to increase economic efficiency, they would try to economise on labour (Pongrácz 1973; Kemeny 1971). In their fear of possible unemployment the planners undertook several provisions to dampen the possible blow of unemployment.

One was the introduction of the maternity care programme (1967), one of whose main purposes was to create job vacancies for female job-seekers. (At the same time this programme had to bring about a more rational utilisation of labour.) 70–80 per cent of the vacancies generated in this way were filled by female job-seekers. Part-time work and work at home were expanded with the aim of creating new jobs for teenagers and women. The admission to training programmes for youth was substantially expanded. The workweek was reduced to 42–4 hours (Vida Horváth 1971). And finally the agreement concluded with East Germany about manpower co-operation, according to which 10 000 young Hungarians would work in Germany to acquire qualifications, was also motivated to a great extent by fear of unemployment (Mátyás 1969).

The worries of the planners did not materialise and employment grew much faster than had been assumed. To understand what happened I will start out with the targets for the third FYP. It was a relatively modest plan; apparently it was designed in an effort to abandon the tradition of obsession with growth. The plan envisaged an increase in national income of 24 per cent, industry 32–6 per cent, gross agricultural output 13–15 per cent, real wages 9–10 per cent and productivity in industry 24–6 per cent (M. Timár 1973, p. 89). As to manpower, the plan visualised an increase in the number of economically active of 180 000 and an increase in employment outside agriculture of 260 000, which means that agriculture had to decline by this difference of 80 000. Taking into consideration the projected number of those retiring and quitting jobs for other reasons (680 000), the demand for new workers was envisaged at 860 000. The number of school-leavers was estimated at 880 000, which was 210 000 more than in the previous FYP (J. Timár 1966). And this fact was a further reason for unemployment worries.

The restructuring of the economy, one of the main objectives of the FYP, primarily focused on fast changes in the sources of energy production in favour of oil and natural gas at the expense of coal-mining[2] (low productivity mines were shut down), faster development of the petrochemical industry (fertilisers and synthetic fibres) and modernisation of the food industry (Ajtai 1966) – was carried out to a great extent without due application of technology; managers relied as before largely on labour-intensive methods. Decentralised investment, which was expanded as a result of NEM, grew much faster than was assumed (one reason being that the development fund increased more than expected) and with it employment (M. Timár 1973, pp. 89, 102–3; Portes 1977, pp. 776–7). Despite deceleration of economic growth in 1968–9 employment grew twice as fast.

The imposition of a 4 per cent wage-increase ceiling on enterprises with the introduction of NEM, which was intended to be a protection against inflation, became a stimulus to hoard labour. The easiest way to circumvent the wage ceiling was by hiring semi-skilled and unskilled workers who could be paid wages below average (Bánki 1971; Kónya 1971).

The profit motive did not offset the negative effect of wage regulation on labour utilisation. Managers soon realised that it was possible to increase profit and employment at the same time by expanding output (Friss 1972). The reduction of the workweek was only partially offset by technical-organisational improvements; thus it also contributed to increased demand for labour (Lázár 1971).

The fast growth of employment – the number of economically active in 1966–71 increased by 7.4 per cent against the planned 3.8 per cent – was combined with several unfavourable features. Due to the elimination of all obstacles to free movement of labour, labour turnover substantially intensified; according to one author at least a third of the turnover was unwarranted from an economic viewpoint (Lázár 1971). There was also a decline in labour discipline, a shift to labour-intensive products, and slow progress in eliminating auxiliary physical work. Labour shortages showed up, mainly in some service branches at a time when industry was overmanned by at least 100 000 workers. The number of white-collar workers continued to grow faster than blue-collar workers, partially the result of the introduction of NEM (Kónya 1971; Rózsa 1971).

The government undertook several provisions aimed at coping with the situation in employment and manpower management: to mention some, it restrained investment, changed the wage-regulation system, introduced a compulsory labour exchange for some workers. The latter two will be discussed in the section dealing with employment regulation.

Despite all the mentioned shortcomings in manpower management and productivity, NEM had a favourable effect on the performance of the economy, mainly by contributing to an equilibrium in the market, and the third FYP was overfulfilled. To mention some figures: national income increased by 39 per cent, industry attained the highest point in the planned range, agriculture exceeded the target slightly and real incomes increased by 18.6 per cent.

In the fourth FYP for 1971–5 mostly higher targets than for the previous FYP were envisaged: for national income 31.3 per cent, industry 31.9 per cent, agriculture 15.9 per cent, investment in the socialist sector 31.9 per cent and real incomes 24.6 per cent (M. Timár 1973, p. 165). The objectives of the FYP were in substance those mentioned for the third FYP.

As to manpower the figures did not vary much from the previous plan: the number of economically active was to increase by 191 000 and employment in the non-agricultural sectors by 320 000–360 000. It was assumed that in agriculture the number of economically active would decline by 150 000. The plan anticipated a much smaller influx of young people to the labour force (780 000 against the actual 952 000 in 1966–71). This was in accordance with the projected substantial decline to 1.5 per cent in increments to the working-age population. As to housewives, their number was to increase minimally (10 000 against the actual 210 000 in 1966–71) since it was felt that the vast majority of women who wanted jobs already had them (Rózsa 1971).

The planners set as a goal full employment and at the same time a more rational utilisation of labour. For this purpose they planned small increases in employment in the material sphere, mainly in industry which was particularly overmanned, and greater increases in the non-material sphere. They also vowed to press for a transfer of workers to more productive jobs. This time they were not worried about unemployment even if they admitted that in the process of structural changes some people would temporarily lose their jobs. They expected that the new wage-regulation system would induce managers to practise greater labour economy (Pál 1970).

The fourth FYP was overfulfilled though not by as great a percentage as the third. What was especially appreciated was that there was an improvement in productivity growth; 90 per cent of the increase in industrial output resulted from increases in productivity. Despite difficulties with foreign trade the plan was overfulfilled (Huszár 1976).

The number of economically active increased by 1.7 per cent (83 000) which was only 44 per cent of the target. What is worth while mentioning is that for the first time the planners managed to implement their goal for the distribution of labour. Employment in the material sphere (without agriculture) increased in 1971–6 by only 4.6 per cent, in industry by only 0.7 per cent (in the previous FYP 10.6 per cent), whereas in the non-material sphere it increased by 14.4 per cent (against 5 per cent in 1966–71). See Table 9.2.

It seems that the new wage-regulation system put into effect in 1971 had a favourable impact on labour hoarding, but did not nearly solve the pressing problems of labour utilisation. Absenteeism, great losses of work time, low labour discipline and high labour turnover persisted (Hoós 1976; Pongrácz 1976).

4 Employment Regulation

This period differs from the previous one in several aspects of employment regulation. The economic reforms adopted in this period eliminated direct limits for employment and introduced new methods to serve employment regulation exclusively, so that employment regulation was no longer left to the wage-regulation system alone. Even in Czechoslovakia, where in 1970 a return to a centralised system of management occurred, indirect methods were also used. The increasing labour shortages and the desire for greater economic efficiency forced the central planners to give greater attention to labour economy. Naturally the changes in the system of employment regulation were not identical since the economic reforms were not identical either.

Though the Czechoslovak planners assumed that the new wage-regulation system – introduced during the economic reform of 1966 which abolished the assignment of the wage-bill from the centre (for more see Adam 1979, pp. 166–7) – would in itself encourage labour economy, they nevertheless also applied an indirect instrument as tax, for controlling growth of wages as well as employment. The so-called stabilisation tax consisted of two divisions: the first was geared to the control of growth of wages and the second targeted the control of employment with the objective of discouraging enterprises from making an excessive use of labour for expansion of output. It was also expected that an increase in labour costs would induce enterprises to substitute capital for labour (Kutálek 1966; *Zásady . . .* 1966).

The formula for the stabilisation tax (T) was

$$T = \frac{30}{100}\left(W - \frac{90}{100}\,wE\right) + \frac{rW}{100}$$

where W is the actual wage-bill of the year for which the tax is payable, w is the planned average wage in the previous year, E is the number of employed in the year for which the tax is payable and r is the growth of employment in the year for which the tax is payable.

From the second part of the equation, which refers to the tax payment for an employment increase, it is clear that for each per cent increase in employment, enterprises were obliged to pay 1 per cent of the wage-bill (or the equivalent of the increased wage costs). There were, however, many exemptions from this rule.[3]

The objective of this tax was to hamper further growth of employment in sectors where overemployment already existed, thus giving sectors short of labour a greater share in the net addition to the labour force. The hopes pinned to the tax did not materialise for two reasons. First, the unsuccessful 1967 wholesale price reform brought about more favourable revenue conditions in enterprises than anticipated. Second, the low tax credit for employment reduction (0.3 per cent for 1 per cent reduction) made enterprises reluctant to release their labour reserves if they felt that they might need them in the future (Bajcura 1969, pp. 63–4).

The Hungarian architects of the reform had many reasons to believe that NEM would stimulate labour economy; they assumed that NEM being based on the profit motive would make enterprises interested in having an optimal number of employees and qualification mix, that managers would endeavour to save labour in order to increase the value of the year-end reward per employee and that increased taxes on the wage-bill making labour more expensive would have a favourable effect on labour economy (Buda and Pongrácz 1968, pp. 172–4).[4]

The planners were so confident of the favourable impact of the provisions mentioned that they even assumed that there might be unemployment. Yet the evolution of employment showed that such assumptions were ill founded. The 4 per cent wage ceiling imposed on enterprises – as an anti-inflationary precaution – generated, as already mentioned, considerable labour hoarding. The distributed bonuses were too small to be a powerful incentive to labour economy. Provisions to make labour more expensive did not have a great effect, for reasons which will be explained when discussing Poland. In order to counter the trend to labour hoarding the government introduced in 1970 a temporary tax on employment increases (Bokor 1973).

In 1971 the wage-regulation system was changed, the main reason being the desire to make the use of labour more efficient. Wage increases were no longer to be paid from the sharing (bonus) fund; they were to be included in costs. Growth of average wages in enterprises was linked to the growth of gross income (wages plus profit) per employee compared to the previous year. On wage increases achieved as a result of this formula, enterprises had to pay a tax amounting to 50 per cent of the additional wage costs. Increases in average wages above the formula hinged on enterprises' willingness and ability to pay additional taxes amounting to 150–400 per cent of the additional wage costs (Buda 1972, pp. 96–8, Flór and Horváth 1972, pp. 103–5).

The new wage-regulation system meant that average wages were regulated (instead of the wage-bill)[5] and that growth of wages was tied to a productivity indicator. The link between wage increases and growth of profit was maintained, though in a weakened form; still taxes for wage increases had to be financed from the sharing fund and growth of gross income depended on profit.

The planners' expectations that the new wage regulation would stimulate maximum gains in productivity only materialised to a certain extent; hoarding of labour did not disappear. There were several reasons for this. The normative was too low to be a powerful stimulus; a 10 per cent increase in gross income per employee was needed in order to achieve a 3 per cent rise in average wages. Increases in wages above the level, enterprises were entitled to on the basis of performance, were prohibitive for most enterprises due to high taxes.

Profit can be increased (by saving materials, shifting to more profitable products, increasing prices, expanding output) without having to economise on labour. In addition the price system[6] made the terms under which enterprises work quite unequal; the price flexibility built into NEM benefited enterprises whose products were sold at free prices. These and other factors prevented profit from being an objective indicator of performance. To mitigate these inequities and the heavy taxation authorities granted needy enterprises subsidies and tax exemptions. Needless to say, the authorities had a hard time determining the extent of the need of individual enterprises, and this enabled enterprises to abuse the system and ensure wages for workers they wanted to keep.[7]

Up to 1973 Poland more or less adhered to the usual methods of employment regulation applied in a centralised system of management. In 1967 for the first time, the central planners resorted to incentives to make enterprises interested in labour savings. 50 per cent of the savings achieved in the wage-bill due to labour-saving could be used for the socioeconomic group, which brought it about, in the form of bonuses or increases in wages, with some limitations (Fick 1970, p. 164).

As in the Hungarian reform the Polish architects of the 1973 reform (which was confined to the so-called initiating enterprises, with the intention of extending it gradually to all enterprises) expected that the new wage-regulation and incentive systems would have a favourable effect on labour economy. In addition they introduced, for the initiating enterprises on top of the 17.5 per cent (of the wage-bill) contribution to social programmes which every enterprise had to pay, a 20 per cent tax on the wage-bill payable from gross profit, in the hope that the tax would be instrumental in speeding up the process of substituting capital for labour (Kabaj 1977, p. 62; Fedorowicz 1977, pp. 137–9).

The new wage-regulation system was similar to the Hungarian in that the growth of wages depended on performance compared with the previous year. Otherwise it differed in many important respects. The wage-bill was subject to regulation, the wage regulator was a net indicator, but not a productivity indicator as it was in Hungary, the normative was intentionally differentiated (in Hungary the underlying principle was uniformity) and finally taxation as an instrument for controlling wage growth was not included in the original concept.

The following formula was used for industry for the formation of the wage-bill (F_n).

$$F_n = F_0 \left(1 + R \, \frac{P_n - P_0}{P_0} \right)$$

F_0 is the wage-bill of the previous year; P_n and P_0 are output added of the current and the base year respectively; R is the incremental normative expressing the rate at which the wage-bill increases with the increase in output added by 1 per cent.

R was supposed to be a long term normative in the range of 0.5–0.9 (Topiński 1975, p. 132). At a given R the smaller the number of employed and thus the higher the growth of labour productivity (output added per employee) then the faster wages per employee can grow. In other words the formula had a built-in stimulus to labour economy. In addition, the authorities could set R for individual enterprises at a level that would encourage enterprises to reduce labour input per unit of output.

The reform brought about a new incentive system for the managerial staff in all enterprises. The bonus fund was fed from profit and its size depended on produced net profit. Progressive taxation was used as regulator of the growth of the bonus fund.[8] One could argue that the incentive system was also stimulative to labour economy.

Despite these stimuli employment continued to grow fast in the initiating enterprises; it grew twice as fast as in units with the old system. There was one good reason for this: the initiating enterprises shared to a greater extent than other enterprises in the huge investment activities. But this was not the only reason. Many enterprises managed to acquire enough funds for wage increases without being under sufficient pressure to be concerned with the level of employment. This was possible due to manipulation of output added: some got away with price increases on new products which were not warranted by the additional costs, while others shifted to more profitable products. Some enterprises managed to turn to their advantage their involvement in foreign trade under inflationary conditions (Holubicki 1977; Gliński 1977, pp. 40–1).

The imposition of the tax on the wage-bill probably did not have an impact on labour economy either. The share of wages in the cost of production is small; in the 1970s it was 16 per cent in Polish industry. In addition, the introduction of a 5 per cent tax on assets and an 8 per cent tax on investment credits offset the impact of the tax on wages. Even if the favourable income conditions of enterprises are disregarded the tax would have had to be much higher to have any effect (Kabaj 1977, pp. 62–3).

To cope with the rapid increase in employment the government reintroduced in 1974 – as already mentioned – limits on employment, and in addition introduced a charge on employment increases and on the portion of the wage-bill exceeding 4 per cent of growth. The charge for an increase in employment of one person was Zł 20 000 (Gliński *et al.* 1975, pp. 59), an amount which corresponded approximately to six months' average wage in 1974. The charge was not identical to a tax; it was surrendered to a new branch reserve fund and the ministry could use it for wage increases and other purposes.

After the scrapping of the economic reform in the CSSR, employment limits binding on enterprises were reintroduced. The central planners, however, did not rely only on directives; they also introduced some incentives. Enterprises which achieved higher labour savings than the plan envisaged were allowed to increase wages by a certain fraction for each percent of saving; yet the effectiveness of this incentive was somehow weakened by introducing a modified version of the 1967 tax on wage increases. In addition the planners introduced a 25 per cent contribution to social insurance from the wages paid out, with the same purpose as in the other two countries (*HN 1969*, no. 50).

5 Placement Policies, Unemployment Benefits and Retraining

The economic reforms brought about further improvements in the freedom of choice of jobs. In Czechoslovakia the free movement of adult workers was instituted; provisions by which enterprises could prevent workers quitting jobs without good reasons were in practice eliminated. The same happened in Hungary. The placement of graduates in Czechoslovakia was also liberalised; plans for the distribution of graduates had only the nature of guidelines and it seems that they were in no way compulsory for individuals. In Poland the placement regulations for university graduates were eased starting with 1971, without changing the substance of the 1964 law (see pp. 130–1). The number of jobs offered to graduates was increased in order to give them a greater choice. The authorities also induced enterprises to expand grants to students with the understanding that after completing their studies they would be employed by the supporting enterprises (*Życie Warszawy* 1970, 3 Nov).

In Hungary the central planners assumed that the compulsory labour exchange would, with the introduction of NEM, be reduced to cover only partially disabled persons (*Népszabadság* 1967, 1 Nov). When, however, labour turnover started to grow rapidly due to NEM the Hungarian authorities gave the county councils permission to go ahead with compulsory labour exchange. A great many of them, mainly in Budapest, took advantage of this, though it was limited to persons who changed jobs at least twice a year or left their job before their notice expired or were fired for labour discipline reasons. Such persons could fill jobs only with the approval of councils; however enterprises were not obliged to employ the people who were suggested to them (L. Horváth 1970).

This provision, which no doubt violates human rights and therefore seems a strange element in NEM, had several purposes. It was hoped that it would reduce labour turnover since people usually do not like to have bureaucrats decide about their employment, all the more because these bureaucrats had to ensure that 'drifters' did not benefit from job changes. Furthermore this provision had to direct labour into sectors and enterprises which suffered from shortages and which, according to the planners, deserved preferential treatment. This was also why the textile industry and construction and some services could hire 'drifters' without the approval of councils (*Népszabadság* 1971, 20 Oct). As could be expected, under conditions of labour shortages compulsory labour exchange could not be very successful (*Pártélet* 1972, Jan).

Judging from the two editions of M. Olędzki's book (1974; 1978) no important changes in labour exchange occurred in Poland in 1966–75.

In Czechoslovakia the scrapping of the economic reform in 1969 also meant changes in placement policies and in the labour code. According to the new uniform system of labour distribution enterprises were not allowed to employ people who changed jobs twice a year without the approval of the district national committees. Otherwise the uniform system essentially took over the provisions of 1958 with regard to recruitment of workers by enterprises and the planning of admission to vocational and high schools and universities and the distribution of their graduates (Murgaš 1971; Blažek 1973). The modified labour code enabled people to be fired simply for political reasons (Nejedlý 1970).

As mentioned all three countries endeavoured to change the structure of the economy, which, in the employment sphere, meant that some workers must be transferred to other jobs within the enterprise, others to other enterprises and some must be dismissed. Transfers and dismissals on a larger scale are politically very sensitive matters and therefore the workers' co-operation is necessary for their smooth implementation and can be brought about only by adequate incentives. Wage differentials alone are not sufficient to make workers move according to the needs of the economy. Unfortunately there is not enough information about the incentives used in the countries under review, except in Czechoslovakia which applied incentives from the beginning of central planning and has the most developed system of incentives for individuals.

In 1967 the CSSR government, in fear of unemployment as a result of the economic reform and the desire to liquidate inefficient and obsolete enterprises, introduced a set of guidelines for the placement of laid-off workers and for their material well-being. Workers who, despite the help of their employer and local government, could not find jobs corresponding to their physical and mental abilities and, as much as possible, to their qualifications, were entitled to an 'allowance', a euphemism for unemployment benefits amounting to 60 per cent of the net earnings achieved in the organisation that dismissed them, up to a maximum of Kčs 1800 which corresponded to more than the average wage in 1967. In addition a dismissed worker could claim severance pay up to six months' average wages. If he accepted a job through recruitment by national committees he was entitled to a hiring bonus and an equalisation supplement (which would bring his wage to the level in the old enterprise) for three months. Should the new job require retraining the equalisation supplement was and is given for six or twelve months (Kudrna 1967).

C   WAGE POLICIES

1   Policy of Wage Increases

In the period under review nominal and real wages continued to grow, but at different rates in individual countries and periods. The pace of growth of real wages was influenced as before by fluctuations in economic growth, internal political development and also by the economic reforms.

For the quinquennium 1966–70 all the countries planned higher targets in money and real wages than they had achieved in the period 1961–5 (see Table A.1, p. 234). Interestingly enough, in this period – unlike the preceding quinquennium – all the countries exceeded the targets. In 1966–70 the economies of the area witnessed relatively high growth rates, and this was one of the reasons why real wages could grow faster than envisaged in the plan. In Hungary the excess was quite substantial; the annual growth rate of real wages amounted to 3.4 per cent, while the plan anticipated a rather modest increase of 1.8 per cent. The pace of real wage growth was quite differentiated; the CSSR with 3.6 per cent took the lead, and Poland with 2.1 per cent ranked last (see Table 9.3). The increases in real wages in Poland were so small that some groups of the population, mainly low-income groups, suffered a decline in real wages because price increases affected consumer staples. The situation was compounded by a government limitation of funds for social purposes (*ESE 1972*, part II, p. 107).

In Czechoslovakia and Hungary the introduction of the reforms had a great impact on wage policy. In these countries the view started to take hold that the previous approach, which viewed consumption as a residual in the process of income distribution, should be abandoned and that the growth rate of wages should be boosted for the sake of improving the standard of living and enhancing the stimulative role of wages. In Czechoslovakia, for the first time, computations were made to find out how big nominal wage increases should be to make the wage an effective stimulus[9] and to be able to carry out a widening of wage differentials. Many economists took the position that the tasks which an accelerated wage growth was called on to fulfil were so important that it was worth implementing them even at the expense of modestly increasing prices. These notions were initially resisted; Novotný's leadership saw in them a threat to the investment drive. Later they were partially integrated into government policy. Wages grew, however, faster than was even envisaged in the changed plans. Political events in 1968 created a suitable climate for upward wage pressure which was difficult to resist; in addition political tension led to a loosening of discipline in enterprises and to a circumvention of government regulations. Pressure for wage increases was strengthened by the fact the trade unions had achieved a certain measure of independence from the communist party and government.

The Hungarian reform of 1968, with its great stress on incentives which manifested itself in the introduction of a separate bonus fund fed from profit, brought about higher money and real-wage increases; in 1969–70 real wages grew annually by 4.6 per cent (see Table 9.3). Unlike

TABLE 9.3 *Evolution of money wages (A), consumer prices (B) and real wages (C)*[a] *1966–75 (annual growth rates)*

		1966	1967	1968	1969	1970	1971	1972	1973	1974	1975	1966–70	1971–5
Poland	A	4.6	4.1	3.8	3.2	2.9	5.4	6.4	11.5	13.8	11.9	3.7	9.7
	B	1.2	1.5	2.4	1.5	1.2	-0.2	0.0	2.6	6.8	3.0	1.6	2.4
	C	3.4	2.5	1.2	1.6	1.7	5.6	6.4	8.7	6.5	8.7	2.1	7.2
CSSR	A	2.7	5.5	8.2	7.5	3.0	3.7	4.1	3.3	3.3	3.2	5.3	3.5
	B	0.3	1.5	1.2	3.6	1.7	-0.4	-0.4	0.2	0.4	0.6	1.6	0.0
	C	2.4	3.9	6.9	3.7	1.3	4.2	4.5	3.1	2.9	2.6	3.6	3.5
Hungary	A	4.0	4.2	2.3	5.9	6.2	4.6	5.0	6.3	7.4	7.6	4.5	6.2
	B	1.8	0.6	0.0	1.2	1.2	2.3	2.8	3.3	2.1	3.6	1.0	2.8
	C	2.4	3.5	2.2	4.4	4.7	2.5	2.0	2.9	5.6	3.5	3.4	3.3

[a] See note [a] of Table 8.3.

SOURCES Poland – *RS 1981*, pp. xxxiv–xxxv.
CSSR – Kazimour 1980, p. 159.
Hungary – *SE 1980*, p. 19.

Czechoslovakia and Hungary, which were determined to abandon the previous strategy of growth, Poland continued it and also subjected its wage policy to it. In order to sustain the pursued rate of growth, Poland had to step up the accumulation ratio. Higher rates of employment expansion were another effect of the extensive growth, though they were also a result of the pressure of the relatively high growth rate of the working-age population. Due to the unchanging growth rate of the global wage-fund (it grew annually by 7.4 per cent) a great portion of its increment (44 per cent) was used for wages for new employees, so that the rate of nominal wage increases could only be modest (Morecka 1974).

Poland planned higher, and the CSSR and Hungary smaller, targets for real-wage increases for 1971–5 than those achieved in the preceding quinquennium. The actual movements of real wages were not substantially different except in Poland. This time Poland achieved the highest tempo in real-wage increases (7.2 per cent annually in 1971–5) which was a remarkable contrast to the 60s. The fast increases in real wages were made possible by the new approach of Gierek's leadership to wages, partially motivated by political considerations, and by the new strategy of growth, which in the initial period, seemed to be very successful, considering performance figures for this period. It is interesting that real wages grew even faster than the revised target allowed for (6.7 per cent), and despite the exceeding of the planned limit for employment.

The invasion of the CSSR and the political events following had a great impact on the wage policy there. Wage growth was put under strict control and prices were frozen, partly in order to eliminate inflation (Tomášek 1971). As a result of these measures real-wage increases dropped to 1.3 per cent in 1970. But soon, without loosening the control over wages the central authorities allowed higher wage increases in order to ease political tension. (In 1971–2 real wages increased annually by 4.3 per cent.) They also made efforts to ensure market equilibrium by importing more consumer goods.

The growth of real wages in Hungary in 1971–5 was not as dynamic as one would expect from the general image of the system. In fear of inflationary pressures Hungary introduced in 1971 a stricter control of wages and put greater limits on wage increases. The normative was fixed at only 0.3 per cent for a 1 per cent increase in gross income per employee. This brought down real-wage increases to an annual 2.5 per cent in 1971–3, a level which, due to the differentiated growth of wages, meant no increase at all or even a decline for some groups of workers. Such small increases cannot be of great stimulative value and usually generate tension. To minimise the potential tension (and also to make corrections in differentials) the government took an apparently unusual step (which is in a sense in conflict with the spirit of NEM) and decreed wage increases, first for manual workers in large enterprises (Dankovits 1973) and then for other workers. And this provision increased real wages to 5.6 per cent in 1974.

2　Wage Determination for Individual Workers

This is a period marked by substantial changes in the tariff system in Hungary and the CSSR. The intention of reducing wage-rate differentials for the same work, which had already been touched off by the first major reforms in the second half of the 50s, got a new boost; the great difference in wage-rates for the same work between heavy industry and light industry was reduced. The tendency to smaller interbranch differentials also enabled the number of wage-rate scales applied in individual countries to be dramatically reduced, a process which had already started in the previous reforms.

Enterprises were given a greater say in the concrete application of the wage-rates. This manifested itself in a conspicuous way in the Hungarian reform of the tariff system in 1971. The preferential treatment of piecework, which was reflected in higher rates than timework, was eliminated.

In the period 1966–9 Czechoslovakia started to make preparations for an overhaul of the tariff system, pay forms and setting of work norms. But no real changes were carried out; the reform of the system of management was scrapped before major changes in the system of remuneration of individual workers could be undertaken.

In 1972 the government decided to gradually overhaul the remuneration system in profit organisations. This was carried out under the slogan 'rationalization of work and of the wage system'. All manual and non-manual workers were reclassified. Classification was carried out on the basis of an analytical point system, applied to typical work activities of both groups.[10] For manual workers nine skill grades (instead of the previous eight) were introduced. The spread between the first and the ninth grades is now 2.75 (instead of the previous 2.4). This in itself shows that the reformers intended to ensure greater skill differentials, and this aim becomes even more obvious in light of the fact that before the change, 90 per cent of jobs were in practice classified in the three middle grades in most branches of industry (*HN 1974*, no. 4).

On the other hand the reform brought about a reduction in

intersectoral differentials by a substantial lowering of the number of wage-rate scales; it is now nine. The first two are supposed to be used for most of the productive sectors and the activities therein. Work in mining, metallurgy, and some other branches with difficult working conditions is classified in the third to seventh wage-rate scales. The remaining two scales are reserved for special cases. Apart from production and working conditions, social factors, including historical relationships, play an important role in the classification. The spread between the ninth and first wage-rate scales is 66 per cent (distributed evenly between the consecutive wage-rate scales) and is smaller than between the previous ones (Šmolcnop 1974). The highest wage-rate (ninth skill grade of the ninth wage-rate scale) is 4.5 times higher than the lowest. Wage-rates were substantially increased to the range of 85 per cent of average wages against 50–60 per cent before.

For non-manual workers seventeen skill grades were introduced and, in addition, three grades for general managers and their deputies in bigger enterprises (more than 2 000 employees). The spread between the first rate and the twentieth (the general manager) is 1 : 7. In contrast to the old system which had separate salary-rate scales for technical staff and administrative staff, the new system has only one common scale for both groups. This new provision aims at eliminating the complaints of the administrative staff who felt that the old system discriminated against them.

In 1971 Hungary introduced a new tariff system, which reclassified all manual workers and salaried employees on the basis of their skills. For manual workers six skill grades were introduced; unskilled workers are classified in the first, semi-skilled in the second and third, and the third to the sixth grades inclusive are used for skilled workers. The third grade is given to workers who perform simple skilled work, whereas the sixth is the most sophisticated. In addition every skill grade has been divided up into four groups according to working conditions: that is, physical arduousness, body position at work, temperature, and health hazard and danger (Kővári 1981, p. 320). In other words all manual workers have been classified into twenty-four groups, a provision which enables the differences in remuneration for the same work to be reduced substantially. The new wage-rates were set in broad spans (Berényi 1974, pp. 29, 107) which are supposed to give managers room to manœuvre and to base wages more on performance.

As to remuneration of non-manual workers, three aggregate groups were set up: the first is for top and middle managers. Top managers and their deputies are now classified in five groups, according to the responsibilities involved, which are evaluated on the basis of the number of employed, the value of output and value of the assets of the enterprise. The second group includes specialists and professionals; they are classified into four skill groups, and each of them into five groups according to length of experience. Finally the third group includes administrative workers. The spread between the lowest basic salary of administrative workers and the salary of the best-paid top manager is 1 : 8 (Bánki and Tóth 1974, pp. 108–11, 122).

In Poland, despite discussions, pledges and preparations, only a limited number of industrial branches went through a reform of the tariff system in the period under review. In 1972 the number of wage-rate scales in engineering, mining and energy were reduced, and enterprises could use two, one for normal working conditions and the other for difficult conditions. Wage-rates were no longer differentiated according to payment forms and were increased (Jacukowicz 1974, p. 57).

10 Employment and Wage Policies since 1976

A INTRODUCTION

In the period discussed the economy took a turn for the worse. In the first half of the 70s all three countries expanded their trade with the West in a desire to put their economy on a higher technological level and make it more efficient. High increases in oil prices, above all in 1979, resulted in worsening terms of trade. The slump in the West accompanied by protectionist tendencies made the competition for Eastern products on Western markets more difficult. All this contributed to balance of payment deficits and to indebtedness *vis-à-vis* the West, particularly in Poland. All three countries tried to grapple with this problem by slowing down economic growth.

The labour market did not develop everywhere and always according to the needs of the economy. Increments in the working-age population reached their nadir, mainly in Hungary which, in the period discussed, registered a decline in the working-age population. The demographic factors added to the labour shortages in Czechoslovakia and hampered economic growth. Their impact in Poland and Hungary was different at different times.

In population growth the trend was not the same. The CSSR managed to slightly increase the growth rates; apparently the pronatal measures had an impact in 1976–80. In Poland the growth rates stabilised, whereas in Hungary they declined slightly (see Table 10.1).

All three countries still planned relatively ambitious growth targets for 1976–80; they had, however, to reconcile themselves to the substantial slowdown in economic growth; in certain years output even declined. The targets for 1981–5 are much more modest, but even they were not fulfilled in 1981–2. Poland's political and economic crisis, which has entailed a huge decline in output, has had a spin-off effect on the other countries.

TABLE 10.1 Growth of the population, working-age population and economically active population [a]

	Poland[c]				CSSR				Hungary			
	A		B		A		B		A		B	
	1980	1982	1976–80	1981–2	1980	1982	1976–80	1981–2	1981	1983	1976–80	1981–82
1. Population	35 700	36 400			15 311	15 369			10 713	10 710		
Index 1975 = 100	104.4	106.4	0.9	1.0	100.4	103.4	0.7	0.2	101.4	100.0	0.3	0.0
2. Working-age population	21 200	21 500			8 709	8 696			6 275	6 104[d]		
Index 1975 = 100	106.0	107.5	1.2	0.7	102.7	99.8	0.5	−0.1	98.5		−0.3	
3. Economically active population	16 492	16 853			7 358	7 435			5 015	4 970		
Index 1975 = 100[b]		99.5	−0.1	−1.2	104.2	101.0	0.8	0.5	98.4	99.1	−0.3	−0.4
4. Participation rates												
(a) 3:1	46.2	46.3			48.1	48.4			46.8	46.4		
(b) 3:2	77.8	78.4			84.5	85.5			79.9			

A – In absolute numbers (in thousands). B – Compounded annual growth rates.

[a] Notes in Table 7.1 except [b] refer to this table too.
[b] Due to the new method of calculation, figure for item 3 of 1982 is not comparable to the previous ones. Growth rate for 1981–2 is calculated from new data for 1980 and 1982.
[c] Index for Hungary 1976 = 100.
[d] Non-comparable with the previous figures due to a new definition of working-age population (15–59 for men and 15–54 for women).

SOURCES Poland – MRS 1983, pp. xxiv, xxv.
CSSR – SRC 1983, pp. 23, 25.
Hungary – SE 1982, pp. 28–30, 53; SE 1980, p. 130.

The FYPs for 1976–80 envisaged increases, though modest ones, in real wages; the plans were not fulfilled. The present FYPs in Czechoslovakia and Hungary promise to retain the existing level of real wages. Poland has serious trouble avoiding further erosion of the standard of living.

The state of the economy again pushed the question of reforms to the forefront. Hungary strengthened its decentralised system by expanding the role of the market mechanism, and the Polish planners embarked on a reform which is supposed to be, in its final stages, even more far-reaching than the Hungarian. One must wait and see whether the Polish leaders will have the courage and stamina to overcome the initial difficulties of the reform which has started in almost chaotic economic conditions. If the past is any guide, the outlook is not good. The Czechoslovak planners' experiments are usually confined to some minor reforms.

In Poland and Hungary the private sector has been given a greater role. Besides political and employment reasons (particularly in Poland) recognition of the need to expand services and small-scale production was very important.

B   EMPLOYMENT POLICIES

1   Poland

The new strategy of economic growth which seemed to be so promising in the first phase has turned out to be a failure. The Polish leaders overestimated the capability of their economy: they stepped up the investment ratio to a level (in 1975, 37.5 per cent) at which they could not even absorb the imported investment goods (Fallenbuchl 1982в). On top of this, investment decisions were made by administrative methods without due regard to export possibilities. At the same time they allowed unprecedented real-wage increases over a long period which, due to the slower growth of consumer goods output caused partially by a crop failure in 1975, generated shortages. The internal disequilibrium was aggravated by a huge balance-of-trade deficit.

In 1976–7 the government undertook several provisions to remedy the situation, but without success. Some changes in the system of management, which was also to blame for the failure, were carried out. One aimed at bringing enterprises and especially their finances under greater control. The government dramatically reduced imports, primarily from capitalist countries, unfortunately in a highly arbitrary manner. As a result output, including that for export, started to decline, and many projects could not be finished which endangered further development. Despite import cuts indebtedness grew; in 1975 Poland owed $7.6 billion to capitalist countries and in 1980, $27 billion.

The still-ambitious FYP for 1976–80 approved at the end of 1976 bore the imprint of the political crisis which has arisen due to the aborted price increases. It put great stress on a renewal of market equilibrium by allowing more funds for investment in consumer goods branches and in agriculture. Stepped-up housing construction was included among the priorities. The renewal of external equilibrium was supposed to be achieved by a 75 per cent increase in exports (an unrealistic target) and only a 25 per cent increase in imports (Chelstowski 1977; Kolos 1980).

The employment plan, for the first time in central planning, attached great importance to the private sector; of the 1 100 000 planned addition to the work force 500 000 were supposed to find employment in the private sector; of those 300 000 in agriculture and the rest in services (Kabaj 1980; Mosóczy 1979, p. 135). Several reasons were instrumental for this policy. Job-creation in the state sector required increasing investment outlays and, in addition, the planners were afraid that the socialist sector would not be able to absorb the new manpower resources. This might also have been the reason for the planners' intention to increase the work force in agriculture, though the expansion of agricultural output was surely also on their minds. Though the increment in the working-age population declined compared to the previous quinquennium, it was still respectable (1 200 000) (see Table 10.1). The expectations that the expansion of the private sector would contribute to a political relaxation also played a role.

What is also of interest is that the greatest part of the increment in the work force was to find employment in services (transportation, trade, health care and education). Industry was supposed to increase by 170 000, which was less than the projected demand as a result of new productive capacities put into operation. Greater allocation of labour was to go to branches producing consumer goods.

The FYP in employment was not fulfilled. The number of economically active declined in 1976–80 by 80 000 instead of increasing. Yet employment in the socialist sector increased, while it declined in the private sector because of agriculture (including forestry) which registered a decline of 11 per cent points (552 000) (see Tables 9.2 and 10.2). Considering the private sector without agriculture it increased by 133 000. Employment in industry remained 75 000 behind the target.

Despite the decline in the number of economically active, particularly in 1979–80 when the economy faltered, Poland was not hit by unemployment. In the period 1976–80 the number of retirees and disabled increased by 474 000 as a result of various provisions aimed at easing retirement. In addition, 263 000 more females were on maternity leave in 1980 than in 1975 (Kabaj 1980). That unemployment did not occur – disregarding some pockets of it – is backed up by the following figures: in 1979 6 400 people were registered as job-seekers for 128 500 openings.

In 1980, when the government introduced hugh price increases, Solidarity appeared on the political scene, and the fight for free trade unions and economic and political reforms entered a new, unprecedented stage in post-war Poland. Solidarity's fight was accompanied by strikes and pressure for higher wages, activities which contributed to a decline in output and to a deepening of market disequilibrium and inflation. The decline in coal output in particular, combined with a reduction in material imports from the West, had a multiplying effect on total production. Already in 1979 and 1980 national income had declined (by 2.3 per cent and 6 per cent respectively) and for the whole quinquennium 1976–80 had increased by only 6 per cent against the planned 40–2 per cent. In 1981 national income produced plummeted by 12 per cent, industrial output by 16 per cent and coal production by 14.8 per cent. The authorities feared the consequences for employment of the decline in production, all the more because they were faced with the usual problem of placing 440 000 graduates (of those, 50 000 with university education). On the other hand they toyed with the idea of giving up the policy of full employment and shutting down 700, later 300 inefficient enterprises, an idea which materialized only to a limited extent. As a result unemployment in the range of one million people was calculated (Krasniewski 1982).

All the fears of unemployment turned out to be ill founded; on the contrary the labour market became tighter than before the crisis. Labour shortages became almost as important a factor as raw material shortages in hampering economic growth. In 1982 there were 248 000 openings against 9 000 job-seekers (Sonntag 1983). There were shortages, primarily of skilled male workers. However, employment did not increase, it actually declined again, this time markedly in the material sphere, particularly in 1982 (*TL 1983*, 3 July). This does not mean that overemployment ceased; it rather worsened, and this was one of the main reasons for labour shortages.

That unemployment did not arise was due to several factors, and the systemic were perhaps the most important. The economic reform of 1982

TABLE 10.2 Growth of the labour force 1976–82[a]

	Poland[b]				CSSR				Hungary			
	A		B		A		B		A		B	
	1980	1982	1976–80	1981–2	1980	1982	1976–80	1981–82	1981	1983	1976–80	1981–2
1. National economy Index 1975 = 100	16 492 99.5	16 853	−0.1	−1.2	7 358 104.2	7 435 105.3	0.8	0.5	5 015 98.5	4 970 97.6	−0.3	0.4
2. Socialist sector Index 1975 = 100	12 718 104.2	12 198 100.0	0.8	−2.1	6 637 106.1	6 725 107.5	1.3	0.6	4 834	4 799		−0.3
3. Material sphere Index 1975 = 100	13 996 97.9	14 216	−0.4	−1.6	5 619 101.9	5 638 102.2	0.4	0.1	4 043 96.1	4 048 96.2	−0.8	0.05
4. Non-material sphere Index 1975 = 100	2 496 109.9	2 637	1.9	3.1	1 740 112.5	1 797 116.2	2.4	1.6	971 109.8	922 104.3	1.9	−2.5
5. Industry Index 1975 = 100	5 245 101.8	5 006 97.2	0.4	−2.3	2 779 102.5	2 806 103.5	0.5	0.5	1 654 92.5	1 577 88.1	−1.5	−2.3
6. Construction Index 1975 = 100	1 337 95.1	1 222 86.9	−1.0	−4.3	641 103.1	625 100.5	0.6	−1.2	393 93.4	373 88.0	−1.3	−2.5
7. Agriculture inclusive of forestry Index 1975 = 100	4 465 90.0	5 170	−2.1	−0.6	953 93.1	946 92.4	−1.4	−0.4	1 033 97.5	1 083 102.3	−0.5	2.4

8. Transport and communications	1 119	1 062	1.2	−2.6		489	494	0.8	0.5		400	393	−0.1	−0.9				
Index 1975 = 100	105.9	100.5				104.3	105.3				99.4	97.8						
9. Trade	1 305	1 316	3.2	4.2		664	675	1.9	0.8		488	498	0.9	1.0				
Index 1975 = 100	106.8	107.7				109.8	111.6				104.3	106.4						
10. Health and social care	703	753	3.3	3.5		334	352	2.4	2.7									
Index 1975 = 100	117.4	125.6				112.5	118.5											
11. Education, culture, physical education	830	903	1.3	4.3		509	544	3.2	3.4									
Index 1975 = 100	106.3	115.6				117.0	125.1											
12. Communal and housing services	602	624	3.9	1.8		222	225	1.0	0.7									
Index 1975 = 100	121.1	125.7				105.2	106.6											
13. Collectivised agriculture	1 139	1 061	3.5	−3.5														
Index 1975 = 100	118.8	110.6																

A – In absolute numbers (in thousands). B – Compounded annual growth rates.

[a] All notes in Table 7.2 except [c] and [f] refer to this table too.
[b] In Poland, due to the change in the method of calculation, data for items 1, 3, 4 and 7 for 1982 are not comparable to the previous ones, and the annual growth rates for 1981–2 are calculated from the new data for 1980 and 1982.
[c] The base year for indexes in Hungary is 1976.

SOURCES   Poland – *MRS 1983*, pp. 38–41; *RS 1981*, p. 64.
           CSSR   – *SRC 1983*, p. 190.
           Hungary – *SE 1982*, pp. 52–3; *SE 1980*, pp. 132–3.

gave enterprises the right to hire labour according to their own considerations, to set their own wage-rates within certain broad parameters and to have a great impact on prices. Indirect methods used for influencing employment, wages and prices did not turn out to be very effective. Later I will discuss this problem in greater detail; here it should be mentioned that taxation of average wages as a way to restrain wage increases and to finance the fund for occupational activation (FAZ) encouraged the hiring of people paid below average wages. Enterprises do not have great difficulty expanding wage-bills at a time when price increases are encouraged by shortages and when competition is non-existent (Pisz 1983).

The huge price increases carried out at the beginning of 1982 reduced the share of labour costs in total costs, and so it became even more advantageous to enterprises to use labour instead of labour-saving equipment (*TL 1982*, 2 Sep). Labour hoarding has also been encouraged by hopes of future availability of raw materials and thus acceleration of output. Furthermore the underutilisation of labour worsened. In 1981 245 hours per worker were lost in industry, an increase of 32 compared with 1979 (*TL 1982*, no. 192; *TL 1983*, 20 Feb). Considering the demand for labour one must also mention the expansion of the private sector.

On the supply side the authorities' underestimation of the number of people who would take advantage of the change in pension law (1981) enabling workers to retire five years earlier on full pension provided they did so by the end of 1981 (Brojewski 1981) played an important role. (Due to the much higher incidence of retirement and the developing labour shortages, the authorities allowed manual workers to return to work for two years without affecting their rights with regard to earlier retirement (*TL 1982*, 30 July).) Furthermore the fact that the number of women on prolonged maternity leave continued to climb, no doubt a result of the 1981 introduction of an allowance for women on such leave, contributed to an avoidance of unemployment.

2   Czechoslovakia

'With the sixth FYP we enter a new phase in which our economy will develop under more demanding internal and external economic conditions. Sources of extensive growth are practically exhausted; it will be necessary to fulfil the higher targets in substance with the present, in some cases with a lower number of workers and a slower growth rate of energy and raw materials consumption.' This is the way G. Husák characterised the economic situation in his report to the XVth Congress of the communist party in 1976 (*Základy* . . . 1979, p. 79).

At the beginning of the 70s there were signs that Czechoslovakia would gradually get away from its unfavourable structure of industry and reduce the growth of material and energy intensive branches. This trend was, however, arrested for some time by the decisions of the CMEA which required Czechoslovakia to continue to develop her capital-intensive branches (Levcik 1981, p. 390). The FYP for 1981–5 again envisaged some reductions in the requirement for fuels and energy, primarily by reducing the growth of the chemical industry (*HN 1981*, no. 16).

In the second half of the 70s the terms of trade worsened and the balance of trade showed a deficit even with CMEA countries (Altmann 1980, p. 157). Needless to say, the slump in the West made the competition for Czechoslovak products harder.

The situation in the labour market was another predicament facing the economy. Labour shortages deepened; due to high participation rates (in 1975–83.2 per cent) employment increases depended to a very great extent on the number of new school graduates (vocational and non-vocational). The number of teenagers who entered the labour force directly from compulsory elementary school was steadily declining; in 1976–80 only 4 per cent of teenagers entered the labour force directly against 8 per cent in the previous quinquennium (Tesařová 1982). And the increment in the working-age population was lower than before (0.5 per cent annually against 0.8 per cent) and in it the female increment was negligible. In addition the service sector had to be supplied with more labour.

The planners allowed for an increase in the number of economically active of 210 000; of this 101 000 in the productive sphere, 66 000 in the non-productive sphere and the rest in reserve. The greatest percentage of the labour for the service sector was supposed to go to trade and catering (30 per cent), less to education (16 per cent) and health and social welfare (18 per cent) (Ujházy 1982).

In reality the number of economically active increased by almost 300 000, 43 per cent more than assumed. Two factors were primarily responsible for this outcome. The number of housewives who joined the labour force exceeded several times the planned figures (137 000 against 11 000). The increase in the number of working retirees also exceeded expectations (54 000 against 11 000) (Ujházy 1982). It seems that the main reason for these changes was the declining standard of living.

The greater increase than expected in housewives' employment had two consequences. It brought about a much higher increase in employment in services than was expected (196 000 against 66 000), whereas industry and agriculture reached the anticipated level. Second, since housewives usually only take jobs which are not too far from their homes, the territorial disequilibrium between demand for and supply of labour, one of the employment problems, could be coped with to a lesser degree than desired.

Though employment limits were exceeded, and fixed assets grew fast, labour shortages persisted.[1] The expectation that workers would be gained for new plants from enterprises scheduled for closure materialised only partially though the targets were modest. Experts estimated that in the long run 20 per cent of the industrial capacity should be eliminated; however the target for 1976–80 was the elimination of 32 000 jobs (approximately 1 per cent of the work force in industry). In 1966–7 only 6 600 jobs were eliminated (66 per cent of the target) (Pick 1979).

Another source of workers for factories short of labour is the huge army of auxiliary workers, which is, in spite of government efforts, still growing. Greater mechanisation, primarily in handling materials (transporting, sorting and shelving) could release many workers (Mikeš and Steinich 1975). Not much progress was achieved, either, in reducing the number of administrative and managerial workers, though new measures were undertaken.

Though the planned size of employment in the material sphere was met, national income growth and, with it, labour productivity remained far behind the target. National income increased by 22 per cent (against the planned 27–9 per cent), industrial production by 27.5 per cent (against 32–4 per cent), agricultural output by 9.5 per cent (against 14–15 per cent) and social labour productivity by 13.8 per cent (against 24.5 per cent). According to the computations of one economist, the economic slowdown was caused by, in addition to the exhaustion of extensive sources of growth (as labour, investment and energy; their share was 41.16 per cent), decreasing economic efficiency (31.57 per cent) and external factors (26.14 per cent) (Šujan 1982).

The final FYP for 1981–5 is much more modest than the previous one. It envisages an increase in national income of 10–14 per cent, in gross industrial output of 18–20 per cent and in gross agricultural output of 7–10 per cent (Altmann 1982). Judging from the 1981–2 results (in 1981 national income produced declined by 0.4 per cent and in 1982 stagnated) it can be assumed that the targets will not be met. Czechoslovakia has been under pressure to reduce its indebtedness to the West, and, as a result, has been forced to restrain imports of consumer goods, and materials and machines for industry. Due to a decline in oil imports in 1982, the CSSR had to invest more in coal production than expected and this affected investment in other sectors. Crop failures in 1981 and 1982 contributed to a deepening of market disequilibrium in consumer goods (Potáč 1983).

Nor is the situation in the labour market favourable for economic growth. The increment in the size of the working-age population in 1981–5 is estimated to be no more than 75 000 (42 per cent of the previous quinquennium) and almost all in Slovakia. The planned net increment in the labour force is predicted to be, of course, higher – 157 000; the shortening of university studies, and thus the appearance of two classes of graduates on the labour market in 1982 and 1983, is one of the factors. As in 1976–80 it is assumed that the majority (101 000) will find jobs in the service sector. However, due to the desire to expand some industrial branches, mainly coal production, the originally intended distribution of labour was changed in 1983 in favour of industry. What is also important, no decline in the work force in agriculture is planned (Ujházy 1982).

3 **Hungary**

The thrust of Hungarian economic policy was to cope with the worsening terms of trade and the increasing deficit in the balance of payments. Hungary was hit more than the other two countries by oil price increases, and the slump in the West also affected its exports. The targets for the FYP for 1976–80 were set against this background; they were a bit more modest than for the previous FYP. What was more important was that a much smaller income for domestic use (23–5 per cent against 30–2 per cent for national income produced) was planned in order to increase exports and thus reduce indebtedness. Industrial production was planned to increase by 33–5 per cent and agricultural production by 14–16 per cent (Mosóczy 1979, p. 188).

It soon turned out that planned growth rates could not be achieved. Terms of trade continued to worsen and efforts to offset them failed because of the existing structure of the economy and the faster than planned domestic use of national income. As a result of these developments indebtedness grew (Csikós-Nagy 1982). At the end of 1977 party authorities decided to slow down economic growth, intensify the trend to structural changes in the economy and modernise industrial branches which could have a long-term comparative advantage (Lázár

1982; Nyitrai 1981, p. 64). Naturally this also meant a change in the structure of investment. Thus Hungary decided to abandon for good the old policy of import substitution and to orient its economy to export possibilities. When the troubles in the economy intensified as a result of huge new oil price increases in 1979, the Hungarian planners made changes in the management system which meant a return to decentralisation, among other things, they introduced in most industrial branches a price system simulating world market prices (Csikós-Nagy 1982).

The 1977 decision, which in practice meant a slashing in imports in order to improve external equilibrium, brought about a substantial decline in economic growth. National income produced increased in 1976–80 by only 17.2 per cent (in 1980 it even declined by 0.8 per cent) while national income distributed increased by 9.2 per cent (in 1979 it declined by 5.5 per cent and in 1980 by 2 per cent). Industrial output increased by 21 per cent.

The main objectives of the FYP for 1981–5 were the same as for 1976–80. Since the situation worsened in the meantime the targets set were modest; national income is supposed to grow by 14–17 per cent, but its domestic use by only 5–6 per cent. Productivity in the material sphere should increase by 18–19 per cent and in producing sectors by 21–2 per cent (Balassa 1981; Havasi 1982). In the first two years of the FYP even those more modest targets could not be fully achieved. However the performance of the economy improved compared to 1980.

Rationalisation of manpower management was an integral part of the strategy mentioned; structural changes in the economy are conditioned by structural changes in employment, a tricky task under socialist conditions, particularly in a tight labour market as is and was the case in Hungary. The working-age population was not expected to grow (and it really declined by 95 000 during 1976–81), and as a result the number of economically active was supposed to grow by only a small amount, 60 000. The employment policy was also influenced by the need to improve and expand services due to the increased standard of living. In light of these considerations industrial employment was planned to remain the same, whereas constructional and transportational employment was to grow moderately. Their growth was supposed to come from labour productivity gains. Agriculture was expected to reduce its work force by 120 000. Services were to absorb the labour released by other sectors.

In order to make sure that the structure of employment would adjust to the planned restructuring of the economy and that priority enterprises would not be short of labour, the planners used administrative methods in addition to economic ones in the first half of the FYP. All enterprises were classified into three categories according to their potential for growth and efficiency. Enterprises scheduled for labour force reduction or liquidation were subject to compulsory placement. To make sure that workers available in the job market would not find their way into white-collar work, a freeze on hiring was imposed which was later modified. Also provisions were undertaken to tighten labour discipline (among other things limitations were imposed on holding two jobs) (Karakas 1976). The shortage of labour was also to be coped with by mechanisation, primarily of arduous manual work (Kónya *et al.* 1978).

Some economists predicted that unemployment would result from the 1977 change in policy (cf. Csikós-Nagy 1982). The prediction did not materialise; yet the number of economically active declined by 78 000 instead of increasing. Total employment in the material sphere decreased too; industry especially was affected by this turnabout (decline by 7.5 per cent). The work force in agriculture declined however, by much less than expected (26 000). Employment in the non-material sphere increased by 87 000 (10 per cent).

The main reason for the decline in the number of economically active (an occurrence which did not really generate unemployment) was a decrease of 85 000 in the number of full-time working retirees, a direct outcome of improved pension benefits. An increase in the number of disabled people of working age due to real or even simulated handicaps (the latter to supplement the pensions by moonlighting) was another factor.

It is not clear to what extent the changes in the wage regulation system and the introduction of administrative methods contributed to the decline in industrial employment. It seems that they did not play a great role. Only 20 per cent of those who left industry in 1980 did so because of dismissal for disciplinary reasons or transfer; the vast majority who left for other jobs did so voluntarily, to a certain degree because of the increased attractiveness of the service sector (Munkácsy 1980; Balogh 1981). The reduction in employment did not affect the growth of industrial output, partly because most branches used the available reserves and partly because there was a rapid growth in the stock of fixed assets (Gyetvai 1982).

The employment plan for 1981–5 reflected the 1976–80 trends, all the more because the working-age population was projected to continue to decline. Employment in the material sphere is envisaged to decline by 2–3 per cent while the service sector is expected to grow (J. Timár 1978; Balassa 1981). In 1981–2 employment did not develop according to the plan; employment in the material sphere stagnated (it continued to decrease in industry but increased in agriculture)[2] whereas in the non-material sphere it declined rather surprisingly. It is not yet clear how the gradual introduction, starting with 1981, of a five-day workweek of 40–2 hours will affect the relationship of demand for and supply of labour (S. Berényi 1982; Gulyás 1981).

The FYP for 1981–5 attaches a greater role to the private sector and for this purpose – as already mentioned – some provisions for its expansion were introduced. The private sector is supposed to participate in the planned, substantial expansion of services, but is not expected to grow as fast as in Poland; if everything proceeds according to the plan the number of economically active there will increase by 25 000 (Gervai 1983).

4   Employment Regulation

Unlike the previous period this period is not marked by new, previously unused methods for the regulation and rationalisation of employment. Hungary and Czechoslovakia continue to use methods from the previous period, though with some important modifications. Again stress has been put on wage regulation; incentives for labour savings have been expanded and the ineffective policy of making labour more expensive has been retained. What is also important to mention is that direct methods were used for the control of white-collar employment in both countries and that in 1982 – to the surprise of many economists – Czechoslovakia abandoned the assignment of compulsory limits for employment at the enterprise level.

In 1976 Hungary started to expand the regulation of the wage-bill (at the expense of average wage regulation), and already in 1978 it had become the most important regulation method. Wage-bill regulation was not applied in its pure form; it was combined with average wage regulation once increases in average wages reached a certain set limit. The growth of the wage-bill was linked to the growth of value added over the previous year; increases in average wages above a level given by the normative or a set limit regardless of performance were controlled by taxes paid from the sharing fund (Gadó 1976, pp. 49–61; Rácz and Pongrácz 1980, pp. 74–8).[3] The planners hoped that the extension of wage-bill regulation would encourage enterprises to practise greater labour economy, since the smaller the work force, the greater the wage-bill per employee could be. This assumption is true if the savings in wages or a great part'of them remain with enterprises for wage increase purposes and if all other conditions remain the same. Yet the planners, in fear of inflation and excessive wage differentials, were not willing to grant enterprises even part of the savings due to labour economy. Not until 1980, when it became clear that wage-bill regulation in itself was not furthering labour economy, did the authorities allow enterprises a tax exemption for a 3 per cent increase in average wage made possible by labour-saving (Rácz and Pongrácz 1980, p. 75).

It soon turned out that the great excitement about wage-bill regulation was ill founded and that even the incentive of a 3 per cent tax exemption did not change enterprises' behaviour much. Many economists felt that wage-bill regulation in its existing form favoured enterprises with great hidden reserves, whereas it put in a disadvantageous position highly efficient enterprises which were not able to increase their value added very much each year (Pongrácz 1982).

As of 1983 average wages in most enterprises are regulated; their growth is linked to the level of profitability (*jövedelmezőség*) calculated as a ratio of produced profit to fixed assets plus the wage-bill. This means that the rate of wage growth no longer depends on performance compared to the previous year, but only on current profitability. The planners hope that this will encourage enterprises to fully utilise reserves. In order to make enterprises interested in labour savings, 30 per cent of the saved wages can be used for wage-increase purposes for the remaining labour force (Borlói 1982). It is necessary to wait and see whether the 30 per cent will be a sufficient incentive; if Czechoslovak experience is any guide, then the answer seems to be negative.

In the CSSR incentives to labour economy are built in primarily in the wage-regulation system introduced in 1970. The size of the wage-bill is, in the spirit of the traditional system, mostly set as a percentage share, since 1981, in the planned net output (before marketed output). Since 1982, when incentives for labour economy were increased, all savings in the wage-bill resulting from labour economy, regardless of whether they were planned or not, belong to enterprises. In addition, the mentioned tax on average wage increases was eliminated (Moravec 1981; Pick 1982).

In 1982 the authorities freed enterprises from compulsory employment limits; such limits are now only indicated to enterprises as information in the hope that, faced with a choice between higher average wages and no change or a reduction in employment, they will opt for the former (Pick 1982; Ujházy 1982). This change is all the more interesting in that even in July 1981 the government confirmed its intention to continue the compulsory limits for employment in 1981–5 (Formánek 1981) and to enforce the law with the help of heavy penalties.

The first evaluations of the 1982 change revealed that enterprises chose increases in employment over increases in average wages (Čáp and Rybnikář 1982). Among the reasons for this situation one can mention the hope of enterprises that the economic slowdown would be only temporary and therefore reserves should be kept for the acceleration of growth. The psychological inhibition of managers against revealing reserves which they tried to hide from the planners (Pick 1982) and also the fear that the rules of the game might be changed and enterprises would find themselves in a disadvantageous position, surely played a role. Probably another factor is the very small wage increases planned for 1981–5. One can only guess what the reaction of the planners will be to this disappointment; it would not be surprising if binding limits for employment were reintroduced.

In the period 1976–82 no major changes occurred in employment regulation in Poland. The 1976–7 modifications in the reform of 1973, which brought about a tightening of wage regulation for a short time, had only a minimal effect on employment growth. As will be shown later, in the second half of 1980 the government lost a large degree of control over wage growth, and therefore it could not affect employment through wages.

In 1982 an economic reform of the system of management was introduced. If its provisions are put into practice, then Poland will have a far-reaching decentralized system. In the reformed system enterprises are supposed to have full autonomy; they are allowed to plan their product mix according to their own interests, and no targets (with some exceptions) from the centre are to be imposed on them. On the other hand, enterprises are obliged to cover all costs of their operations by self-financing (Golinowski 1982; Król 1982).

An integral part of the economic autonomy is that enterprises are allowed to determine the wage-bill, the size of the work force and its skill structure without any administrative interference from the centre. It is assumed that the principle of self-financing will induce enterprises to have a rational employment policy and that enterprises will try to manage operations with the minimum work force possible. In order to ensure some control over wage growth, authorities imposed for a while a progressive charge (a quasi-tax) on average wages, whose yield still accrues to a special fund for occupational activation (FAZ). In the case of a work-force reduction compared to the previous year, a charge discount is granted (Meller 1982).

It very soon became clear that, contrary to the expectations of the planners, the new rules encouraged growth of employment. By hiring people with wages below average enterprises can reduce the pace of growth of wages and thus ease the charge payments. Funds for wages can be produced by juggling prices; the imposition of a heavy progressive tax on gross income is no great obstacle. Yielding to the overall criticism of the taxation of average wages the planners changed the rules; starting with 1983 the wage-bill is burdened by a charge in favour of FAZ (Król 1982). The planners' hope that this charge will make labour more expensive and thus induce managers to practise greater labour economy could be justified if the principle of self-financing were implemented and the price system were rational; in a situation where no great chances are that self-financing will materialise and where enterprises can juggle prices – despite limitations imposed in connection with a new campaign against inflation (*TL 1983*, 19 May) – it cannot be expected that the taxation will be very helpful.

In different periods all three countries applied administrative methods aimed at curbing the growth of white-collar workers, primarily administrative and managerial staff. In 1976 the Hungarian government imposed a freeze on hiring new workers in government and other organisations financed from the budget; in profit-making enterprises the freeze referred to administrative and managerial staff. Vacated jobs could be filled exceptionally, and the rule did not apply to new graduates of universities and high schools (Karakas 1976; Szabó 1976). Starting with 1977 the freeze was lifted and replaced by a limitation of the number of administrative workers to the ratio achieved by the end of 1975 (Vincze 1976). Later the whole provision was dropped, apparently in connection with greater stress on market forces.[4]

Since 1975 the Czechoslovak government has been experimenting with a twofold approach: on the one hand it has applied short-term provisions (orders for reduction in the administrative apparatus by a certain percentage) and, on the other, it has been trying to work out a permanent mechanism in the form of an establishment of norms for the size of the white-collar labour force and its structure (cf. Adam and Cekota 1980). It seems that the latter approach has not been very successful, since, for 1981–5, targets have been set for the reduction of the administrative and managerial staff in the material and non-material spheres. If enterprises and organisations overfulfil the targets they can keep the money savings so achieved (Starecký 1982; Pick 1982).

5   Placement Policies, Unemployment Benefits and Retraining

Disregarding Poland's situation under martial law (when the restriction of human rights also affected employment) it can be said that a further step has been taken to expand the freedom of choice of job. In 1980, in the spirit of the trend to give market forces a growing role, Hungary abolished compulsory placement (Szatmári 1982). As a result of this development, labour exchange takes on a new content and becomes primarily informational.

Judging from the objectives of the Polish reform, one would expect that Poland will go this way too, though there are signs that a return to compulsory placement – for a transitional period – as a way of ensuring manpower for enterprises producing goods in short supply, is again in the cards (*TL 1983*, 15 Aug). It seems that in Czechoslovakia no change has occurred in placement policies; the 1958 recruitment law of workers for priority enterprises is still in force (Kováčová 1980, p. 47).

Placement regulation of graduates of universities and high schools has changed only in Poland, which was the only country to apply the known rule of three years' work at an assigned job, combined with penalties for violators up to the end of 1982. Now all graduates are freed from any limitations to employment; and they can take jobs even in the private sector (*TL 1982*, 12 Dec; *TL 1983*, 1 Feb). The new policy is a result of the new economic reform as well as of the circumstance that the authorities can no longer ensure every graduate a job corresponding to his qualifications.

In Hungary the 1957 provisions about unemployment benefits (see p. 131) with some modifications in 1958 and 1972 are still on the books; they were until recently, when they were increased, very low. In Czechoslovakia unemployment benefits are still available in the same amount as in 1967 despite the fact that in the meantime the average wage has increased by 60 per cent.

In Poland unemployment benefits financed from FAZ are available for those who have been employed at least two years. The benefits range from the minimum wage to double that amount depending on the length of unemployment. Other unemployed are entitled to a benefit equal to the minimum wage. Workers who support a family or have passed the age of 55 (women 50) are entitled to the highest benefits in the range mentioned (Borkowski 1982).

In the application of incentives for a redistribution of workers according to the needs of the economy, no great changes occurred except in Poland. In Hungary the determination of incentives for individuals who are affected by the redistribution are left to the initiative of enterprises and are financed by them (Gyetvai 1980). Lost incomes during retraining which can last up to twelve months are borne by the government (*Munkaügyi Közlöny* 1983, no. 7). In the CSSR the already-mentioned incentives have been expanded by a special provision of 1979 designed primarily for the transfer of workers from closed factories to existing, expanding factories, where growth is to be achieved by increasing the shift coefficient, and to newly constructed factories as a part of the centralised investment. Such workers qualify automatically for a recruitment bonus (other workers qualify only if they move to jobs for which they are recruited by national committees) for a maximum of three months. If they are willing to contract to work at least five years in the new job they can obtain an increased recruitment bonus equivalent to a maximum of six months' gross earnings. (However, for each un-justifiably missed shift, 1/60 of the recruitment bonus is deducted.) In addition, such workers have a preferential claim to housing and placement of their children in preschool facilities (*HN 1979*, nos 4 and 5).

In Poland funds from FAZ can be used for financing of training and retraining, and for equalization supplements for workers who are transferred to new jobs. These supplements can be given for a period of three months and under certain conditions for six months (Borkowski 1982).

C   WAGE POLICY

1   Policy of Wage Increases

The policy of wage increases is as before conditioned by the development of the economy and internal political developments. The latter refers primarily to Poland. With the worsening of the economy it was clear that the countries would not be able to continue the previous levels of wage increases. Indeed the planned increases in real wages for 1976–80 were much smaller than before, in the range of 2.5–3.4 per cent annually, the Polish being the highest – 3.0–3.4 per cent (see Table A.1, p. 234). But even these modest targets were not achieved and, as a result, some groups of workers saw their real wages decline. The prospects for 1981–5 are even worse.

Considering the Polish economic situation and its post-war history, one could bet that the wage targets would not be fulfilled. One suspects that the planners knew it from the beginning. In June 1976 the government attempted to carry out huge price increases which, had they materialised, would have increased the cost of living by 16 per cent. It is doubtful whether the compensation offered in wages and pensions was of the same magnitude as the price increases (for more see Adam 1979, p. 28). The failure to increase prices deepened market disequilibrium and increased food subsidies. True, the government tried to compensate at least partially for the aborted price increases by opening 'commercial stores' where goods could be obtained at higher prices (Szafar 1981). In addition, enterprises used the loop-holes in the system of management for achieving higher prices. They did so also because they were under strong pressure from their employees who were looking for higher wages. As a result of these developments a price–wage spiral – not at a very high level – came into being, fuelled by employment increases in the socialist sector.

After 1976 government wage policy was marked by a great deal of improvisation. The plan for 1976–80 envisaged that the main source of wage increases in enterprises would be increases in labour productivity and that the government would not use wage-funds from the centre for regulation of wages as it usually did (Czajka 1981). However, in a situation where the economy was entering a critical stage and the applied regulators were less than effective, it could not be expected that wages would develop according to the wishes of the planners and in a structure that would act as an incentive. Even greater disorders in wages arose in connection with their adjustments at the end of 1980 as a result of an agreement with Solidarity; the adjustments were namely influenced by various social aspects, and therefore lost almost all connection with productivity increases. In addition, they brought about new disparities in wage differentials (Przywara 1982; Spotan 1982). During 1976–80 real wages increased by 9.7 per cent; 4 per cent of this was the consequence of the 1980 adjustment resulting from Solidarity's political pressure.

The FYP for 1981–5, which was scrapped, envisaged an increase in real wages of 9–11 per cent (Czajka 1981). In reality real wages stagnated in 1981, and in 1982 due to a doubling of prices on the average at the beginning of the year when martial law started, real wages declined dramatically. The Polish leaders felt that by crippling Solidarity a political situation came about in which wage policy could be shaped simply by economic necessities as they understood them. According to the plan for 1983 no further decline is expected (*TL 1982*, 5 Dec), which is not a very realistic assumption.

The Czechoslovak FYP for 1976–80 visualised an increase in average nominal wages of 13–15 per cent depending on labour productivity (Ujházy 1982). Since the planners followed a rigid price policy, targets in

TABLE 10.3 *Evolution of money wages (A), consumer prices (B) and real wages (C)[a] 1976–82 (annual growth rates)*

		1976	1977	1978	1979	1980	1981	1982	1976–80	1981–2
Poland	A	8.8	7.2	5.8	8.9	13.4	27.4	51.0	8.8	39.2
	B	4.7	4.9	8.7	6.7	9.1	24.4	101.5	6.8	62.9
	C	3.9	2.3	-2.7	2.1	4.0	2.5	-25.1	1.9	-14.4
CSSR	A	2.8	3.2	3.0	2.4	2.5	1.6	2.0	2.8	1.8
	B	1.0	1.3	1.6	3.5	3.0	0.9		2.1	0.9[b]
	C	1.8	1.9	1.4	-0.6	-1.0	0.8		0.7	0.8[b]
Hungary	A	5.2	7.8	7.8	7.0	7.2	5.8	5.5	7.0	5.6
	B	5.0	3.8	4.6	8.8	9.3	4.6	6.8	6.3	5.7
	C	0.4	3.8	2.9	-1.6	-2.0	1.1	-1.2	0.7	-0.1

[a] See note [a] of Table 8.3.
[b] Refers to 1981.

SOURCES Poland – *RS 1983*, pp. xxxiv–xxxv.
CSSR – *SRC 1983*, p. 25.
Hungary – *SE 1980*, p. 19, and *Magyar Statisztikai Zsebkönyv, 1982*, p. 35.

nominal wages were assumed to be translated into equal increases in real wages. Such a policy required that employment increases be kept within the limits of the plan, not an easy task when central planners have behaved almost schizophrenically in considering employment policy. On the one hand they were frightened of possible increases in employment above the plan which might bring about an overfulfilment of the planned global wage-fund, and, on the other, they endeavoured to attain maximum possible increases in employment in order to tackle labour shortages. To solve this contradiction, they tried desperately to bring about improvements in labour productivity. For this purpose they unfolded a major action for the rationlisation of employment and norm-setting which aimed, in substance, at a better utilisation of labour and thus at labour-saving. Statistically the action was successful, but in practice it did not help much (Hrdlička 1982; Hamerník 1982).

In 1976–80 average nominal wages increased by 14.7 per cent and the target for the growth of the global wage-fund was met (20.8 per cent against 21.2 per cent). The higher increase in employment than anticipated in the plan was in services where the government has a tight control (mainly in non-profit organisations) over wages, and therefore wage increases in services lagged behind increases in the national economy (Ujházy 1982).

The cost of living did not evolve according to expectation; in 1976–80 it crept up for employees' households by 7.6 per cent, and thus real wages remained much below the plan target; they increased by 3.5 per cent only. In 1979–80 the cost of living grew even faster than average nominal wages.

In view of the development in 1979–80 and output plans for 1981–5, the targets for 1981–5 are modest – a 1 per cent annual increase in nominal wages. Their final level, and also whether there will be a raise for workers in non-profit organisations, will depend on how effective the endeavour to achieve labour-saving and increase output is (Ujházy 1982). If the first two years, when wages are supposed to grow faster, are any guide, then the prospects are not good. Employment is growing faster than assumed. In addition in the beginning of 1982 the CSSR was forced to increase retail prices which had, despite compensation given, an unfavourable effect on real wages.

The policy of wage increases in Hungary was conditioned by several factors. As in the other two countries, the worsening economic situation did not allow for a significant increase in real wages. Hungary, more than the other countries, was committed not to allow an erosion of market equilibrium for consumer goods, nor to maintain it at a cost of high rates of inflation. To allow the undermining of market equilibrium would mean giving up what is the most characteristic feature of the Hungarian success story. Neither can Hungary give up its flexible price policy if it wants to continue adjusting price relativities to increasing costs and changes in demand. Therefore the Hungarians have tried to achieve a delicate balance between wage and price increases and to continue the old policy of planned price increases without evoking a price–wage spiral. Furthermore the authorities faced the problem of making services suffering from labour shortages (mainly health care, education, culture) more attractive in terms of pay so that new workers could be lured to them.

For 1976–80 the planners envisaged a 2.7–3 per cent annual increase in real wages. Nominal wages were to grow much faster; it was assumed that productive enterprises would increase wages from their own resources by $4\frac{1}{2}$ per cent, and that the government would top the increase according to its considerations. Starting from 1976 all producing enterprises were for some time allowed to increase wages by $1\frac{1}{2}$ per cent – as a compensation for expected inflation – regardless of their performance (Buda 1976).

Wage targets for 1976–80 were not met; the cost of living grew faster than anticipated. When the economy started to stagnate (1979–80) the cost of living reached relatively high levels (8.8 per cent and 9.3 per cent) and overtook nominal wage increases, and real wages consequently declined. As a result of this development real wages grew in 1976–80 on the average by only 0.7 per cent annually (see Table 10.3).

The FYP for 1981–5 sets as a goal the maintenance of at least the level of real wages in 1980 (a goal which, in the light of recent inflationary development, has no great chance for success). Enterprises will have to earn the fund for wages; only very little will be available for wage preferences. No money will be available for central adjustment of wages (Balassa 1981; Lökkös 1981).

Needless to say, Hungary is going through a difficult stage, and the authorities will have to try hard not to let real wages slip much; otherwise the trust of the population may erode (Hámori 1980).

2   Determination of Wages of Individual Workers

In the tariff system no great changes occurred in Hungary and Czechoslovakia. In Hungary the upper limits of wage-rates were increased several times in order to bring them into line with the increase in average wages. The Hungarian tariff system has thus retained its flexibility, a feature which the Czechoslovak system still does not have and the Polish system is in the process of introducing. At the adjustment in 1981 greater increases were set for highly skilled work, arduous work and work performed under difficult conditions. The basic salaries of top managers were also increased more than average since, in the preceding years, they had remained behind other groups (Szávai 1981).

In 1982 some minor changes were instituted in the Czechoslovak tariff system, the most important being the introduction of a supplementary payment for work in the second shift in order to make it more attractive (Šmolcnop 1982).

During the political and economic developments in the period under review the Polish tariff system was entirely disorganised. For some time it had needed a substantial overhaul, since the main part of the existing tariff system had its origins in the beginning of the 60s. There were changes made in wage-rates, mainly after the huge price and wage adjustments of 1980, but they were not large enough; in addition they were made without any macroeconomic conception and therefore could be rightfully characterised as patchwork. As a result, wage-rates lost their true functions and disorganised the work norms (Czajka 1982; Studniarek 1982).

In the spirit of the new economic reform the government decided in 1982 to overhaul in two stages the system of wage determination for individual workers. In the first stage, which was supposed to start instantly, enterprises were given the right to set wage-rates within the broad parameters determined by the centre. The upper limits are much higher than at present, and enterprises can use them provided they have the funds. In order to make the wage-rates more flexible, compensation for price increases will be dealt with separately. Other elements of the system will be determined in the next stage (Czajka 1982).

Enterprises in all three countries have the right to determine payment forms. It seems that piece-rates which, in the previous period, lost much of their importance are regaining significance. This is true not only in Poland where piecework in recent years has substantially spread as a result of a tacit understanding between workers and the authorities (Czajka 1982); workers in general see in it a good way to achieve higher wages in the face of growing prices, and the planners do not object for lack of other tools of motivation. It can be assumed that this tacit understanding will continue. Judging from the labour ministry's document on wage policy, it seems that the Hungarian government would also not mind a greater spread of piecework (*MSz 1982*, no 11).

11 Wage Differential Policies

1 INTRODUCTION

To begin with it is useful to discuss briefly some of the methodological problems one encounters in conducting research into wage differentials. Naturally the most important problem is what to compare in order to receive a genuine picture of the state of wage differentials. The most frequently used method in the literature is to compare average wages of large groups, say for the whole economy, sectors of the economy or socioeconomic groups. It is obvious that this method is used because figures for such a comparison are readily available, and time-series figures for a comparison of employees' earnings in certain occupations which might give a deeper insight into the evolution of wage differentials are missing. However it must be clear that comparisons with largely aggregated figures can serve only as a rough indication of the direction of development, particularly if they refer to a long period. Namely such figures are usually influenced by factors which are not necessarily a result of changes intended to affect wage differentials. The dynamics and structure of employment have an impact on the evolution of average wages. If the number of employed grows fast, say because of the rapidly expanding employment of women, most of whom in the past were unskilled and therefore belonged to the low-paid groups, this depresses average wages. Statistical figures are not available in such aggregations that an elimination of this influence can be made. The fact that the advances in qualifications are not equal in the figures to be compared is another disturbing element. Despite these shortcomings I will have to use average wages for large aggregates. Further on in the text I will examine intersectoral and intraindustrial wage differentials as well as differentials for socioeconomic groups. The first phase in which dramatic changes in wage differentials came about will be discussed separately with the remaining phases being examined together.

191

2   WAGE DIFFERENTIAL POLICIES IN THE POST-WAR PERIOD UP TO 1955

The narrowing of wage differentials which started during the Second World War and continued after the war was dramatically accelerated with the advent of the communists to power. It is difficult to demonstrate precisely the profoundness of the changes since appropriate figures for the period when the great changes occurred – from the start of the fight for political power and its seizure by the communists up to 1953 – were officially published only in some countries of the Soviet bloc. Taking 1950, for example, as a base year, as some publications do for lack of proper figures or from unwillingness to face facts, cannot capture the dramatic evolution in wage differentials.

The research work by L. Beskid (1963; 1964) with the help of M. Kalecki indirectly confirms my statement about dramatic changes in wage differentials. Kalecki (1964, pp. 91–101), who summarised the joint research work in his own publication, shows that real incomes of manual workers in Poland increased during 1937–60 by 75 per cent, whereas those of non-manual workers declined to 74 per cent of the 1937 figure. Nominal incomes of non-manual workers in 1937 exceeded those of manual workers by 160 per cent, but this difference had shrunk to 18 per cent in 1960. Since no great changes occurred in the differentials in the period 1955–60, it can be assumed that the dramatic change occurred prior to this time.

In addition, thanks to the work of J. Hron (1968), proper figures are available for Czechoslovakia, and they can to a great degree be regarded as indicative of the other countries. Yet a qualification is warranted, since it is known that Czechoslovakia took the narrowing of differentials to greater extremes than the other countries did.

In 1948–53 a great narrowing of intersectoral wage differentials occurred; this was largely the result of a narrowing of occupational wage differentials, mainly between blue- and white-collar workers. Nominal wages in industry and construction grew faster than wages in the national economy, which necessarily meant that in some other sectors, principally the non-material sectors where white-collar workers prevail (but also in agriculture), wage growth lagged behind that of the national economy (see Table 11.1).

For the non-material sphere only figures for Czechoslovakia and Poland are available. As Table 11.1 shows, in Czechoslovakia in 1948 average wages in education and culture, and health and welfare exceeded the average wages in the national economy by 24.7 per cent

TABLE 11.1 *Intersectoral wage differentials 1948–56*[a]

	Czechoslovakia			Hungary		Poland A		Poland B	
	1948	1953	1955	1949	1953	1951	1956	1951	1956
National economy	100	100	100	100	100				
Industry	92.7	108.5	107.8	102.5	107.8	36.7	14.9	0.58	2.96
Agriculture	80.2	70.6	75.3	65.7	81.3	73.2[b]	44.0[b]	0.02[b]	0.50[b]
Construction	101.2	115.6	113.8	104.9	101.2	28.5	13.7	2.77	3.78
Transport	109.4	107.0	106.4	100.4	109.8	52.5	14.7	0.26	1.15
Communications	80.0	89.6	85.9			28.9	26.7	0.11	0.16
Trade	102.5	77.3	83.1	90.5	88.6				
Education and culture	124.7	88.9	87.4						
Health and welfare	120.8	88.6	83.0						
Cultural and social institutions						38.4	46.3	1.30	0.89
Government administration						21.1	31.8	4.38	1.53
Financial institutions	134.5	104.3	99.5			22.1	24.4	0.22	0.10

[a] In Czechoslovakia and Poland the figures refer to gross wages and in Hungary probably to net.
[b] Including forestry.

A = Percentage of employed with earnings up to Zl 800 monthly.
B = Percentage of employed with earnings above Zl 3 000 monthly.

SOURCES   CSSR   – Hron 1968, appendix x/1; *SRC 1967*, p. 112.
Hungary – *SE 1949–55*, p. 58.
Poland   – *Ekonomista*, 1958, no. 3.

and 20.8 per cent respectively. In 1953 the average wages in the same sectors declined to 88.9 per cent and 88.6 per cent of the level in the national economy. What is no less important, they even declined absolutely (in education and culture from Kčs 1022 monthly to Kčs 965 and in health and welfare from 990 to 961) at a time when consumer prices were growing rapidly. The real wages in the sectors mentioned must have fallen dramatically. There was a similar situation in Poland.

Heavy industry and construction were given preferential treatment in regard to wages in order to make these sectors attractive to job-seekers. Wages in industry as a whole would have grown even faster if not for the slow growth of wages in light industry and in food-processing. Simultaneously with the narrowing of intersectoral wage differentials, a widening of intraindustrial wage differentials occurred. Available figures for Poland and Czechoslovakia demonstrate this without a doubt. They show that wages in the branches which make up heavy industry grew much faster than wages in light industry and food-processing. The textile branch in the CSSR was an exception, for unknown reasons (see Table 11.2).

As to occupational differentials the only figures available are for the

TABLE 11.2   *Intraindustrial wage differentials in Poland and CSSR 1948–56 (wages in clothing industry = 100)*

Industry	Poland			CSSR	
	1948	1952	1956	1949	1953
Mining	128.4	174.5	183.2	88.8	120.9
Metallurgy	105.9	149.1	150.5	91.4	111.5
Metal and electro-technical branch	102.9	145.3	134.7	90.5[a]	102.7[a]
Building materials	91.2	117.9	120.8	94.8	110.2
Printing and publishing	153.9	120.8	119.8	86.2	96.6
Chemical branch	109.8	128.3	121.8	93.1	106.8
Food	134.3	117.0	104.0	89.6	90.5
Paper	89.2	107.5	106.9	94.8	104.1
Wood	119.6	113.2	117.8	91.4	98.0
Leather	149.0	116.0	111.9	90.5	89.8
Textile	98.0	94.0	99.0	100.0	119.6

[a] Refers to machinery branch.

SOURCES   Poland   – B. Fick, 1959.
                  Czechoslovakia – Hron, 1968, appendix x/4.

three known socioeconomic categories in industry, and only for Czechoslovakia for the whole period (see Table 11.3). The figures show that, in all three countries, wages of manual workers grew much faster than those of the other two categories. Again in Czechoslovakia the changes were the most dramatic. In 1948 wages of engineering-technical personnel were on the average 65 per cent higher than those of manual workers; in 1955 the difference had shrunk to 26 per cent. In 1948 wages of administrative and clerical personnel were ahead by 25 per cent on the average, whereas in 1955 they were 15 points lower than those of manual workers.[1]

Narrowing of wage differentials after the seizure of political power by the communists was not only a result of ideological and social considerations (as, for example, the desire to improve the material situation of low-paid groups). The governments were confronted with a serious problem: how to distribute the growing investment and armament burden among the employees of the socialist sector. It was clear that agriculture alone could not foot the bill. To distribute the burden evenly, thus affecting badly paid income groups and blue-collar workers too, would have badly hurt the communist parties in political terms. It was only natural that the parties tried to solve the problem at the expense of higher income groups which happened at the same time to be the most vulnerable. Shifting more of the burden on to the shoulders of white-collar workers had two advantages. The communist governments could demonstrate that they were favouring the interests of manual workers, who after all constituted the political base of their rule. Such a distribution of income had a partly appeasing effect on manual workers since their 'rivals' (white-collar workers) fared even worse.

The mentioned approach to income distribution was, of course, reflected in policies which had a direct or indirect impact on wage differentials. (It would, however, be wrong not to see that part of the narrowing was spontaneous, with the reluctant approval or even against the wishes of the authorities.) The compensations for price increases carried out at the currency or quasi-currency reforms were mostly set inversely to the level of earnings. In Hungary in December 1951 low wages were increased by 21 per cent, medium by 18 per cent and high by 15 per cent as a compensation for huge price increases (Pongrácz 1970). In Czechoslovakia the compensation for price increases in 1953 favoured manual workers over white-collar workers. The same happened with the transition to the new wage-tax in January 1953; since the new tax was lower than the previous one, white-collar workers' salaries were accordingly reduced, whereas wages of blue-collar workers were not

TABLE 11.3 *Wage differentials between industrial employees by type of occupation*[1] *1948–55*
(*wages of manual workers = 100*)

	Poland			Czechoslovakia			Hungary		
	1950	*1953*	*1955*	*1948*	*1953*	*1955*	*1949*	*1953*	*1955*
Engineering and technical personnel	176.6	149.5	156.3	165	132	126.4	193.9	177.5	174.8
Administrative and clerical personnel	117.1	96.2	97.7	125	91	85.1	140.6	107.0	104.8

[1] Refers to state industry

SOURCES   Poland – Morecka 1965.
   CSSR   – Hron 1968, appendix x/3; *SRC 1967*, p. 28.
   Hungary – Kisházi 1958, p. 66, quoted according to Pongrácz 1975, p. 85.

touched (Hron 1968, p. 42). In addition, blue-collar workers enjoyed up to 1953 a tax exemption on earnings from overtime work and overfulfilment of work norms.

Wage differentials in the material sphere and those sectors of the non-material sphere which are financed from state revenues were, as mentioned, influenced by the different assignment of the wage-bill and its control. In profit-making enterprises the actual wage-bill was at that time – and still is in administrative systems – dependent on the extent of fulfilment of output targets. This built-in incentive enabled enterprises to a certain degree to evade central control over wages. Enterprises had, particularly in the period under review, a few devices which allowed them to manipulate the fulfilment of plan targets; in this way they could receive additional funds for wage increases.

In the budget-financed organisations there was and is no such built-in flexibility; the actual wage-bill can exceed the planned only if the supervising authorities explicitly agree. Therefore the authorities can exert tight control over wage growth.

What has been said about profit- and non-profit-making enterprises is also true of the regulation of wages of white- and blue-collar workers. Most of the latter were and a large percentage still are remunerated on the basis of piecework, which means that their earnings depended on the extent of fulfilment of work norms, which were not unchangeable. Despite pressure to tighten norms, pieceworkers, mainly the experienced ones, could always find ways to maintain soft norms which could be overfulfilled. This development was certainly not to the liking of the authorities since it contributed to a spontaneous narrowing of wage differentials between blue-collar workers and engineering-technical staff and also upset the wage differentials between pieceworkers and time-workers (Upława and Dębniak 1958). For political reasons the governments could not do much about this.

On the other hand the basic salaries of white-collar workers were set by the authorities and could be changed only by them. True, managers, mainly in profit-making enterprises, could increase salaries of individual workers by reclassifying them into a higher skill groups, but relatively narrow limits were set to this manœuvring.

The process of narrowing wage differentials was supported by fast-growing employment and the great demand for unskilled workers. Various provisions aimed at increasing wages in poorly paid jobs acted in the same direction.

3   WAGE DIFFERENTIAL POLICIES SINCE 1956

When the tremendous pressure for fast industrialisation abated, and greater attention started to be devoted to economic efficiency, calls for changes in differentials became louder and louder. It was argued that the preceding period had brought about many disparities in wage differentials which hurt the economy. Such calls were repeated many times in the three countries during the last three decades. The politicians more or less concurred with the critical evaluation of wage differentials. Yet the wage differentials, discussed in the preceding section, were, with some exceptions, more or less retained in the way they evolved during the first medium-term plans.

First the evolution of intersectoral, intraindustrial differentials and differentials between socioeconomic groups in the last three decades will be discussed. In this connection also an examination will be made of how political crises and their aftermaths as well as economic reforms affected wage differentials. Then an analysis of the reasons for the relative stability of wage differentials will be given.

(a) **Intersectoral Wage Differentials**

I start out with the material sphere, but, before doing so, a warning is in order. Figures indicated in Table 11.4, which are limited to every fifth year, do not reflect precisely the evolution of differentials for the following reason in addition to the reasons already mentioned. In the sectors of the economy which receive funds for wage purposes from the state budget, adjustments in average wages are made at different intervals; therefore the figures for every fifth year do not reflect entirely accurately the state of differentials in individual sectors.

At first glance it is clear that no dramatic changes occurred, with one exception – agriculture. In all three countries agriculture (see note [a] to Table 11.4) substantially improved its position. In Czechoslovakia in 1955, average wages[2] in agriculture made up only 75 per cent of the wages of the whole national economy. In subsequent years wages in agriculture grew much faster than in the national economy, to achieve almost parity (97 per cent) in 1980. In Polish state farms and collective farms, which constitute only a small portion of total agriculture, the rate of average wage growth was even greater; it reached 104 per cent in 1979. In Hungary wages in agriculture had already reached almost parity in 1970, to decline later as a result of a deliberate decision (in 1980, 94 per cent).

TABLE 11.4 *Intersectoral wage differentials 1955–80[a,b]*

	CSSR						Poland						Hungary[d]					
	1956	1960	1965	1970	1975	1980	1955	1960	1965	1970	1975	1980	1955	1960	1965	1970	1975	1980
1. National economy	100	100	100	100	100	100	100	100	100	100	100	100	100	100	100	100	100	100
2. Industry	108	106	106	102	101	103	109	110	109	107	105	107	107	106	103	99	100	100
3. Construction	114	112	116	113	111	109	122	116	118	120	119	110	105	107	107	110	110	106
4. Agriculture	75	82	89	93	96	97	76	80	81	84	99	104	81	90	90	100	93	94
5. Forestry	90	94	98	98	101	102	66	70	73	73	84	83	:					
6. Transport	106	109	111	117	116	119							97	98	102	103	104	104
7. Communication	86	88	88	92	88	89	100	96	100	102	102	106	88	93	92	94	89	88
8. Trade	83	81	83	85	:	...	84	84	86	87	84	82						
8a. External trade					112	114				122	115	102						
8b. Internal trade					83	82				86	83	89[b]						
9. Communal services	83	77	73	78	77	77	89	94	92	96	97	107						
10. Housing services	53	57	62	65	69	71					84[b]	89[b]						
11. Science and techno.	121	114	119	116	113	113				122	111	107						
12. Education	87[c]	91[c]	88[c]	95[c]	96	95				86	81	84						
13. Culture and arts					89	70				95	85	85			97			
14. Health care	83	85	80	92	99	95	70[c]	77[c]	77[c]	78[c]	82	82						
15. Social welfare					82	79												
16. Administration and justice	101	102	104	106	107	106	95	92	98	100	102	98						
17. Banking	99	97	83	112	104	102	91	92	91	98	93	93						
18. Insurance						105												
19. Non-material sphere	93	93	91	96	97	95							97	97	99	98	100	101

a In CSSR the figures refer to the socialist sector (without collective farms and apprentices), in Poland to the socialist sector and in Hungary to the state sector.
b Czechoslovak figures refer to monthly gross wages, Polish with exception of 1955, 1960 and 1965 to net wages and Hungarian net inclusive premiums for social security and military charge.
c Sports are included in Poland in health care and in CSSR in culture.
d Starting with 1968 the Hungarian statistics distinguish wages and earnings. The latter include bonuses. In substance, however, earnings up to 1968 corresponded to previous average wages. The figures for 1970, 1975 and 1980 refer to earnings. Starting with 1970 a new classification came into being and therefore the figures for 1970, 1975 and 1980 are not entirely comparable with the previous.

SOURCES   CSSR   – SRC 1976, p. 112, 1976, p. 122, and 1981, p. 203.
            Poland   – Rocznik Statystyczny Pracy 1945–68, pp. 414–15; RS 1980, p. 111; and MRS 1981, p. 70.
            Hungary – Incomes in . . . 1967, ch. 8, p. 67; A lakosság jövedelme és fogyasztása 1960–1980 (Budapest, 1982) p. 22.

In all three countries the relative position of industry with regard to average wages had partially eroded. The same is true of construction, which had been ranked first among the material sphere sectors.

In Hungary average wages in the non-material sphere grew in the long run slightly faster than in the national economy. In Czechoslovakia there was a similar development, with the difference that in 1975–80 a reversal occurred, when the government used all its reserves in the global wage-fund for the priority sectors in the material sphere (Ujházy 1982).

(b) Intraindustrial Wage Differentials

The figures indicated in Table 11.5 are not entirely comparable since the classification of branches has slightly changed during the last twenty-five years. Nevertheless they give a good insight into the evolution of intraindustrial differentials. They show that with some exceptions wage differentials remained stable; changes which occurred before 1955 have not been reversed. The key branches of heavy industry, such as coal-mining and ferrous metallurgy, have managed to retain their relative wage position. In Poland, and to a lesser degree in Hungary, relative wages in coal-mining even increased. (It is, however, not clear how the decline in relative wages in the production of fuel in Poland fits into this picture. Is this due to a change in classification or to an error?) Textiles and clothing slightly improved their relative position in Poland and Czechoslovakia, and the food industry in Hungary.

Intraindustrial wage differentials are the only one of the three aggregates followed here for which figures comparable with those of Western countries exist. This is thanks to the *Yearbook of Industrial Statistics*. Figures for 1978 show several important differences between intraindustrial wage differentials in the East and the West.[3] On the whole intraindustrial wage differentials seem to be wider in the West (this can be positively stated about Great Britain and Austria) than in the East. Coal-mining is first in ranking order with regard to average wages in the three East European countries, whereas in the West (mainly the UK and Austria) production of oil and gas is first. Average wages in light industry and in the food industry are much lower in both blocs than in other branches of manufacturing. In the West this is less consistently applied than in the East (e.g. in the paper and paper-products industry average wages in Canada, the USA and Austria were above wages in manufacturing).

TABLE 11.5 Intraindustrial wage differentials 1955–80[a,b]

	Poland						CSSR						Hungary[d]					
	1955	1960	1965	1970	1975	1980	1955c	1960	1965	1970	1975	1980	1955	1960	1965	1970	1975	1980
1. Industrial total	100	100	100	100	100	100	100	100	100	100	100	100	100	100	100	100	100	100
2. Production of fuel and energy				145	160	153												
2.1. Coal-mining[f]	145	150	147	157	179	170	139	138	136	136	134	137	132	141	140	142	141	148
2.2. Production of fuels	140	146	143	104	103	104	115	109	110	110	109	112						
2.3. Production of energy[h]	101	113	118	114	107	103												
3. Metallurgy				124	129	131	126	120	120	117	120	119	99	100	102	103	98	103
3.1. Ferrous metallurgy	125	123	125	123	126	128	104	103	102	101	101	101	113	106	106	105	112	112
4. Engineering indus.				100	98	96												
4.1. Metal products industry	101	98	97	94	89	90					92e	91e			100	98	98	95
4.2. Production of machinery	108	106	106	104	103	100					105	105			97			
5. Chemicals and rubber indus.							101	99	100	100	100	101	105	100	104	101	101	97
5.1. Chemical indus.	96	96	97	96	94	93	106	103	103	105	105	102	93	93	97	97	102	104
6. Building materials	95	91	93	94	96	93		89	89	92	92	90	93	95	94	98	94	94
7. Wood-working indus.	83	83	84	84	88	84							89	91	90	92	89	87
8. Textiles	76	84	82	84	82	87	75	78	80	81	81	82	80	82	83	88	87	88
9. Clothing	72	70	73	78	74	80	70	71	74	76	75	77	83	84	82	79	78	78
10. Food industry	84	83	84	85	85	86	90	90	88	95	95	91	82	87	88	92	94	98

a Figures refer to socialist industry in Poland, industry in Czechoslovakia and state industry in Hungary.

b Polish figures with exception of 1955, 1960 and 1965 refer to monthly net wages. Czechoslovak to gross wages and Hungarian to net wages (probably including premiums for social security).

c Refers only to manual workers.

d Figures for 1970, 1975 and 1980 refer to earnings. See note d of Table 11.4.

e Includes also electrotechnical industry.

f In Hungary it refers to mining.

g In Czechoslovakia it refers also to coal and petroleum products in 1955, 1960, 1965 and 1970.

h Refers to electric energy.

SOURCES Poland – Rocznik Statystyczny Pracy 1945–68, pp. 419–21; RS 1980, pp. 158–60; MRS 1981, p. 115.
CSSR – Incomes in . . . 1967, ch. 8, p. 68; SRC 1976, p. 247, and 1981, p. 358.
Hungary – Incomes in . . . 1967, ch. 8, p. 69; SE (English version) 1965, p. 91, and 1975, p. 148; SE 1970, p. 158, and 1980, p. 189.

TABLE 11.6 *Wage differentials between industrial employees by type of occupation 1955–80[a, b]*
(wage of manual workers = 100)

	Poland[c]		CSSR[d]		Hungary[e]	
	ETP	ACP	ETP	ACP	ETP	ACP
1955	156	99	126	85	172	104
1960	159	104	133	87	156	95
1965	164	107	135	86	155	96
1966	161	105	140	89		
1967	160	104	142	90		
1968	158	102	141	89	152	97
1969	154	101	140	88	152 (163)	96 (102)
1970	150	103	135	86	151 (161)	96 (100)
1971	148	102	133	86	150 (160)	97 (101)
1972	146	101	131	85	148 (160)	97 (102)
1973	144	100	119		142 (154)	92 (97)
1974	141	97	120		144 (155)	93 (98)
					Technicians	*Other Non-manual workers*
1975	138 (130)	94 (89)	117		140 (150)	117 (125)
1976	131	89	118		139 (147)	117 (124)

1977	132	88	116	136(143)	117(122)
1978	132	87	116	135(141)	115(120)
1979	129	85	115	136(140)	115(120)
1980	129	86		137(141)	117(121)

ETP = engineering technical personnel; *ACP* = administrative and clerical personnel.

a Polish figures refer to socialist industry and Hungarian up to 1974 to state industry and from 1975 to socialist industry.

b Polish figures refer up to 1969 (inclusive) to monthly gross wages and the rest to net wages. The Czechoslovak refer to gross wages and the Hungarian probably to net wages including social insurances premiums.

c Figures starting with 1976 are not comparable with the previous due to a new classification. For 1975 figures in brackets are according to the new classification.

d Starting with 1973 Czechoslovakia replaced the old grouping by one called technical-managerial personnel which seems to include the vast majority of the previous ETP and ACP. The figures in the middle refer to the new category.

e Starting with 1975 Hungary publishes figures only for manual, non-manual workers and technicians; the last corresponds roughly to the former ETP. In 1969 Hungarian statistics started to distinguish average and earnings (see note d of Table 11.4). Figures in brackets refer to earnings.

SOURCES Poland – *Rocznik Statystyczny Pracy 1945–1968*, p. 419; *Rocznik Statystyczny Przemyshu 1980*,
p. 243; *RS 1972*, p. 159, *1980*, p. 158.
CSSR – *SRC 1967*, p. 28; *1973*, p. 243, *1980*, p. 31.
Hungary – *SE 1956*, p. 78, *1973*, p. 175, *1980*, p. 189.

(c) **Wage Differentials between Industrial Employees by Type of Occupation**

As in the first phase I here confine myself to differentials between the three socioeconomic groups. These have undergone much greater changes than the differentials previously discussed. The reason for the difference is not entirely clear. Perhaps changes leading to a narrowing in the former differentials which are the most aggregated cannot assert themselves due to offsetting trends.

Figures for the three countries clearly show that in the long run the tendency to a narrowing of differentials, which was so profound in the first phase, is continuing (see Table 11.6). After 1955 Czechoslovakia and Poland experienced a slight reversal of this trend, though in Czechoslovakia only for engineering-technical staff. At the same time in Hungary an opposite development took effect, perhaps because Hungary in 1955 had less compressed differentials (average wages for engineering-technical staff exceeded by 75 per cent the average wages of manual workers against 56 per cent in Poland and 26 per cent in Czechoslovakia). In the 70s Poland went through a substantial narrowing, whereas in the CSSR there was only a slight one. In Hungary the narrowing trend started in 1972.

(d) **The Effect of Political Crises and Economic Reforms on Differentials**

We have seen in the preceding chapters that political crises and economic reforms acted as a boost to wage increases. The question is – how did the two events affect wage differentials?

The political crisis question refers primarily to Poland and to a lesser extent to Hungary. There was a lot of pressure in Poland for widening wage differentials, mainly during the political crisis of 1956 and its aftermath, all the more because the crisis brought into being some short-lived reforms in the system of management. Polish economists blamed the wage disparities which had arisen between pieceworkers and timeworkers and between manual workers and engineering-technical staff on the excessive and inadequate use of piecework and on deficiencies in norm-setting (Upława and Dębniak 1958).

Some other economists called for improving the lot of low-income groups which, despite a great narrowing of wages, experienced hardship. It should not be forgotten that average wages compared to *per capita* national income were low in all three countries. The level of wages was at least as much of a problem as wage differentials, but this belonged somehow to the taboo topics in all three countries. Politicians did not mind the occasional criticism of the state of wage differentials which they also exercised from time to time, but were reluctant to allow criticism of the level of wages since this meant indirect disapproval of the strategy of economic development. The Polish government tried to move in two directions: on the one hand, to increase low wages (in this connection a minimum wage was introduced (Jaworski 1956) and, on the other hand, to bring about some corrections in wage differentials. For the purpose of the latter goal the Polish plan for 1956–60 envisaged a differentiated annual average increase in wages of 5.4 per cent in industry, 2.3 per cent in construction, 7.2 per cent in forestry, 5.2 per cent in trade and 6.0 per cent in administration. The actual increases were, however, little differentiated. In industry wages increased annually by 9.2 per cent, in construction 8.1 per cent, in forestry 9.6 per cent, in trade 8.7 per cent and in administration 10.8 per cent (Czajka 1981). There was, however, a slight widening of differentials between engineering-technical staff and manual workers. In brief, judging from aggregate figures, it is safe to say that the political crisis did not bring about important changes in wage differentials. The introduction of minimum wages contributed to this situation.

I have not come across adequate figures for Hungary. L. Pongrácz (1970) maintains that 1957 wage increases eliminated some wage disparities. On the other hand, it seems that the process of narrowing wage differentials between engineering-technical staff and manual workers continued. Here, as in Poland, the introduction of the minimum wage had a narrowing effect.

More wage figures are available for the period after the political crisis in 1970 in Poland. What they show without doubt is that the process of compressing wages continued. The revised FYP for 1971–5, which bore the imprints of the forthcoming reform, envisaged a partial widening of wage differentials, but this did not materialise. The best example is what happened with wages in education. At the end of the FYP education was to advance from tenth place in the ranking of average wages to fourth (behind science, construction and industry), but in 1976 it found itself in twelfth place (Czajka 1981).

The computations of W. Krencik (1980), which are confined to wage differentials between non-manual and manual workers, show the same trend. They reveal that in 1970 wages of fully employed non-manual workers in the first decile (10 per cent of workers with the lowest income) were 21 per cent higher than those of manual workers in the first decile, and in the ninth decile the difference was 11 per cent. In 1976 the difference was 16 per cent and 5 per cent respectively, and in 1978 12 per cent and 2 per cent.

The political crisis in the 80s has perhaps had an even greater narrowing impact on wage differentials than previous political crises. It has already been mentioned that the wage adjustment in 1980 had a compressing impact. The huge price increase in 1982 acted in the same direction. Compensation for price increases was differentiated: workers with lower incomes received higher compensation and workers above a certain income no compensation at all (*TL 1982*, 28 June).

As to the effects of economic reforms on differentials I will concentrate on two reforms: the Czechoslovak and the Hungarian. In both countries the reformers included widening of wage differentials among the most important tasks of the reforms, quasi an important precondition for making the reform workable.[4] In the period 1965–6 the Czechoslovak officials promised to start widening wage differentials by adjusting wages in the non-material sphere. Soon this approach was abandoned; it was argued that for the sake of creating an adequate political and social atmosphere, widening of wage differentials must start within individual categories and groups of employees and occupations in the material sphere. It was reasoned that manual workers would have a better understanding of the need for greater differentiation if they saw the impact of this action on their own occupation or category. The political changes in 1968 did not bring about a substantial change in the approach to wage differentials. Only after the occupation of Czechoslovakia did the collective agreement between the government and trade unions envisaged in 1969 a faster growth of wages in the non-productive sphere than in the productive (*PaM 1968*, no. 11). Thanks mainly to wage increases in 1969, health and welfare, and education were able to improve their relative position.

Wage differentials between socioeconomic groups in the material sphere in 1966–9 developed in favour of non-manual workers. This was mainly due to an increase in the amount of bonuses which accrued to managers and to engineers in a greater proportion than to manual workers.

In the first phase of NEM in Hungary (1968–72) a slight widening in wage differentials between industrial manual and non-manual workers occurred. As in Czechoslovakia this was the result of the increased role of bonuses in earnings. As follows from Table 11.6, the basic salaries of engineering-technical staff in 1970 were 51 per cent higher than the average wages of manual workers, whereas earnings including bonuses were 61 per cent. Top managers were the greatest beneficiaries of this trend; in the period 1965–9 their earnings increased by 57 per cent (approximately three times faster than those of other employees) (Szávai 1975). Due to the popular dissatisfaction the government undertook several actions which reversed this trend. As already mentioned, the rules for the distribution of bonuses were changed, and wages of manual workers were increased preferentially.

From the foregoing it is clear that political crises have not turned out to be conducive to widening wage differentials. This experience is in line with what one could expect if the role of different social groups in the political structure is considered. It would be almost suicidal for politicians to engage in wage policies which might antagonise the social groups on which their survival depends. And this is also why decompressing wage differentials during economic reforms can be – as experience shows – only a temporary phenomenon. Once widening of wage differentials start to affect manual workers, tremendous pressure is exercised on politicians to reverse the course with only one possible effect.

4 Concluding Remarks

It has been mentioned that politicians have vowed many times in different forms to bring about greater wage differentiation. In practice, as has been shown, the opposite has happened. The question is warranted: have the politicians' pledges been only lip service, aimed at pacifying dissatisfied people, or have they not been able, despite good intentions, to honour their promises? It seems that the truth is somewhere in the middle. The politicians have been caught in a great dilemma that in practice hampers them in pursuing a consistent policy. They know that non-monetary incentives alone cannot create the conditions needed for a more efficient economy. They also know that coping with the current stagnation in economic growth is conditional on, among other things, greater incentives and widening of wage differentials. On the other hand they are under popular pressure not to allow widening of wage differentials. On the whole people have recently become more resentful of what they regard as wide wage differentials as they show up in consumption in a more conspicuous way than in the past. In the past high-income receivers could afford better food, clothing and furniture than other people, whereas nowadays, due to a generally higher standard of living, they can afford cars, country houses, trips abroad, etc. (Szikra 1975).

It has already been indicated that the working of the wage system in the first phase favoured narrowing of wage differentials. In the period which was elapsed since 1955 not much has changed in this direction. The control of wages of pieceworkers – though their number has relatively declined – is as difficult as before, or maybe even more so due to enterprises' increased say in remuneration. On the other hand average wages in non-profit organisations are still under the strict control of the centre. Since 1953 all three countries have attached increased importance to market equilibrium for consumer goods and have endeavoured to avert inflation; therefore, when equilibrium is threatened and inflation looms on the horizon, planned wage increases for groups in non-profit organisations have often been postponed. For similar reasons the salaries of university teachers and employees, in Czechoslovakia for example, were not adjusted for eleven years (from 1954–65), though at the same time money wages grew on the average by 25 per cent, and real wages even more. (For more see also Adam 1972.)

In the second half of the 70s, and more markedly in the early 80s when economic growth started to slow down, restrictive wage policy had to be applied. Again workers in non-profit organisations, whose wages can best be controlled, first felt the pinch.

Labour shortages, which are especially pronounced with regard to auxiliary workers in physically arduous work, have also contributed to a narrowing of wage differentials. When jobs are abundant workers shun jobs with difficult working conditions unless they are well paid. On the other hand there is an oversupply of certain groups of administrative workers and certain professionals (Révész 1981, p. 243).

12 Labour Productivity, Wages and Employment

In Chs 7–10 some important topics, such as the role of quality improvement in the labour force (education), the relationship of growth of wages to productivity growth, and structural changes in employment, have been deliberately left out. I felt that the reader would benefit more if these problems were discussed in a separate chapter. I will start out with a brief discussion of the growth of labour productivity and its role in economic growth, and then discuss the mentioned problems.

1 LABOUR PRODUCTIVITY

In socialist countries productivity on the macroeconomic level is measured by what is called the 'social productivity of labour', which is national income per person employed in the material sphere (including agriculture). This is not the most suitable measure for the purpose of this study, since it does not cover the steadily growing non-material sphere. In addition, figures on wages in the material sphere as a whole are not available for all three countries. Therefore I resort to a compromise. When discussing labour productivity as a factor of economic growth I limit myself solely to the material sphere, whereas, when I deal with average wages and productivity, the latter is defined as national income per person employed in the national economy.

Social labour productivity depends not only on the productivity of individual sectors but also on structural changes in the economy. The move of labour from lower productivity sectors to higher ones, a phenomenon characteristic of economic development, adds to productivity gains. I do not intend to elaborate on this problem other than to mention that the Hungarian economist, K. Szikra (1967), who studied the impact of structural changes on labour productivity in the period 1951–65, maintains that they grew in importance.

At first glance the record in the growth of social labour productivity seems to be good. With the exception of 1976–80 when the growth rate substantially declined in all three countries and 1961–5 in Czechoslovakia, it was on a relatively high level, but, of course, fluctuating through the period under review. (See Table 12.1). The effort to make growth of national income depend primarily on labour productivity, an important task in light of the decreasing labour supply, was on the whole successful. Already in the period 1951–65 the countries had managed to increase to 80 per cent the percentage share of labour productivity in the generation of national income. Since 1965 the share has increased even more, mainly in 1976–80 when the growth rate of national income plummeted. The increased role of labour productivity means that labour–output ratio (the amount of labour needed for the production of a unit of output) declined. Social labour productivity looks different if the costs incurred in its achievement are accounted for, mainly if capital expenditure is considered. Labour productivity namely depends to a large degree on capital intensity (on the amount of fixed assets available per person employed in the material sphere) and capital productivity (output per unit of fixed capital in the material sphere).

A glance at Table 12.1 shows clearly that the growth rate of the stock of fixed assets accelerated in the period under review. This is most obvious in Poland, where the rate grew from one quinquennium to another; in 1951–5 it was 3.4 per cent and in 1976–80, 8 per cent. Efforts to increase shift work in order to reduce the need for fixed assets and/or to make their use more efficient were not successful. In 1960 the shift coefficient was 1.57 in Poland, 1.38 in the CSSR and 1.47 in Hungary (in 1965). After some fluctuations the shift coefficient declined to 1.37 in Poland and 1.32 in the CSSR in 1981, and to 1.38 in Hungary in 1980. Understandably workers prefer not to work in shifts, and labour shortages enable an increasing number to avoid such work. With the increase in the stock of fixed capital, capital intensity grew, all the more because the growth rate of employment in the material sphere slowed down on the whole.

Yet the evolution of capital productivity reveals a bleak picture, mainly in 1976–80 when fixed assets grew at a much higher rate than national income, in Poland even more than six times. In the article mentioned K. Szikra (1967) complains that, while in CMEA countries in 1951–65 social labour productivity compared to employment accounted for 80 per cent of the national income growth, the contribution of capital productivity compared to the stock of capital did not reach 50 per cent in any country. Since then the situation has become much worse; capital

TABLE 12.1 Selected productivity indicators 1951–80 (growth rates in per cent)

	Poland						Czechoslovakia						Hungary					
	1951 –5	1956 –60	1961 –5	1966 –70	1971 –5	1976 –80	1951 –5	1956 –60	1961 –5	1966 –70	1971 –5	1976 –80	1951 –5	1956 –60	1961 –5	1966 –70	1971 –5	1976 –80
National income produced	8.6	6.5	6.2	6.0	9.8	1.2	8.1	7.0	2.0	6.9	5.7	3.6	5.7	6.0	4.1	6.8	6.2	3.2
Employment[a]			1.5	1.8	1.5	-0.4	1.0	-0.1	0.4	1.2	0.3	0.4	1.8	0.9	-0.4	1.5	-0.1	-0.7
Fixed capital stock[b]	3.4	4.0	4.4	6.1	8.1	8.0	3.9	4.7	4.9	4.4	5.8	6.2	5.1	4.1	4.9	5.5	6.7	6.7
Social labour productivity			4.6	4.0	8.1	1.6	7.0	7.2	1.6	5.6	5.4	3.2	3.8	5.1	4.5	5.2	6.3	3.9
Capital intensity			2.8	4.1	6.5	8.4	2.8	4.8	4.5	3.2	5.4	5.8	3.2	3.1	5.3	4.0	6.7	7.4
Capital productivity	5.0	2.4	1.7	-0.1	1.5	-6.3	4.0	2.2	-2.8	2.3	0.0	-2.4	0.6	1.9	-0.8	1.2	-0.4	-1.0
Factor productivity	6.1	4.5	3.8	2.9	6.6	-0.6	5.8	5.4	-0.3	4.4	3.6	1.2	3.1	4.6	2.5	4.1	4.0	2.2

a Refers solely to the material sphere.
b Refers to gross capital stock in the material sphere.
c Capital elasticity 0.3 and labour ealsticity 0.7 are assumed.

SOURCES   National income – Rocznik Statystyczny Przemysłu 1981, pp. xl–xli; SRC 1982, pp. 22–3; SE 1980, pp. 5.
Employment – Tables 7.2, 8.2, 9.2 and 10.2.
Capital stock – MRS 1983, p. 114; RS 1980, pp. xxxiv–xxxv; SRC 1977, p. 212; SRC 1982, pp. 22, 26–7, 239; SE 1972, p. 87; SE 1980, p. 103.

productivity growth was negative through most of the three quinquennia, but mainly in 1976–80. This also means that the capital output ratio, which was anyhow high in 1971–5, increased in 1976–80 and can be expected to increase even more in 1981–5. Due to the evolution of capital productivity, factor productivity was declining in all three countries.

2 ROLE OF EDUCATION

When discussing the labour force in the preceding chapters I have considered it in terms of quantity and mostly disregarded its quality. It is known that the quality of the labour force permanently improves; the current labour force is much more qualified than that, say, of the 50s. Young newcomers to the labour force have on the whole better qualifications than people who are about to retire. Qualifications as such can hardly be quantified, and therefore research is confined to education which is the most important element of qualification.

All three countries have achieved remarkable progress in the expansion of education. The number of workers with university education has increased dramatically. In Hungary in 1949–80 the percentage of economically active people with university education increased 4.3 times; in the CSSR in 1950–78 the corresponding figure is 7.25 and in Poland, 1958–81, 2.2 (see Table 12.2). The great difference between Hungary and the CSSR in the growth of the number of university graduates is due to the fact that universities in the Czech lands were closed throughout the war (this was also true to Poland), so that post-war enrolment in universities was very high. And this also is one of the main reasons why the number of university graduates increased 3.5 times during 1950–60.

What is surprising is that Czechoslovakia has a lower percentage of university graduates than Hungary; as Table 12.2 shows, in 1978 it was 5.8 per cent of the total number of economically active against 8.2 per cent in Hungary (in 1980). (The higher figures for Poland (8.1 per cent in 1981) result apparently from the fact that they refer only to the socialist sector.) One explanation seems to be that in Hungary graduates of schools which are somewhere between high school and university (measured by Czechoslovak standards) are included as university graduates.

Great changes have also occurred in the structure of the blue-collar labour force. The number of skilled workers has increased dramatically, absolutely and relatively. For example, in the CSSR in 1950, 11.3 per

TABLE 12.2 The evolution of the level of education of economically active persons 1950–81 (in per cent)

	Poland[a]			Czechoslovakia				Hungary[a]			
	1958	1970	1981	1950	1960	1970	1978	1940	1960	1970	1980
Economically active	100	100	100	100	100	100	100	100	100	100	100
University graduates	3.8	5.3	8.3	0.8	2.6	3.9	5.8	1.9	3.2	5.1	8.2
Technical high schools graduates	6.9	13.6	21.5	4.6	10.7	15.3	18.3	4.3	7.2	13.9	20.9
High schools graduates	4.3	5.6	6.4								
Vocational schools graduates	8.2	17.0	24.8	11.3	20.1	25.5	28.3			7.8	16.9
Rest	76.8	58.5	39.0	83.5	66.6	55.3	47.6			73.2	54.0

[a] Refers to the socialist sector.

Sources Poland – RS 1962, p. 51; RS 1982, p. 59.
        CSSR   – Průcha and Kalinová 1981, p. 62.
        Hungary – SE 1980, p. 135; Olajos 1978, p. 60.

cent of the total labour force were skilled workers and in 1978, 28.3 per cent.

The figures mentioned do not express fully the extent of progress achieved in education. In all three countries compulsory education was extended. A great number of people are improving their qualifications in various schools and courses which do not lead to degrees.

E. Denison (1967, p. 83) calculates the contribution of education to labour input primarily with the aid of wage differentials. He assumes that 'three-fifths of the reported income differential between each of the other groups and the group with 8 years of education represented differences in earnings due to differences in education as distinguished from other associated characteristics'. In socialist countries studies have also been undertaken to measure the contribution of education to labour input. In the CSSR the authors who deal with this problem reject the use of wage differentials as a gauge; they apparently believe that wage differentials in the socialist countries do not correctly reflect differences in education. Instead they use reproduction costs of different degrees of education. Assuming that the completion of elementary education involves reproduction costs valued as one, then all education degrees are related to it by an added coefficient reflecting increased reproduction costs. A Czech author indicates the following coefficients for education in the CSSR: vocational school 1.37, high school 1.49, university 2.68 and a scientific degree (equivalent to a Ph.D.) 3.0 (Kalinová 1977). The difference between the values attached to education by Denison and Kalinová is not huge.

In applying the coefficients to the evolution of the structure of education during 1958–78 in the CSSR, we obtain an increase in the size of the labour force (or, as it is termed in East European literature, the labour fund) of 19.3 per cent. This figure, of course, does not take into consideration the extension of compulsory education, the increase in the number of people who have completed elementary schooling and the increase in the number of semi-skilled workers.

In computing the labour fund it is also necessary to take into account that all three countries have reduced the workweek. The best way to calculate this is to compare the number of days worked by an average worker at the beginning and the end of the period under review. I have data for the Czechoslovakian industry which is fairly representative of the whole economy; in 1955 the average worker worked 269.8 days and in 1981 43.2 less, 226.4 days. Overtime work in industry has not changed very much; at present it is lower than in the 50s (in 1979–81 it ranged between 5.6 and 5.9 per cent and in 1953–5 6.6–6.7 per cent of the total hours worked) and higher than in the 60s (1965–7, 4.6–4.8 per cent).

The two figures indicated (19.3 per cent and 19.2 per cent), combined with what has been said about education expansion, allows me to conclude that progress in education probably adds more to labour input than the shortening of the workweek deducts from it, all the more because it can be assumed that each new class of graduates is better equipped with knowledge than the previous.

Progress in education has had, no doubt, a favourable impact on labour productivity growth, but not enough to avert a continuing decline in factor productivity.

3   LABOUR PRODUCTIVITY AND WAGES

It has already been mentioned that socialist countries have followed a policy of low wages and why they have done so. This policy has been reflected in the rule adopted at the beginning of central planning that average wage growth should lag far behind the growth of the social productivity of labour. The word 'social' should be stressed since what the planners had primarily in mind was a macroeconomic relationship. Growth of average wages including incomes in collective farms (assuming constant prices) was related to the growth of national income per employee in the material sphere (including agriculture). Some economists believe that this rule was a rather empirical instrument for ensuring equilibrium between growth of wages and growth of output of consumer goods and services (Levcik 1969, p. 32). Probably this was not the only rationale; another, perhaps even more important, was to make sure that enough funds for maximum economic growth were available, even if the returns on investment projects tended to decline. Regardless of the real reason for adopting this rule, official theory tried to justify it by arguing that the faster growth of productivity than of wages is a prerequisite for economic growth (Derco and Kotlaba 1976; Krencik 1976).

This rule relating wage growth to productivity growth reveals that the planners had a tendency to perceive this relationship as one-sided. They only stressed the dependence of wage growth on productivity growth, without really taking into consideration that growth of productivity to a certain extent depends on growth of wages. They were apparently reluctant to rely on feedback from wage increases; they were afraid that if the incentive did not work as expected the investment drive might be endangered.

The question is: to what extent has practice followed the rule? First it must be recalled that the rule mentioned is a macroeconomic one and is not intended to be applied to individual sectors of the economy and industrial branches in the sense that wages should be raised in direct relation to productivity growth. And, indeed, many examples of deviations could be listed, the most notorious being the much faster growth of wages in heavy industry than in light industry in the first phase of the planning era, though productivity did not grow in the same relationship. In fixing the growth rates of wages for individual sectors and industrial branches the planners' ideas about what were desirable differentials played an important role. Had wages been increased in direct relationship to productivity they would have grown quickly in some sectors, branches and enterprises, and slowly in others. However productivity growth is to great degree beyond the control of enterprises. The planners took this into consideration in order to avoid adverse political repercussions (cf. Levcik 1969).

To answer the question two sets of productivity figures and data on real wages are given (see Table 12.3). National income per employee is not the most suitable gauge for measuring productivity; the numerator is confined to the material sphere and disregards most of the activities in the service sector which is growing the fastest. The denominator includes, however, all employees and it is thus constructed as the denominator of average real wages, and this is why I prefer it over social labour productivity. The figures on industrial productivity have the advantage that the numerator and the denominator are in accord, yet they are based on gross output (with the exception of Poland) and the number of employees (instead of manhours). Here both sets of figures on growth of productivity are compared only with growth of wages,[1] since the examination is focused on the benefits workers obtain from gains in productivity.

The rule that wages should lag behind productivity was implemented in a pronounced way in the initial period of central planning in all three countries. Table 7.3 reveals that real wages in 1950–3 declined substantially (figures for 1951–5 in Table 12.3 also include the 'consumption period' of 1954–5) and this happened at a time when, it is known, productivity grew relatively fast.

It has already been mentioned that the evolution of real wages, after the initial industrial drive abated, was, *inter alia*, influenced by political crises and their aftermath, economic development and economic reforms; the question is to what extent such factors brought about a change in the relationship between real wages and productivity in deviation

TABLE 12.3 National income per employee (A),[a] average real wages (B) and labour productivity in industry (C)[b]
1951–80
(annual growth rates in per cent)

	Poland					Czechoslovakia					Hungary				
	A	B	C	B/A	B/C	A	B	C	B/A	B/C	A	B	C	B/A	B/C
1951–5	1.5	2.1	..	1.40	..	5.0	1.9	10.1	0.38	0.19	0.9	0.9	3.9	1.00	0.23
1956–60	5.3	5.2	7.0	0.98	0.74	4.4	4.5	8.1	1.02	0.56	3.7	8.0	4.1	2.16	1.95
1961–5	2.6	1.5	5.8	0.58	0.26	−0.2	1.2	3.4	−6.00	0.35	1.6	1.7	5.0	1.06	0.34
1966–70	2.0	2.1	4.4	1.05	0.48	4.9	3.6	5.4	0.73	0.67	4.9	3.4	3.7	0.69	0.92
1971–5	6.2	7.2	8.0	1.16	0.90	4.4	3.5	6.0	0.79	0.58	5.0	3.3	6.2	0.66	0.53
1976–80	0.4	1.9	2.0	4.75	0.95	2.5	0.7	3.9	0.28	0.18	3.0	0.7	4.5	0.23	0.16

[a] Refers to national income produced at constant prices and to employment in the socialist sector in Poland and Czechoslovakia (in the latter without collective farms) and in the state sector in Hungary.
[b] Refers in Poland to net industrial output per employee (in 1956–60 per manual worker) and in Hungary and the CSSR to gross industrial output per employee (in the latter in 1951–60 per manual worker).

SOURCES For A and B – Tables 7.2, 8.2, 9.2, 10.2, 7.3, 8.3, 9.3, 10.3 and 12.1.
For C –Poland: *Rocznik Statystyczny Pracy 1945–68*, p. 342; *Rocznik Statystyczny Przemysłu 1981*, p. 211.
CSSR: *SRC 1975*, p. 259; *SRC 1982*, p. 370.
Hungary: *SE 1980*, p. 7.

from the rule. The best example for the effect of political crises is Hungary in 1956–60 (Poland quickly managed to largely undo the fast increases in real wages 1956–7) and, of course, Poland in the 70s. Real wages grew faster than productivity in both concepts in Hungary in 1956–60, and almost as fast as national income per employee in Poland, as Table 12.3 shows. Economic reforms did not have such a pronounced effect, since at the same time they contributed to an increase in productivity (see the CSSR in 1966–70, Hungary 1966–70). In Poland the change in the strategy of economic growth combined with economic reform in the first half of the 70s brought about a substantial increase in productivity, which moderated the effect of the political crisis on the growth relationship between real wages and productivity. The downturn in economic growth in 1976–80 brought about a substantial decline in real-wage growth as a percentage of productivity growth in the CSSR as well as in Hungary. In Poland the effect of the political crisis turned out to be stronger than the effect of the economic downturn, primarily due to 1980 wage increases.

Of the three countries Czechoslovakia followed the most consistently the principle of letting wages lag behind productivity, and this becomes clearer when industrial productivity is considered. National income per employee as a productivity indicator usually suffers from distortions, and more so when employment in the service sector grows fast as it did in 1961–5, and this is also why the share of real-wage growth in the two productivity formulae differed so much at that period. In Czechoslovakia in the period 1951–80 average real wages of industrial workers grew on the average at the ratio of 42 per cent of industrial productivity, in Hungary 69 per cent and in Poland 67 per cent (in 1956–80). These are, of course, very rough figures without any claim to accuracy.

4   CHANGES IN THE STRUCTURE OF THE LABOUR FORCE

In the more than three decades which are covered in this book great changes have occurred in the structure of the labour force considered from the viewpoint of the known theory of three sectors. In all three countries the number of economically active in the primary sector (agriculture and forestry) has dramatically declined. In 1980 in Poland only 27.1 per cent of the economically active were in agriculture and forestry against 54.5 per cent in 1950; in Czechoslovakia the figures are 14.2 per cent against 37.2 per cent and in Hungary 20.6 per cent (in 1981) and 49.6 per cent (in 1951).[2] At the same time employment in the secondary sector (industry plus construction) increased dramatically, particularly in Hungary: from 23.8 per cent in 1951 to 40.8 per cent in 1981. In Poland the figures are 25.7 per cent in 1950 and 39.9 per cent in 1980, and in Czechoslovakia 35.8 per cent and 46.5 per cent. Employment in the tertiary sector (services) grew even faster (with the exception of Hungary) for the whole period, mainly due to its extraordinarily fast growth in the last fifteen years when the secondary sector grew slowly; yet employment in services is still below the level of the secondary sector. See Figure 12.1.

On the whole changes in the employment structure went in the same direction as in advanced capitalist countries; yet there are differences in levels. In all three countries the primary sector has a much greater share and the tertiary sector a much smaller one. The number of economically active in the primary sector is especially high in Poland because of the prevailing private ownership and limits on concentration, but it is also high in Hungary. One could argue that the two countries are still far from the level of economic development in advanced countries, and therefore the primary sector must have so much weight. If one accepts this explanation then one is confronted with the question of why the secondary sector is close to the level of advanced capitalist countries. E. Ehrlich and J. Timár (1981) give an acceptable explanation; they maintain that in Britain, which embarked on the process of industrialisation first, employment in industry was high and was not accompanied by a simultaneous, high increase in employment in services. Countries which embarked on the process of industrialisation later and therefore could take advantage of the technology developed in the meantime have a lower employment in industry (e.g. the USA) and this process is accompanied by a fast rise in employment in services. The two authors believe rightly that industrialisation in the socialist countries proceeded according to the first model, and one can add that the high share of the secondary sector in employment is the result of the industrialisation drive, which was carried out largely by intensive methods, by increasing capital and labour input.

The smaller employment in services is also due to the Marxist methodology of national income computation, which regards services, with the exception of material services, as non-productive (not generating national income), and therefore leads to an underestimation of services for the development of the economy. In view of the obsession with economic growth (computed in terms of national income) till recently, it is no wonder that non-productive services have been

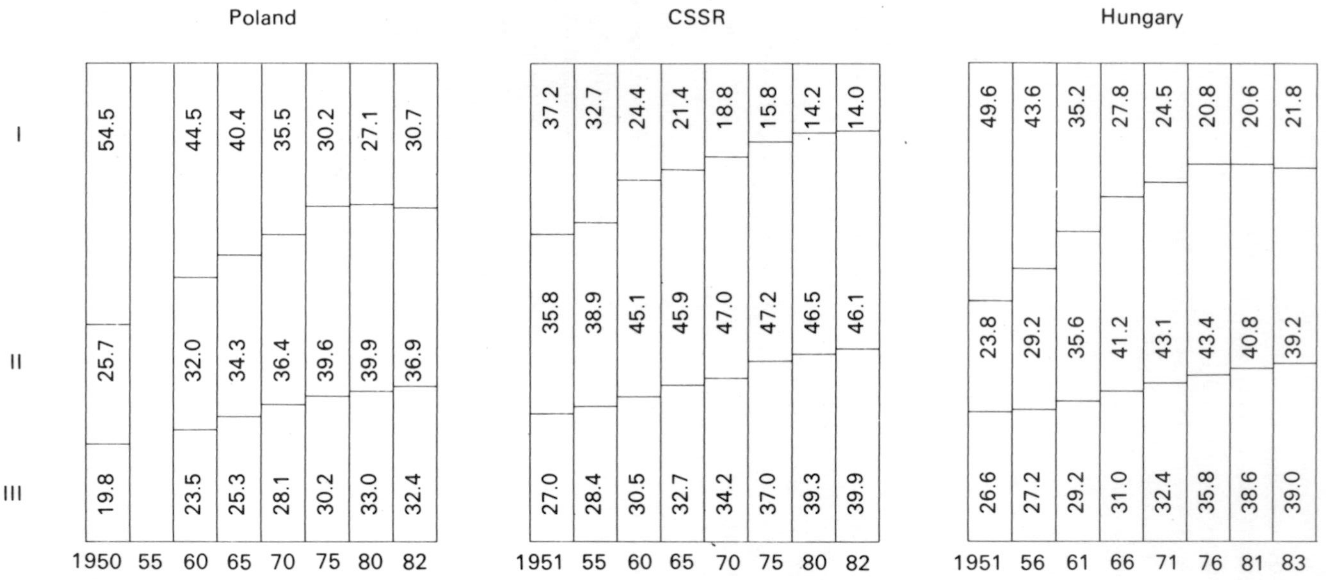

Hungary

Year	I	II	III
1951	49.6	23.8	26.6
56	43.6	29.2	27.2
61	35.2	35.6	29.2
66	27.8	41.2	31.0
71	24.5	43.1	32.4
76	20.8	43.4	35.8
81	20.6	40.8	38.6
83	21.8	39.2	39.0

CSSR

Year	I	II	III
1951	37.2	35.8	27.0
55	32.7	38.9	28.4
60	24.4	45.1	30.5
65	21.4	45.9	32.7
70	18.8	47.0	34.2
75	15.8	47.2	37.0
80	14.2	46.5	39.3
82	14.0	46.1	39.9

Poland

Year	I	II	III
1950	54.5	25.7	19.8
55			
60	44.5	32.0	23.5
65	40.4	34.3	25.3
70	35.5	36.4	28.1
75	30.2	39.6	30.2
80	27.1	39.9	33.0
82	30.7	36.9	32.4

I = primary sector, II = secondary sector, III = tertiary sector

SOURCES   Tables 7.2, 8.2, 9.2 and 10.2

FIGURE 12.1   *Evolution of the structure of the labour force 1950–83*

neglected. Such a tendency was strengthened by the fact that most of the non-productive services are unpaid, and thus the expansion of employment there means greater government spending.

If one accepts the structure of employment in advanced capitalist countries as a pattern for the socialist countries, and it seems that most economists in the countries under review accept this, then it is clear how further changes should develop. On the one hand the number of economically active must be reduced in the primary sector, and on the other, increased in the service sector. It is also necessary to reduce industrial employment, perhaps only temporarily, in order to get rid of overemployment. In Hungary and Czechoslovakia the share of the secondary sector had already declined (in 1976–80).

It can be expected that structural changes will proceed much more slowly than in the past. For 1981–5 no country plans declines in the work force in agriculture and, as already mentioned, Poland even planned for 1976–80 a relatively large increase. Since industrial employment is stagnating or declining, it becomes more difficult for workers who aspire to work in industry to quit agriculture. The situation will become even worse if the countries go ahead with a greater mechanisation of auxiliary processes in industry. There is, and for a long time will be, plenty of positions in services; however many require skills.

There was also a change in the sex structure of the labour force; the percentage share of females in the labour force increased substantially, primarily in Hungary where the female labour force grew the fastest. In 1949–81 it increased by 90.9 per cent; the corresponding figure in the CSSR (1948–80) is 59.9 per cent and in Poland (for 1950–81) 42.2 per cent. (The Polish figure would also be higher if it could be compared with earlier data than 1950.)

The growth in the number of economically active women was not even through the period under review. It grew the fastest in the beginning of the planning period, especially in the socialist sector. In the period 1950–5 it increased in Poland by 27 per cent in the socialist sector, and its share in the total employment went up from 31.8 per cent to 33.3 per cent. In Czechoslovakia female economic activity in the national economy (figures for the socialist sector are not available) increased by 20.8 per cent in 1948–55, and its share increased from 38.4 per cent to 42.7 per cent. In Hungary the corresponding figures for 1949–55 were 23.5 per cent and from 29.3 per cent to 32.3 per cent. In the 60s female economic activity again grew fast, whereas in the 70s a slowdown occurred. As a result of this slowdown the participation rates in Poland and the CSSR declined. In 1970 in the two countries the percentage share of women in the total number of economically active reached 47 per cent, to decline in 1981 to 46 per cent in Poland and 45 per cent (1980) in the CSSR. The decline is due primarily to the introduction of a prolonged maternity leave programme in 1968 and 1970 respectively. In Hungary, where the total number of economically active as well as the number of women on prolonged maternity leave declined in 1981, the participation rate of women, which reached 42 per cent in 1970, continued to grow, to achieve the same level as in the CSSR (see Table 12.4).

The evolution of the structure of the female labour force reflects the evolution mentioned in the three sectors. There are, however, some differences. In Poland women are nowadays more represented in agriculture than men, whereas in Czechoslovakia and Hungary the opposite is true. The tertiary sector employs relatively more women than men, whereas the situation is the reverse in the secondary sector.

TABLE 12.4 Evolution of the female labour force 1948–81[a]

	Poland				Czechoslovakia				Hungary			
	1950	1960	1970	1981	1948[a]	1960	1970	1980[b]	1949	1960	1970	1981
National economy (in thousands)	5 546.0	6 154.7	7 671.6	7 888.4	2 095.0	2 608.0	3 286.0	3 349.3	1 181.0	1 717.3	2 079.5	2 254.1
Indexes	100	111.0	138.3	142.2	100	124.5	156.8	159.9	100	145.4	176.1	190.9
Primary sector in %	68.2	58.8	46.5	31.4	55.6	29.8	18.7	12.9				17.6
Secondary sector in %	13.7	17.0			22.8	35.9	38.6	36.6		29.2	40.0	35.8
Tertiary sector in %	18.1	24.2	53.5	68.6	22.2	34.3	42.7	50.5				46.6
Participation rates[b]	0.45	0.44	0.47	0.46	0.38	0.43	0.47	0.45	0.30	0.36	0.42	0.45

[a] Women on maternity leave are not included except in Czechoslovakia up to 1970 inclusive.
[b] Ratio of economically active women to the total number of economically active.

SOURCES Poland   – RS 1982 pp. 38, 51; RS 1967, pp. 42, 47.
Czechoslovakia – SRC 1982 pp. 22, 23, 25, 205; SRC 1981, p. 22; SRC 1976, p. 113; SRC 1972, p. 131; SRC 1968, pp. 44, 62.
Hungary   – SE 1980, pp. 4, 29, 53, 130; SE 1979, pp. 28, 29; Szilágyi, 1966.

Conclusion

All three countries have not only managed to liquidate unemployment, but they even suffer from labour shortages. They have managed to avoid unemployment even at a time when the economy has stagnated or declined. Poland's economic situation is a case in point; despite great declines in output, resulting largely from shortages of raw materials, unemployment has not arisen. On the contrary, labour shortages are felt in various sectors.

This success is, no doubt, a product of the economic system. This is not to say that this has been an automatic outcome of the working of the system. It has been shown that the planners have interfered in the economy in different periods with the sole purpose of eliminating or averting the spectre of unemployment. Very often investment policy has been influenced or even changed substantially in order to meet goals in employment. A lot of funds have been spent on retraining. What is of great significance is that the governments have had at their disposal quite powerful instruments for the maintaining of full employment. They can regulate the size of the post-productive labour force by adapting the conditions of work of retirees to the needs of the economy, regulate the size of the female work force through changes in long-term maternity leave and regulate the size of the private sector. As has been shown, Poland has largely avoided unemployment just by regulating these tools.

In considering the factors which will protect the economies against unemployment it is also important to remember that the countries still have great job opportunities in the service sector which has been quite neglected. In addition, in all three countries, the growth rates in the working-age population in 1981–5 continue to decline (in Poland also in 1986–90). Finally they can resort to shortening the workweek.

The three countries have been less successful in coping with the central problem of employment policy – rational utilisation of labour. As has already been shown, only little progress has been made in the solution of this problem. Overemployment, particularly in industry, still plagues all

224

three countries at a time when labour shortages exist in several sectors. Contrary to the wishes of the central planners, many obsolete and inefficient enterprises survive, often using skilled manpower which could be put to better use in thriving or labour-deficient enterprises. Mechanisation of administrative work and auxiliary production processes proceeds slowly. Losses in working time are still horrendous. Labour discipline in all its aspects is still low.

Considering from a historical viewpoint the methods used for coping with the problems mentioned, it can be said that they have become more sophisticated. There is no doubt that the central planners try – though slowly – to learn from the experience gained during the application of the methods. They have come to realise that mandatory employment limits cannot bring about a better utilisation of labour. As long as enterprises are not interested in labour economy, the imposition of administrative employment limits cannot be very effective. Even the CSSR, which still sticks to the centralised system of management, has dropped mandatory employment limits (perhaps only temporarily).

Wage regulation, combined with incentives for labour-saving, is the method mostly used to bring growth of employment into line with the objectives of the planners, to restrain overemployment and to better utilise labour. Its effects are not very encouraging, and this is not surprising. The wage-regulation system has to serve several functions and is difficult to design in a way that serves all functions equally well, all the more because some aspects of the functions may conflict. And this is also why the planners were long reluctant to leave with enterprises a great portion of the money savings achieved by better labour economy. But now all the countries have reconciled themselves to such a solution; yet enterprises still do not try hard to achieve labour-savings. It seems that managers value the possibility of having some labour reserves more than tiny increases in average wages. They may feel that, in view of the present restrained wage policy, the central planners will not tolerate any more substantial increases in wages.

The restructuring of employment according to the needs of the economy (an important step in the direction towards the solution to the problem of labour shortages) proceeds slowly, because it depends primarily on the decisions of workers. Wage incentives for such a restructuring are not strong enough, particularly now when real wages stagnate so that the possibilities for wage increases in priority sectors and branches are limited. In addition, in the considerations about a job change, many other factors, especially the availability of housing, which is in short supply, play an important role. Of course the transfer of labour from less efficient enterprises and the shutdown of obsolete enterprises could be speeded up if the governments could apply the methods used by private enterprises in a capitalist economy. A socialist government cannot, even if it wished to, resort to a massive dismissal of workers in the hope that they will find jobs where the economy needs them, and risk that many will be without jobs for some time. Such a policy would undermine the credibility and the political base of the system. In addition, it is doubtful whether managers under existing conditions would be excited about being the executors of such a policy; their material interest in economic efficiency is not strong enough to eclipse the worries which would be generated by a policy of massive dismissal. After all, in the real socialist system, the position of managers depends on the goodwill of workers to a much greater extent than in private enterprises.

From time to time ideas pop up about allowing some unemployment as an instrument for handling labour discipline. It is an idea which may be economically attractive, but, since it hides political dangers, it has no chance to be implemented under existing conditions. The political leaders are committed to full employment and, as has been shown, whenever the spectre of unemployment looms up, they try to avoid it.

The question may be posed: can there be a substantial turnaround in labour economy? In the author's view the turnaround hinges on three conditions: enterprises' finances must depend as much as possible on their own performance, there must be a rational price system and a level of labour cost which will encourage a substitution of capital for labour. A consistent application of the first condition in the sense that enterprises' finances would be fully dependent on their performance would necessarily mean a change in the economic system and the creation of unemployment. Yet if the idea of self-financing is pushed as much as possible, without affecting the centre's ability to co-ordinate the economy effectively, pressure may be exerted on enterprises in the direction of greater labour economy. Such pressure can, however, be effective only if the other two conditions are met. Self-financing cannot be effective if enterprises are able to juggle prices and/or if they have access to cheap labour. The latter can only be handled by taxes at present. Again the tax can fulfil its role only if it affects palpably the finances of enterprises, and this is only possible under conditions of self-financing.

For a long time increases in consumption were treated as a residual; consumption was low on the list of priorities. Under such conditions the policy of wage increases was one-sidedly subordinated to other considerations, economic growth being the most important. This was especially true during the first medium-term plans, whose primary goal was the promotion of a fast industrialisation drive. Such a policy was reflected in a decline in real wages, which was mitigated by a slight growth in consumption as a result of fast growth in employment.

The experience of 1949–53 brought about gradual changes in the approach to wage policy. The leaders of the communist parties started to realise that for the sake of the survival of the regime greater attention must be devoted to the material interest of the population. This new approach began to be reflected in practical wage policy in the CSSR and Hungary, particularly in the second half of the 60s, and in Poland in the first half of the 70s.

On the whole growth of real wages fluctuated greatly, mainly under the impact of three factors – pace of economic growth, including employment, economic reforms and internal political conditions. Rapid economic growth, especially if it was greater than envisaged in the plan, brought about mostly higher real wages (as in 1965–70 and 1971–5) and vice versa (as in the first half of the 60s). If employment grew fast, particularly if it grew much faster than anticipated in the plan, it had an unfavourable effect on the growth of real wages. Economic reforms usually have a favourable influence on real-wage increases, since their purpose is to increase economic efficiency, a goal which it is possible to achieve by greater incentives, among other things. Political tension (as in Hungary in 1956 and Poland in 1956, 1970 and 1980) contributed to real wage increases, since the increases granted were used as an instrument of tension management.

The development in real wages makes unrealistic expectations of and demands for a widening of wage differentials in order to make changes in the management system (as in Hungary and Poland) more workable.

The various elements of the system of wage determination for individual workers underwent changes of varying extent. Yet in no country, with the exception of Hungary, did significant changes occur in the period under review. The central element of the classical Soviet system – the assigning of binding wage-rates from the centre and their rigidity over a long period – has been in substance retained in Czechoslovakia. Though Poland has undertaken some steps in the direction of doing away with this, only Hungary has partially got away from it, by setting the wage-rate as a span within which enterprises' managers can manœuver and by changing the wage-rates frequently.

Notes

Chapter 1

1. The term 'rational' is explained in connection with rational employment. See p. 8. It is also used interchangeably with the term 'efficient' as long as this refers to labour utilisation.
2. In my opinion the two terms should be distinguished. To put it briefly: 'economic development' is a broader term which includes structural changes as well as economic growth, while 'economic growth' is simply a quantifiable increase (cf. Flammang 1979).

Chapter 2

1. In 1979 a debate on labour shortages (see *KSz*, no. 9, 1979) revolved primarily around R. I. Gábor's paper (1979B) in which he argued that labour shortages are caused by macro- and microeconomic factors. At the macro level they occur because, under socialism, it is worth while to expand employment to a point at which it is still possible to increase national income. At the micro level – to put it briefly – market forces not determining the behaviour of enterprises are the cause.
2. According to M. Pick (1980) computations made in Czechoslovakia have shown that labour costs at the given wages are underestimated by 44 per cent compared to prices of machinery. Another clue to the cheapness of labour is given by the share of wage costs in the total cost of industrial production. In the middle of the 60s it was 15 per cent in Hungary (Ballai 1968) and 16 per cent in Poland (Kabaj 1977, p. 62).
3. Figures indicated in this book without reference are taken from national statistical yearbooks and related sources.
4. The term 'manual workers' is used interchangeably with blue-collar workers, and 'non-manual' with white-collar workers or salaried workers.

Chapter 3

1. Persons who move from one job to another.
2. In Hungary the prolonged maternity leave is extended to three years for each child, in the CSSR only up to two years for the second child, and in Poland up

to four years for each child (Pachl 1976; Abonyi 1979, pp. 230–1 and Glapa, 1979).

3. Czechoslovak figures were as follows: 151 750 in 1970 and 391 757 in 1980. However they are not comparable with Hungarian and Polish figures since they also include mothers on short-term maternity leave.

4. 'Private small-scale entrepreneurship has its justification in the sphere of services' – reads the Action Program of the Communist Party of 1968 (*Rok* . . . 1969, p. 129).

Chapter 4

1. I have tested the statement by several computations, the most important being a comparison of average wages as a ratio of *per capita* national income (in Poland, the CSSR and Hungary of net material product, and Austria, Canada, Greece, Italy, Spain, the UK and West Germany of national income in market prices). Of course, the findings can be regarded as only a very rough indication about the ratios since, in the two systems, average wages and national income are differently computed. The figures obtained show that with the exception of Greece (?) in all other non-socialist countries the ratios are much higher than in the socialist. This only confirms what is generally accepted in informed circles in East European countries.

Chapter 5

1. By 'consumption of the population' is meant personal consumption plus social services in cash and kind.

2. I am reluctant to use the word 'control' here since it has the connotation of a negative action, whereas wage policy is intended not only to avert certain phenomena,'but also to make others happen.

3. By 'incomes' I understand wages including bonuses plus social services in cash.

4. I have discussed this point in my book *Wage Control* . . . 1979.

5. By 'qualification' I mean formal education and experience gained in practical application of the education (cf. Jacukowicz 1974, p. 225).

6. In the Marxist concept of national income accounting only the material sphere, which includes all sectors of the economy producing physical goods or material services (services which bring the process of production to completion, that is, transport and communications) generates national income.

Chapter 7

1. The final version of the Polish plan was of 1950, and therefore no further great modifications were undertaken.

2. 'During the whole period of the Plan – it is written in the Reconstruction plan – the objective will be to maintain full employment' (*Polish* . . . 1946, p. 23).

3. This stagnation resulted from a former uneven evolution of the population, mainly from the low birth-rates during the Great Depression.
4. Based on information from a reliable source.
5. Soon after the war all three countries created a legal framework which allowed governments to allocate people to important sectors of the economy. In Czechoslovakia the coalition government (before February 1948) made very little use of this legislation (*Průběh* . . . 1948, pp. 241–4). In Poland, however, the authorities took advantage of this legislation (Brus 1981, p. 1/33).
6. In Czechoslovakia the local governments are called 'national committees', whereas in Poland and Hungary they are 'national councils'. When talking generally about local governments the term 'council' is used; otherwise the term is used according to the country in question.
7. This is an annual average calculated from the twelve months' averages of workers.

Chapter 8

1. According to Tables 7.2 and 8.2 the increase in the socialist sector was even smaller (404 000 – 5.9 per cent). I have listed A. Rajkiewicz's figures since they compare performance with the plan.
2. The extent of shortages in the coal industry is best characterised by the following figures: in 1956 in the coalfield Ostrava-Karvin only 64.5 per cent of the total production work force was permanent, in 1957 only 59.9 per cent. During one year the turnover of workers was 50 per cent (Čech 1959, p. 121).
3. Employment in the service sector – trade, catering, health and social welfare, education and culture – increased by 185 000 against 70 000 in 1956–60.
4. The fund was used for year-end rewards and was not allowed to exceed 8.5 per cent of the wage-bill (Fick 1967, pp. 116–17).
5. For example, in 1948 in Czechoslovakia wage-rates for piecework in the machine industry comprised 79 per cent of the earnings, in 1955 only 48 per cent. At the same time the overfulfilment of norms increased from 127 per cent to 207 per cent respectively (Razga and Hronský 1958).
6. The reform started in Hungary in 1957, in Czechoslovakia in 1958 and in Poland in 1962 (some modifications were made earlier).
7. It should be mentioned that this was also the case in Poland in a limited number of branches (Krencik 1972, pp. 78–81).

Chapter 9

1. The planned figures are taken from Kubik and Rendl (1965).
2. J. Hoós (1980, p. 54) maintains that change in the sources of energy production was the most important factor in the success achieved in the economy in the period 1966–75. The changes made available relatively cheap energy and reduced production costs.
3. New enterprises as well as increased employment of the partially disabled were tax exempt. Districts with low participation rates were tax exempt or

enjoyed a tax deduction. Some sectors (construction, services) paid a reduced tax.

4. The main purpose of these taxes – 25 per cent of the wage-bill, of which 8 per cent was payroll tax and 17 per cent a contribution to social insurance – was to provide revenue for the state to finance social services.
5. In a few sectors (food industry, agriculture) wage-bill regulation was kept.
6. For information about the price system see Csikós-Nagy (1971).
7. On the other hand, granting of subsidies was an opportune tool for influencing enterprises' activity.
8. For more on wage-regulation system and incentives see Adam (1979, pp. 143–50).
9. It should be borne in mind that part of what statistics refer to as average wage increases is in fact a reward for increases in qualifications and for overfulfilment of work norms.
10. In the case of manual workers the following criteria were considered: theoretical knowledge, experience, responsibility, physical strenuousness and danger of injuries.

Chapter 10

1. J. Mihalik (1982, p. 90) maintains that in the 70s the Czechoslovak industry was short of half a million workers if one assumes a regime of two shifts.
2. Figures on agriculture should be taken with reservations; they also include collective farmers who are mostly engaged in sideline activities.
3. In some sectors and branches wages were directly regulated from the centre.
4. Based on information obtained during my research stay in Hungary.

Chapter 11

1. In 1937 salaries of technicians and clerical staff together exceeded wage earners' average wages by 177.7 per cent, whereas in 1948 they were only 47.7 per cent greater (Hron 1968, appendix x/2).
2. Here average wages mean incomes of collective farmers together with wages of employees of state farms.
3. The comparison is limited to the following five Western countries: Canada, USA, UK, West Germany and Austria.
4. In the CSSR the Action Programme of the communist party, adopted in April 1968, perhaps took the clearest stand. 'The Party has several times criticised egalitarian views but in practice egalitarianism (*nivelizace*) spread to an unusual extent and became one of the main obstacles to intensive economic growth and to an increase in standard of living. . . .' (*Rok* . . . 1969, pp. 111–12). In Hungary see Buda and Pongrácz (1966).

Chapter 12

1. Special real-wage figures for industry are not available. However, the average real wages reflect quite well industrial real wages since industrial nominal

wages do not deviate much from average wages in the national economy (see Tables 11.1 and 11.4).
2. For comparative purposes I use figures for 1980, since Polish figures for 1982 are not comparable with previous years because of a change in classification (see Table 10.2).

Appendix

TABLE A.1 Planned and actual growth of employment and real wages 1950–80
(annual growth rates)

	1950–5[a] P	A	1956–60 P	A	1961–5 P	A	1966–70 P	A	1971–5 P	A	1976–80 P	A
Total employment (without co-operative and private agriculture)[b]												
Poland	8.0	8.3	3.7	1.7	2.3	3.2		2.0	1.6	3.4	1.3	0.2
CSSR	4.6	5.9	1.6	2.5	1.7	2.6		1.2	0.2	0.3	0.5	0.4
Hungary				3.0	4.2	3.0	3.3	1.5	0.9	0.0		−0.5
Industrial employment[c]												
Poland	8.7	8.3 (5.8)	4.2	2.1 (2.5)	1.7	4.1 (3.4)	2.5	3.3 (3.6)	2.5	2.8 (2.9)	0.6–0.7	0.4 (0.4)
CSSR	1.4	4.1 (3.1)	1.2	3.4 (3.0)	1.4	1.9 (1.7)	0.8	1.3 (1.5)	0.7	0.5 (0.6)	0.6	0.7 (0.5)
Hungary	11.2	9.2 (6.6)	1.7	3.2 (4.3)	2.5	2.3 (3.0)	1.4	2.7 (2.0)	0.5	0.2 (0.1)		−1.1 (−1.5)
Real wages[d]												
Poland			5.4	5.2	4.2	1.5	1.9	2.1	3.2–3.4	7.2	3.0–3.4	1.9
CSSR			5.4	4.5	4.6	1.2	3.4–3.5	3.6	2.5–3.0[e]	3.5	2.5–2.8[e]	0.7
Hungary			4.6	8.0	3.0–3.2[f]	1.7	1.7–1.9	3.4	3.0–3.4	3.3	2.7–3.0	0.7

P – planned; A – actual

[a] CSSR figures refer to 1949–53 and Hungarian to 1950–4; [b] All figures starting with 1961–5 (actual) refer to the material sphere; [c] Figures in brackets are official figures; [d] Actual figures are official figures; [e] Refer to nominal wages; [f] Refer to real incomes.

SOURCES *Planned figures* for 1950–65 including actual figures for total employment – *Incomes* . . . 1967, ch. 7, pp. 11 and 29; for the rest – *ESE 1971*, part II, pp. 115 and 121; *ESE 1975*, p. 148; *ESE 1976*, part II, pp. 19 and 71; *ESE 1981*, p. 135.
Actual figures: Non-official for industrial employment – *Incomes* . . . 1967, p. 11; *ESE 1971*, part II, p. 11; *ESE 1971*, part II, p. 121, *ESE 1976*, part II, p. 121. Official figures for industrial employment – *Incomes* . . . 1967, part II, p. 71; *ESE 1976*, part II, p. 119; *ESE 1980*, p. 71; *ESE 1980*, p. 119; *ESE 1981*, p. 219. Official figures from Tables 7.2, 8.2, 9.2, 10.2, 7.3, 8.3, 9.3 and 10.3

Bibliography*

Abonyi, G. (1979) *A társadalombiztositási törvény és gyakorlata* (Budapest).

Adam, J. (1972) 'Wage Differentials in Czechoslovakia', *Industrial Relations*, no. 2, May.

Adam, J. (1973) 'The Incentive System in the USSR', *Industrial and Labor Relations Review*, no. 1, Oct.

Adam, J. (1974) *Wage, Price and Taxation Policy in Czechoslovakia in 1948–70* (Berlin).

Adam, J. (1979) *Wage Control and Inflation in Soviet Bloc Countries* (London, Macmillan; New York, Praeger Publishers, 1980).

Adam, J. (1982) 'Similarities and Differences in the Treatment of Labour Shortages', in Adam, J. (ed.), *Employment Policies in the Soviet Union and Eastern Europe* (London, Macmillan; New York, St Martin's Press).

Adam, J. (1983) 'Old Age Pension System in Eastern Europe: A Case Study of Czechoslovak and Hungarian Experience', *Osteuropa Wirtschaft*, no. 4.

Adam, J. (1984) 'Regulation of Labour Supply in Poland, Czechoslovakia and Hungary', *Soviet Studies*, no. 1.

Adam, J., Cekota, J. (1980) *Revue d'Études Comparatives Est–Ouest*, no. 4.

Ajtai, M. (1966) *TSz*, no. 7–8.

Altmann, F. L. (1980) 'Czechoslovakia: Economic Prospects for the 1980's', in *Economic Reforms in Eastern Europe and Prospects for the 80's* (NATO, Colloquium).

Altmann, F. L. (1982) 'Wachstumpause oder Krise?', *Working Paper of the Osteuropa Institut* (Munich), no. 85.

Bajcura, A. (1969) *Hmotná zainteresovanosť v priemysle* (Bratislava).

Bajszczak, Z., Obodowski, J. (1964A) *PiZs*, no. 7–8.

Bajszczak, Z., Obodowski, J. (1964B) *PiZS*, no. 9.

Baka, W., Gora, S., Knysiak, Z., Porwit, K. (1975) *Planowanie gospodarki narodowej* (Warsaw).

Baka, W. (1979) *GP*, no. 6.

Bakič, R. (1971) *PH*, no. 10.

Balassa, A. (1981) *KSz*, no. 4.

Bálint, J. (1983) *Társadalmi rétegeződés és jövedelmek* (Budapest).

Ballai, L. (1968) *TSz*, Aug–Sep.

Balogh, J. (1981) *MSz*, no. 9.

* For space reasons only full references to books, regardless of the language in which they are published, are listed. References to periodical and newspaper articles are listed without titles unless they are published in English.

Balogh, S., Jakab, S. (eds) (1978) *A magyar népi demokrácia története, 1944–1962* (Budapest).

Bánki, P. (1971) *MSz*, no. 4.

Bánki, P. (1973) *KSz*, no. 2.

Bánki, P. Tóth, G. (1974), in *Tarifnye sistemy oplaty truda v promyshlennosti stran chlenov SEV* (Moscow).

Berend, I. T. (1974) *A szocialista gazdaság fejlődése Magyarországon, 1945–1968* (Budapest).

Berend, I. T. (1979) *A szocialista gazdaság fejlődése Magyarországon, 1945–1975* (Budapest).

Berényi, J. (1967) *Foglalkoztatottság és életszínvonal* (Budapest).

Berényi, J. (1974) *Lohnsystem und Lohnstruktur in Österreich und Ungarn* (Vienna).

Berényi, S. (1982) *MSz*, no. 4.

Bernášek, M. (1969) 'The Czechoslovak Economic Recession, 1962–65', *Soviet Studies*, no. 4.

Beskid, L. (1963) *Przegląd Statystyczny*, no. 3.

Beskid, L. (1964) *Przegląd Statystyczny*, no. 1.

Blažek, J. (1973) *PH*, no. 8.

Bobošiková, M. (1981) *PaM*, no. 12.

Bokor, J. (1965) *KSz*, no. 3.

Bokor, J. (1973) *Pénzügyi Szemle*, no. 12.

Borcz, L. (1970) *Prawo podziału według pracy* (Warsaw).

Borcz L. (1978), in Krencik, W. (ed.) *Płaca w ustroju socjalistycznym* (Warsaw).

Borkowski, R. (1982) *PiZS*, no. 10.

Borloi, R. (1982) *Figyelő*, no. 48.

Bornstein, M. (1978) 'Unemployment in Capitalist Regulated Market Economies and in Socialist Centrally Planned Economies', *American Economic Review*, May.

Brčák, J. (1974) *Politická ekonomie*, no. 2.

Brojewski, M. (1980) *PiZS*, no. 5.

Brojewski, M. (1981) *PiZS*, no. 10–11.

Brus, W. (1981) *Economic History of Communist Eastern Europe*, MS (Oxford University Press, forthcoming).

Buda, I. (1965A) *Népszabadság*, 28 Mar.

Buda, I. (1965B) *KSz*, no. 4.

Buda, I. (1972) 'Wage Regulation and Manpower Management', in Gado, O. (ed.), *Reform of the Economic Mechanism in Hungary* (Budapest).

Buda, I. (1976) *MSz*, no. 1.

Buda, I., Pongrácz, L. (1966) *KSz*, no. 1.

Buda, I., Pongrácz, L. (1968) *Személyi jövedelmek, anyagi érdekeltség, munkaerő-gazdálkodás* (Budapest).

Buda, I., Timár, J. (1963) *Népszabadság*, 22 Oct.

Burdová, E. (1976) Supplement to *HN*, no. 20.

Čáp, V., Rybníkář, K. (1982) *PH*, no.9.

Čech, J. (1959) *Plánovité rozmisťování pracovních sil v ČSR* (Prague).

Černý, S., Rufert, S. (eds) (1970) *Pracovní síly v československém hospodářství* (Prague).

Chelstowski, S. (1977) *TL*, 17 Jan.

Csikós-Nagy, B. (1971) *Magyar gazdaságpolitika* (Budapest).
Csikós-Nagy, B. (1974) *Valóság*, no. 4.
Csikós-Nagy, B. (1982) *KSz*, no. 12.
Czajka, Z. (1981) *PiZS*, no. 10–11.
Czajka, Z. (1982) *PiZS*, no. 5.
Dankovits, L. (1973) *Munka*, no. 2.
Daskiewicz, W. (1955) *Nowe Drogi*, no. 6.
Denison, E. (1967) *Why Growth Rates Differ* (Washington).
Derco, M., Kotlaba, M. (1976) *PH*, no. 12.
Ehrlich, E., Timár, J. (1981) *Gazdaság*, no. 2.
Ellman, M. (1979) 'Full Employment – Lessons from State Socialism', *De Economist*, no. 4.
Fallenbuchl, Z. (1982A) 'Employment Policies in Poland', in Adam, J. (ed.), *Employment Policies in the Soviet Union and Eastern Europe* (London).
Fallenbuchl, Z. (1982B) 'Poland's Economic Crisis', *Problems of Communism*, Mar–Apr.
Fedorowicz, Z. (1977) *Finanse organizacji gospodarczych* (Warsaw).
Feuer, L. S. (ed.), (1959) Marx and Engels, *Basic Writings in Politics and Philosophy* (Anchor Books).
Fick, B. (1959) *Finanse*, no. 9.
Fick, B. (1964) *ZG*, no. 1.
Fick, B. (1965) *Bodźce ekonomiczne w przemyśle* (Warsaw).
Fick, B. (1966) *ZG*, no. 13.
Fick, B. (1967) *Fundusz zakladowy* (Warsaw).
Fick, B. (1970) *Polityka zatrudnienia, a płace i bodźce* (Warsaw).
Fick, B. (1971) *ZG*, no. 44.
First Czechoslovak Economic Five-Year Plan (1949) (Prague).
Flammang, R. A. (1979) 'Economic Growth and Economic Development: Counterparts or Competitors?', *Economic Development and Cultural Change*, no. 1, Oct.
Flór, F., Horváth, S. (1972) *Iparvállalatok jövedelem – és munkaerőgazdálkodása* (Budapest).
Fonal, S. (1956) *KSz*, no. 11–12.
Formánek, K. (1981) *PH*, no. 11.
Formánek, K., Pick, M. (1965) *PH*, no. 7–8.
Frankowski, K. (1952) *GP*, no. 5.
Friss, I. (1972) *Acta Oeconomica*, vol. 8, no. 2–3.
Gábor, I. R. (1979A) 'The Second Economy', *Acta Oeconomica*, vol. 22, no. 3–4.
Gábor, I. R. (1979B) *KSz*, no. 2.
Gábor, I. R., Galasi, P. (1981) *A 'második' gazdaság* (Budapest).
Gadó, O. (1976) *Közgazdasági szabályozó rendszerünk 1976–ban* (Budapest).
Galenson, W., Fox, A. (1967) 'Earnings and Employment in Eastern Europe, 1957 to 1963', *Quarterly Journal of Economics*, no. 1.
Gerloch, V. (1962) *Mzda a její význam za socialismu* (Prague).
Gervai, B. (1983) *KSz*, no. 3.
Glapa, Z. (1979) *GP*, no. 6.
Gliński, B., Kierczyński, T., Topiński, A. (1975) *Zmiany w systemie zarządzania przemysłem* (Warsaw).
Gliński, B. (1977) *System funkcjonowania gospodarki* (Warsaw).

Goldman, J. (1964). *PH*, no. 9, 11.
Goldman, J., Kouba, K. (1967) *Hospodářský růst v ČSSR* (Prague).
Gołębiowski, J. W. (1977), in Ciepielewski, J. (ed.), *Kraje socjalistyczne po drugiej wojnie światowej, 1944–74* (Warsaw).
Gołębiowski, J. W. (1978), in Dobieszewski, A., Gołębiowski, J. W. (eds), *PZPR (1948–78)* (Warsaw).
Golinowski, K. (1982) *GP*, no. 9.
Gulyás, K. (1981), *MSz*, no. 9.
Gyetvai, L. (1980) *MSz*, no. 4.
Gyetvai, L. (1982). *Gazdaság*, no. 2.
Hamerník, E. (1982). *PaM*, no. 10.
Hámori, A. (1980) *Munka*, no. 12.
Hatlacki, J. (1976) *MSz*, no. 1.
Havasi, F. (1982) *TSz*, no. 1.
Havránek, O. (1960). *PH*, no. 3.
Hegedűs, A. (1960) *KSz*, no. 4.
Herner, E. (1982) *Figyelő*, no. 22.
Hoffman, P. (1966) *Ekonomický časopis*, no. 2.
Höhmann, H. H., Seidenstecher, G. (1977), in Höhmann, H. H. (ed.), *Arbeitsmarkt und Wirtschaftsplannung* (Cologne).
Holubicki, B. (1977) *GP*, no. 6, 9.
Hoós, J. (1976) *Pártélet*, no. 3.
Hoós, J. (1980) *Gazdaság és gazdaság-politika* (Budapest).
Horváth, L. (1970) *Figyelő*, Oct. 7.
Hrdlička, L. (1982) *PaM*, no. 7, 8.
Hron, J. (1968) *Změny v oblasti mezd v období 1945–1953* (Prague).
Hudák, I. (1978) *PH*, no. 10.
'The Hungarian Three-Year Plan (1947–49)' (1947) *Hungarian Bulletin.*
Hungary's Five-Year Plan, January 1, 1950–December 31, 1954 (?) (Budapest)
Huszár, J. (1976) *KSz*, no. 3.
Incomes in Postwar Europe: A Study of Policies, Growth and Distribution (1967) (Geneva).
Jacukowicz, Z. (1974) *Proporcje płac w Polsce* (Warsaw).
Jaworski, T. (1956) *ZG*, no. 12.
Jędruszczak, H. (1972) *Zatrudnienie a przemiany społeczne w Polsce w latach 1944–60* (Warsaw).
Jędrychowski, S. (1966) *GP*, no. 7.
Jędrychowski, S. (1967) *Nowe Drogi*, no. 1.
Jezierski, A., Petz, B. (1980) *Historia gospodarcza Polski Ludowej 1944–1975* (Warsaw).
Kabaj, M. (1960) *Ekonomista*, no. 1.
Kabaj, M. (1962), in *Polityka gospodarcza Polski Ludowej*, vol. 1, 2nd edition (Warsaw).
Kabaj, M. (1972) *Elementy pełnego i racjonalnego zatrudnienia w gospodarce socjalistycznej* (Warsaw).
Kabaj, M. (1972ᴀ) *TL*, 12 Dec.
Kabaj, M. (1975) *Nowe Drogi*, no. 2.
Kabaj, M. (1977), in Sajkiewicz, A. (ed.), *Ekonomika pracy* (Warsaw).
Kabaj, M. (1980) *PiZS*, no. 1.

Bibliography 239

Kačmarik, K. (1959) *HN*, no. 22.
Kalecki, M. (1964) *Z zagadnien gospodarczo-spolecznych Polski Ludowej* (Warsaw).
Kalinová, L. (1977) *Politická ekonomie*, no. 9.
Kalinová, L. (1979) *Máme nedostatek pracovních sil?* (Prague).
Karakas, L. (1976) *MSz*, no. 1.
Karpiński, A. (1967) *GP*, no. 1.
Karpiński, A. (1974), in Secomski, K. (ed.), *30 lat gospodarki Polski Ludowej* (Warsaw).
Kazimour, J. (1980) *Hospodářský vývoj Československa* (Prague).
Kemeny, A. (1971) *PaM*, no. 3.
Képzettség és kereset (1971) A Study of the Hungarian Statistical Board, vol. II (Budapest).
Kisházi, Ö. (1958) *Bérrendszerünk* (Budapest).
Kocanda, R. (1965) *Způsoby plánovitého rozdělování pracovních sil* (Prague).
Kocanda, R. (1966) *Ekonomický časopis*, no. 9.
Kochanowicz, T., Obodowski, J. (1958) *Nowe Drogi*, no. 5.
Kolos, M. (1980) *KSz, no. 10*.
Kontra, M. (1982) *Politická ekonomie*, no. 6.
Kónya, L. (1971) 'Further Improvement of the System of Enterprise Income and Wage Regulation', *Acta Oeconomica*, vol. 7, no. 1.
Kónya, L., Lökkös, J., Tóth, L. (1978) *MSz*, no. 12.
Kordaszewski, J. (1960) *Kwalifikowanie pracy robotnikow przemysłowych* (Warsaw).
Kornai, J. (1980) *Economics of Shortage* (Amsterdam), vol. A.
Kosta, J. (1978) *Abriss der sozialökonomischen Entwicklung der Tschechoslowakei, 1945–1977* (Frankfurt).
Kouba, K., Sokol, M., Turek, O. (1966) *PH*, no. 1.
Kováčová, E. (1980) *Pracovné sily, ich rozmiesťovanie a kvalifikácia v sociálno-ekonomickom rozvoji* (Bratislava).
Kovács, J. (1974) *KSz*, no. 7–8.
Kovács, J. (1977) *Gazdaság*, no. 1.
Kővári, Gy. (1981) in Timár, J. (ed.) *Munkagazdaságtan* (Budapest).
Kozár, A. (1977) *PaM*, no. 1.
Kožušnik, Č. (1964) *Problémy teorie hodnoty a ceny za socializmu* (Prague).
Krajewska, A. (1974) *Wykształcenie a zróznicowanie płac* (Warsaw).
Krasniewski, J. (1982) *TL*, 2 Sep.
Krencik, W. (1972) *Podstawy i kierunki polityki płac w PRL* (Warsaw).
Krencik, W. (1976) *GP*, no. 6.
Krencik, W. (1980) *GP*, no. 4.
Krogulski, F. (1959) *Przegląd Ubezpieczen Spolecznych*, no. 2.
Król, H. (1982) *Nowe Drogi*, no. 12.
Kruczkowska, G. (1979) *Egalitaryzm a płace* (Warsaw).
Kubík, J. Rendl, V. (1965) *PH*, no. 7–8.
Kucharski, M. (1972) *Pieniądz, dochód, proporcje wzrostu* (Warsaw).
Kudrna, A. (1967) *PaM*, no. 7.
Kutálek, Z. (1966) *PH*, no. 8–9.
Kutálek, Z. (1976) *PH*, no. 4.
Kuziński, S. (1956) *Nowe Drogi*, no. 9.

Kynstetr, P. (1981) *Politická ekonomie*, no. 12.

Lázár, Gy. (1971) *TSz*, no. 1.

Lázár, Gy. (1982) *KSz*, no. 12.

Lengyel, L. (1958) *Statisztikai Szemle*, Aug–Sep.

Levcik, F. (1969) 'Wage Policy and Wage Planning in Czechoslovakia' un-published study).

Levcik, F. (1981) 'Economic Performance in the Post-Reform Period and Prospects for the 1980's', *East European Economic Assessment*, part I, JEC.

Lökkös, J. (1981) *MSz*, Supplement, no. I–II.

Lukeš, V., Rybnikář, K. (1968) *PH*, no. 12.

Maier, V. (1963) *Zarabotnaia plata v period perekhoda v kommunizm* (Moscow).

Markó, I. (1980) *TSz*, no. 11.

Mátyás, P. (1969) *MSz*, no. 2.

Melich, A. (1978) *Problemy płac w Polsce* (Warsaw).

Meller, J. (1977) *Płace a planowanie gospodarcze w Polsce, 1950–1975* (Warsaw).

Meller, J. (1982) *PiZS*, no. 8–9.

Mihalik, J. (1959) *Ekonomický časopis*, no. 2.

Mihalik, J. (1982) *Práca a sociálny rozvoj v pätročnici* (Bratislava).

Mikeš, E., Steinich, J. (1975) *PH*, no. 11.

Mikeš, E., Steinich, J. (1976) *PH*, no. 9.

Minc, H. (1950), in B. Bierut, *The Six-Year Plan of Economic Development* (Warsaw).

Moravec, E. (1981) *PH*, no. 9.

Morecka, Z. (1960), in Lange, O. (ed.), *Zagadnienia ekonomii politycznej socjalizmu* (Warsaw), 3rd edition.

Morecka, Z. (1965) 'Economic Expansion and Wage Structure in a Socialist Country: A Study of Polish Experience', *International Labour Review*, vol. 91, no. 6, June.

Morecka, Z. (1974) *Ekonomista*, no. 3.

Mosóczy, R. (1979) *A KGST – országok gazdaság-politikája (1976–1980)* (Budapest).

Munkácsy, F. (1978) *MSz*, no. 8.

Munkácsy, F. (1980) *MSz*, no. 12.

Murgaš, M. (1971) *PaM*, no. 10.

Nejedlý, M. (1970) *PaM*, no. 5.

Nyitrai, F. (1981) *A magyar gazdaság és társadalom a hetvenes években* (Budapest).

Obodowski, J. (1966) *Nowe Drogi*, no. 5.

Olajos, A. (1978) *Szakképzés és foglalkoztatás* (Budapest).

Olajos, A. (1981) *Gazdaság*, no. 1.

Olędzki, M. (1974) *Polityka zatrudnienia* (Warsaw), 1st edition.

Olędzki, M. (1978) *Polityka zatrudnienia* (Warsaw), 2nd edition.

Olšovský, R., Průcha, V. (eds) (1969) *Stručný hospodářský vývoj Československa do roku 1955* (Prague).

Pachl, Z. (1976) *PH*, no. 12.

Pál, I. (1970) *Népszabadság*, 26 Aug.

Palotai, L. (1962) *GP*, no. 9–10.

Penc, J. (1977) *PiZS*, no. 12.

Penc, J. (1980) *Ekonomika i Organizacja Pracy*, no. 12.

Phelps Brown, H. (1977) *The Inequality of Pay* (Oxford).
Piątek, K. (1980) *PiZS*, no. 6.
Pick, M. (1959) *PH*, no. 3.
Pick, M. (1974) *Politická ekonomie*, no. 4.
Pick, M. (1979) *HN*, Supplement, no. 4.
Pick, M. (1980) *HN*, no. 18.
Pick, M. (1982) *PaM*, no. 10.
Pisz, Z. (1983) *ZG*, no. 9.
Plichta, J. (1959) *HN*, no. 33.
Pogány, Gy. (1969) *Foglalkoztatás-politika és munkaerőgazdálkodás* (Budapest).
Pokorná, Z. (1979) *PaM*, no. 9.
Polish National Economic Plan (1946) (Warsaw).
Pongrácz, L. (1970) *MSz*, no. 4.
Pongrácz, L. (1973) *TSz*, no. 4.
Pongrácz, L. (1975) *A kereseti arányok távlati fejlesztése* (Budapest).
Pongrácz, L. (1976) *Gazdaság*, Sep.
Pongrácz, L. (1982) *MSz*, no. 8.
Popper, L. (1981) *MSz*, no. 11.
Portes, R. (1977) 'Economic Performance, Policy and Prospects', in *East European Economies Post-Helsinki*, JEC.
Potáč, S. (1983) *PH*, no. 1.
Preobrazhenski, E. (1965) *The New Economies* (Oxford). Translation from Russian.
'Productivity in Planned Economies of Eastern Europe' (1956) *International Labour Review*, no. 2, Aug.
Průběh plnění hospodářského plánu, rok 1947 (1948) (Prague).
Průcha, V. (ed.) (1974) *Hospodářské dějiny Československa* (Prague).
Průcha, V., et al. (1977) *Hospodářské dějiny evropských socialistických zemí* (Prague).
Průcha, V., Kalinová, L. (1981) *Dlouhodobé tendence ve vývoji struktury československého hospodářství* (Prague).
Průša, J. (1969) *Ekonomické řízeni a mzdové soustavy* (Prague).
Przywara, B. (1982) *GP*, no. 12.
Pudlík, S. (1953) *GP*, no. 7–8.
Rajkiewicz, A. (1957) *ZG*, nos 9 and 10.
Rajkiewicz, A. (1965) *Zatrudnienie w Polsce Ludowej w latach 1950–70* (Warsaw).
Rácz, A., Pongrácz, L. (1980), in Horváth, L. (ed.), *Gazdasági szabályozók 1980* (Budapest).
Razga, V., Hronský, M. (1958) *Nová mysl*, no. 10.
Révész, G. (1981) in Timár, J. (ed.) *Munkagazdaságtan* (Budapest).
Révész, G. (1983), in *Kereseti és bérviszonyok* (Budapest).
Rok šedesátý osmý v usneseních a dokumentech ÚV KSČ (1969) (Prague).
Rózsa, J. (1965) *KSz*, no. 12.
Rózsa, J. (1971) *KSz*, no. 3.
Rózsa, J. (1978) *Szociálpolitika Magyarországon* (Budapest).
Rózsa, J., Farkasinszky, T. (1970) *MSz*, no. 4.
Rybovičová, D. (1978) *PaM*, no. 2.
Schmidt, O. (1975) *PaM*, no. 8.

Schönwald, P. (1980) *A dolgozók élet- és munkakörülményeinek alakulása a munkajog szabályainak tükrében 1951–56* (Budapest).
Secomski, K. (1977) *Polityka społeczno-ekonomiczna* (Warsaw).
Sedlák, M. (1961) *Ekonomický časopis*, no. 4.
Seidl, V. (1979) *PH*, no. 8.
Shaffer, H. G. (1965) 'The Labor Shortage in Czechoslovakia', *Osteuropa Wirtschaft*, no. 4.
Sielunin, W. (1971) *Reforma gospodarcza w ZSRR* (Warsaw). Translation from Russian.
Sipos, B. (1980) *MSz*, no. 3.
Skarzyński, R. (1981) *Finanse*, no. 12.
Šmolcnop, V. (1974) *PH*, no. 1.
Šmolcnop, V. (1982) *PaM*, no. 3.
Sociální jistoty ČSSR (1975) (Prague). Collective work.
Sokol, M. (1965) *PH*, no. 12.
Sokol, M. (1969) *PH*, no. 11.
'Some Aspects of Wage Policy in the Planned Economies of Eastern Europe' (1959), *International Labour Review*, no. 1, Jan.
Somogyi, M. (1978) *Figyelő*, no. 33.
Sonntag, K. (1983) *TL*, 14 Feb.
Spis kadrowy 1977 (1979) Publication of the Polish Statistical Board (Warsaw).
Spotan, S. (1982) *Ekonomika i Organizacja Pracy*, no. 7.
Starecký, V. (1982) *PaM*, no. 8.
Studniarek, Z. (1982) *PiZS*, no. 8–9.
Sucharda, B. (1967) *Ekonomicky mysliet a konat* (Bratislava).
Šujan, I. (1982) *Politická ekonomie*, no. 6.
Swiątkowski, A. (1982) *PiZS*, no. 11–12.
Sýkora, J. (1964) *Život strany*, no. 2.
Szabó, S. (1976) *MSz*, no. 2.
Szafar, T. (1981) *Osteuropa: Zeitschrift für Gegenwartsfragen des Ostens*, no. 4.
Szatmári, J. (1982) *MSz*, no. 3.
Szávai, A. (1975) *MSz*, no. 8.
Szávai, A. (1979) *MSz*, no. 9.
Szávai, A. (1981) *MSz*, no. 2.
Szikra Falusné, K (1967). *KSz*, no. 12.
Szikra Falusné, K. (1975) 'Some Aspects of Material Stimulation', *Acta Oeconomica*, vol. 14, no. 2–3.
Szikra Falusné, K. (1978) *KSz*, no. 3.
Szikra Falusné, K. (1979) *Munkabér, ösztönzés, elosztás* (Budapest).
Szilágyi, L. (1966) *Statisztikai Szemle*, no. 1.
Takács, F. (1967) *MSz*, no. 2.
Tesařová, D. (1972) *Statistika*, no. 5.
Tesařová, D. (1976) *Světové hospodářství*, 6 May.
Tesařová, D. (1982) *Statistika*, no. 1.
Timár, J. (1966) *Népszabadság*, 10 Sep.
Timár, J. (1976) *KSz*, no. 12.
Timár, J. (1978) *Gazdaság*, no. 1.
Timár, J. (ed.) (1981) *Munkagazdaságtan* (Budapest).
Timár, M. (1973) *Gazdaságpolitika Magyarországon (1967–1973)* (Budapest).

Tomášek, P. (1967) *Odměňování v nových podminkách řizeni* (Prague).

Tomášek, P. (1971) *Nová mysl*, no. 8–9.

Topiński, A. (1975), in Gliński, B. (ed.) *Zarys systemu funkcjonowania przemysłowych jednostek inicjujących* (Warsaw).

Triska, J. (1980) 'Workers' Assertiveness and Soviet Policy Choices', in Triska, J. F., and Gati, Ch. (eds), *Blue Collar Workers in Eastern Europe* (London).

Ujházy, K. (1982) *PH*, no. 8.

Ungvárszki, M. (1976), in Friss *et al.* (eds), *Gazdaságpolitikánk tapasztalatai és tanulságai, 1957–1960* (Budapest).

Upława, S., Dębniak, W. (1958) *Przegląd zagadnien socjalnych*, no. 10.

Vachel, J. (1965) *PH*, no. 5.

Vacić, A. (1978) *KSz*, no. 4.

Vais, T. (1981) 'Manpower Policy', in *East European Economic Assessment*, part 2, JEC.

Venyige, Molnárné J. (1975), in Venyige, M. J., Józsa, O., Gyetvai, L., *Munkaerő-szerkezet és mobilitás* (Budapest).

Vértes, Cs. (1981) *Figyelő*, no. 39.

Vida Horváth, A. (1971) *MSz*, no. 9.

Vincze, E. (1976) *MSz*, no. 12.

Vlach, P. (1968) *HN*, no. 36.

Voborník, B. (1952) *PH*, no. 10.

Votava, V. (1979) *PH*, no. 3.

Weber, H. (1964) *ZG*, no. 32.

Wilcsek, J. (1970) *Pénzügyi Szemle*, no. 3–4.

Zagorski, K. (1976), in *Przemiany struktury społecznej w ZSSR i Polsce* (Warsaw). Collective work.

Základy hospodárskej politiky KSČ (1979) (Bratislava).

Zásady urychlené realizace nové soustavy řízení (1966) (Prague).

Zelko, L. (1976) *KSz*, no. 12.

Index

(The letter 'd' stands for 'defined'.)